The Enterprising Mr MacGregor

Stockbreeder & Pioneer Pastoralist

Duncan MacGregor, c.1905
Leckie Archive

The Enterprising Mr MacGregor

Stockbreeder & Pioneer Pastoralist

FAY WOODHOUSE

ARCADIA

© Fay Woodhouse 2016

First published 2016 by ARCADIA
the general books' imprint of
Australian Scholarly Publishing Pty Ltd
7 Lt Lothian Street North, North Melbourne, Victoria 3051
tel: 9329 6963 / fax: 9329 5452 / www.scholarly.info

ISBN 978-1-925333-87-9

ALL RIGHTS RESERVED

Contents

Foreword vii
Acknowledgements viii

1 – Sailing for a Foreign Land   1

A ticket to Australia 2 • The MacGregor family 2 • Arriving in the great 'Metropolis of the Southern Hemisphere' 10 • Finding family and making friends 12 • Sober and industrious, 1857–1867 13 • Burke & Wills and a family story 17 • Steady in his habits – working in outback New South Wales 19 • Mount Murchison Station 20 • Donald McRae and Caulpaulin Station – a brief family history 23 • Working and wedding in New South Wales, 1842 25 • The McRae family reunited, 1853 26 • A run of his own – Caulpaulin Station, 1855 27 • Clunie at Chintin, 1865 32 • Maggie McRae and Duncan MacGregor – an 1868 wedding 34 • Death and disruption in the McRae family, 1867 36

2 – The Estate of the Late Donald McRae   39

Maintaining Mount Margaret, Caulpaulin and Clunie 42 • A man in a hurry – Inverauld at Riddells Creek, 1869 44 • A new home for a growing family – Glengyle at Coburg, 1873 49 • The Three Rivers 53 • A partnership saga – Macdonald, MacGregor & Mailer, 1872–1874 54 • Dreaming of draining the Koo-wee-rup Swamp, 1875 65 • A thorn in their side – Annie McRae, 1878 67

3 – Eyes on the Prize: Cattle Breeding, 1878–1888   70

The Booth Shorthorn 71 • Leicester and Border Leicester sheep 74 • Clydesdale horses 76 • Working the stations 77 • From drought to deluge – Koo-wee-rup, 1875 82 • The vast estate – a jigsaw puzzle of leases and partnerships 83 • Taking risks with high finance 84 • The role of a trustee – a lesson in family arguments 87 • The death of Christina McRae, 1887 89

4 – Of Droughts and Flooding Rains, 1888–1901   **93**

The federation drought, 1895–1903 – compounding the problem **96** • Annie and Kenneth McKenzie, 1892 **98** • Out into the world **100** • The Boer War **112** • A sudden death in the year of Federation **115**

5 – 'My Heart is Most Sad and Sore', 1902–1916   **117**

Maintaining a stout heart **127** • Relinquishing the McRae estate, 1904–1910 **129** • The enterprising Mr MacGregor **138**

MacGregor Family Tree   **140**

Vignettes   **141**

Jessie (1869–1933) and Donald Macrae Stewart (1862–1933) **141** • Margaret (Goodie) MacGregor (1870–1901) **144** • John (Jack) (1872–1942) and Alexina (Zena) (1891–1960) MacGregor **146** • Isabella (Tottie) (1874–1957) and William Pestell (1896–1950) **148** • Annie (Cissie) (1876–1947) and Frederick Hutchings (1879–1926) **151** • Christina (Pearl) (1879–1941) and Ernest Wood (1877–1951) **154** • Donald McRae MacGregor (1882–1950), Christina Rogers (1879–1921) and Maud Hannan (1886–1969) **156** • Annie McRae (1853–1939), Kenneth McKenzie (1842–1892) and Phillip Ernest Forster (1868–1946) **158**

Bibliography   163
Notes   171
Index   187

Foreword

From his youngest days, Ian Leckie has known the story of his great-grandfather, Duncan MacGregor (1835–1916), a prominent pastoralist, stockbreeder and explorer. The tales of Duncan MacGregor's exploits have always formed part of the family history and Ian Leckie and other members of his family have been researching their family history for over half a century. This book pays tribute to their intense interest in their grandfather's work and their desire to document his importance as an Australian pastoralist.

The story of Duncan's success owed much to another Scottish immigrant, Donald McRae, who had arrived in Australia in the 1830s. McRae gave MacGregor work and eventually became his father-in-law. His story provides the context to MacGregor's experience and underpins his ultimate prosperity; McRae's life is told in the first chapter.

MacGregor left Scotland for Australia in 1857, arriving when gold fever was still gripping Victoria and the pastoral industry was in its ascendancy. Duncan's skills as a shepherd and manager of stock were in demand and he quickly gained experience in the pastoral industry in Victoria, New South Wales and Queensland. This thoroughly researched and engaging biography charts his path of exploration and enterprising ventures in three Australian colonies. MacGregor was working in New South Wales in 1860 and his descendants have always believed that he assisted Burke and Wills find their way to Cooper Creek. This family anecdote is challenged and discussed in detail.

Duncan MacGregor was ambitious and talented and his life was based on a series of extremes of successes and failures. Fay Woodhouse's interpretation of his life provides the reader with an exciting and highly readable view of his remarkable life.

Peter Yule
Historian

Acknowledgements

Firstly, I would like to acknowledge my grateful thanks to Ian Leckie, great-grandson of Duncan MacGregor, and his wife Janet for instigating the writing of this important biography. The research was made possible by my use of family papers and those held in the State Library of Victoria. Reading through these extensive collections inspired Ian Leckie to proceed with this project.

Family members who have also contributed to this project include Ross and the late Prue Leckie and Susan and John Vale. These family members have read the manuscript and contributed their knowledge of their family history. Others who have contributed vital details of their family histories include Christine Morrison in Edinburgh, Scott MacGregor in England, Margaret Thompson in Traralgon and Tina Terry in Tasmania.

The Leckies and the Vales would like to acknowledge the extraordinary amount of research undertaken by Bernard MacGregor, particularly in the 1970s, long before the Internet, *Trove* and the ready access to family history we take for granted in 2016.

So much research for a work of this nature is undertaken in archival collections. Without access to the MacGregor Collection in the State Library this book could never have been written. I am extremely grateful for the assistance of the knowledgeable and helpful librarians, archivists and specialist manuscript librarians Sandra Burt, Des Cowley, Gerard Hayes, Helena Lozanovski, Kevin Malloy, Lois McEvey, Madelaine Say, Lucy Shedden and Mike Thomas.

I am particularly grateful to Stephen Ford for his research into the New South Wales Archives for property ownership by McRae and MacGregor and to Judith Nissen for her research into the labyrinth of Queensland properties. Together they assisted in the complex property research.

I have also had the pleasure of talking to Archivists in public and private collections throughout Victoria while researching this project. In particular I acknowledge and thank most sincerely Geoff Laurenson, Archivist at Geelong Grammar School, Dr Patricia Macwhirter, at

Harewood House Museum in Koo-wee-rup; Robyn Gross and Kylie McKay at the Romsey and Lancefield Historical Society; the Gisborne Historical Society; the Coburg Historical Society and the Koo-wee-rup Historical Society. My special thanks go to Gerard Cunningham for the use of his Honours Thesis and my tour of the Koo-wee-rup Swamp and its kilometres of drains built by Duncan MacGregor.

My very special thanks go to Mike Sleurink at Lands Victoria for his phenomenal assistance in finding titles to the large number of Victorian properties owned by Duncan MacGregor and his children. His speedy response to my enquiries was a treat to behold and made my research so much easier. Mike, your efforts were very much appreciated.

Colin Pike of Magnetic North Design researched and produced the marvellous maps of the pathways travelled by Donald McRae and Duncan MacGregor. These maps provide a comprehensive visual record of the journeys undertaken by these men and illuminate the extent of the properties they held.

I thank Tony Kelly of Archiva Lucida for his expertise and magnificent production of digital imaging of the historic photographs. I also thank Peter Yule and Geoff Burrows for their input and sound advice on a method of disentangling the jigsaw puzzle of properties owned, leased or mortgaged by Duncan MacGregor et al. We thank Marshall Baillieu for his assistance regarding the Gowan Lea property at Koo-wee-rup, and Lady Susannah Clarke at Bolinda Vale for her insight into the work of Robert Clarke. Special thanks go to Dr Val Noone for his advice on the Gaelic language.

To the friends and family who have lived the MacGregor story with me, especially Christine Walker and Ian Macleod who happily engaged in endless discussions around their dinner table, I thank you all.

— 1 —
Sailing for a Foreign Land

In 1857 the 22-year-old Duncan MacGregor made the first important strategic decision of his life. He understood that in Scotland his opportunities for advancement were slight. After six years working as a shepherd, 'with a view to better his condition and circumstances', he made up his mind to leave Scotland and emigrate to Australia.[1] Others he knew had done so and their letters suggested that it was possible to prosper there. And so with driving ambition he booked his passage and sailed to Melbourne, where a cousin was then living, in June 1857.

The young Duncan was somewhat brash on the one hand, and serious and high-minded on the other. His Presbyterian faith played a major role in his view of the world. He respected others with faith yet was intolerant of those without demonstrable religious beliefs. His understanding of his fellow passengers was limited, and he viewed them as a rabble beneath his notice. He occupied himself during the long voyage by associating with a select group of passengers of his own class, largely ignoring other passengers and the crew. The journal of the youthful Duncan exposes many of the characteristics of the man who matured in the Australian landscape. Although he did not yet know it, throughout his life his superior attitude would often be at odds with the circumstances he had to deal with.

Sober and serious, Duncan found work first in Victoria and then in New South Wales. With each move he took opportunities as they arose. His experience working for well-known and respected pastoralists enabled him to take on more responsible jobs as he travelled through the settled and unsettled districts of the Australian bush. As he worked on various pastoral properties he retained his annual notebooks and many papers, enabling historians to trace his movements. They have become an invaluable resource.

A ticket to Australia

During the late eighteenth and early nineteenth century, Scotland endured great social upheaval and poverty caused by the Agrarian and Industrial Revolutions. Emigration became a viable option for the ambitious, the disenfranchised and the poor. The United States of America, Canada and Australia were favoured destinations[2] in the 1830s when both government and private emigration schemes were devised to relieve Scotland's poverty.

A Presbyterian clergyman, the Reverend John Dunmore Lang, played a major role in these emigration schemes. Lang had emigrated to Australia in 1822 and became the first Presbyterian minister in Sydney. Motivated by religious fervour, he believed that attracting some of the surplus population of Scotland to the colonies would provide labour for their development. He also hoped the immigrants would raise the moral tone of the settlement; in his eyes the convicts indulged in licentious behaviour. His agitation for free immigration therefore had strong a moral purpose. With a grant of £1,500 reputedly 'wheedled out of the Colonial Secretary', Lang selected 140 Scots tradesmen and their families who agreed to repay their fares once they began working in Australia. The arrival of Lang's 'Scotch mechanics' on the *Stirling Castle* in 1831 was applauded.[3]

Between 1837 and 1857, when Duncan travelled, thousands of Scots left behind a crumbling social order, hoping to establish self-contained, family-based, communal agricultural settlements overseas. Historians and economists quantify migration flows by 'push' and 'pull' factors. The famine in Scotland became a major push factor while in Australia the demand for labour to produce wool pulled strongly.[4]

The MacGregor family

Duncan MacGregor was the first son and the third of 13 children born to John (b. 1793) and Janet (née Sinclair, b. 1816) MacGregor. He was born at Liaran, Rannoch, Perthshire, Scotland on 26 February 1835.[5] His siblings were Margaret (b. 1831), Janet (b. 1833), Catherine (b. 1837), James (1838), Ann (b. 1840), Eliza (b. 1842), Donald (b. 1844), Gregor (b. 1846), Ellen (b. 1847), John (1850), Isabella (1852), and Malcolm (b. 1855).[6]

Duncan was nearly 10 years old when the family moved about 100 miles west from Liaran to the other side of Scotland. His father was a tenant farmer and they resettled at Ewich Farm, Tyndrum, in the Parish of Strathfillan in the Highlands. This was one of the wettest parts of Scotland and made farming difficult and challenging. Ewich Farm was a property of 982 acres of arable pasture, with three labourers and two household servants. Their house of twelve rooms was both indicative of their social status and necessary to accommodate the large family. According to the 1851 census, a 16-year-old Duncan was being educated at home.[7]

In 1857, Duncan arranged his passage to Australia, informed his family and sought letters of introduction to assist him to find employment. He carried with him two character references from local ministers of religion and one from his employer. The Reverend John Campbell of Strathfillan wrote that Duncan was a man 'o whom I entertain the most favourable opinion', emphasising that he was 'active, sensible and enterprising … [with] a good knowledge of sheep and cattle and farming operations'. Perhaps equally important, he worshipped in the parish church, was regular in his attendance on the Sabbath and was 'steady in his habits and correct in his deportment'.[8] The Reverend Campbell concluded that it would 'afford him great satisfaction' to hear that Duncan had prospered in whatever part of the world he 'cast his lot'. He had much pleasure in recommending him. The other letters of introduction followed the same theme. The Minister Alex MacKinnon reiterated that Duncan was an honest young man of 'sober and industrious habits' and of good 'moral character'. His employer, the farmer Michael Grieves, also wrote glowingly that MacGregor was an 'exemplary' young man. He was well acquainted with the rearing of cattle and management of stock and worthy of the attention of any gentleman as a manager in 'a forin land'.[9] Those who knew MacGregor's character agreed he was solid, steady and sober: they wished him well.

On 23 May 1857 the American and Australian Packet Office in London wrote to Duncan confirming his place on a passenger ship, the *Marco Polo*, which was due to sail from Liverpool to Australia on Sunday 7 June 1857.[10] Duncan was an unassisted migrant; this meant he had enough money to pay his fare and to take some money with him to Australia. While the census indicates his father spelt his name 'McGregor', this spelling may have been incorrect because official papers and the ship's register show that Duncan spelt his name 'MacGregor'. Duncan took a keen interest in his family history and the name MacGregor. A large, handwritten family tree showing his father and mother and their forebears is amongst his papers.[11]

After bidding farewell to as many members of his family as he could, Duncan MacGregor left Strathfillan on Tuesday 2 June and spent his first night in Glasgow. This may have been the first time he had been away from home. The following day he travelled to Liverpool to join the ship. He had to board the *Marco Polo* two days before it was due to sail.

The *Marco Polo,* named after the Venetian explorer, was a three-masted wooden clipper of 1,625 tons. She was launched in 1851 at Saint John, New Brunswick, Canada. In 1852 she was purchased by the Black Ball Line and converted to become a passenger service between England and Australia. On her first voyage in 1852 she made record time in sailing to Australia in 76 days, and then returning to England also in 76 days.[12] In June 1857, bound for Melbourne, she sailed under Captain James Clarke. Although described as a medium clipper, by today's standards she was a very small ship, just 184 ft in length, with three decks, the height between each being only 8 ft. She sailed with nearly 500 passengers and crew. Only four families enjoyed Saloon accommodation, the remaining 420 were Intermediate and Steerage passengers.[13]

By 1857, travelling from England to Australia was slightly more comfortable than it had been in the 1830s and 1840s, but no less dangerous.[14] The shipping route of the 1850s ran from west to east through the Southern Ocean in order to make use of the strong westerly winds of the Roaring Forties. From England to Australia and New Zealand, returning via Cape Horn, the route at the time made for the fastest circumnavigation of the world. This was a lucrative course for ship-owners as clippers returning home could be loaded with grains, wool and gold. Notwithstanding the financial benefits, the route posed major risks, exposing ships to the hazards of fierce winds, huge waves, and icebergs. This combination of the fastest ships, the highest risks, and the greatest rewards combined to give this route a particular aura of romance and drama.[15]

When he left Liverpool, MacGregor began writing a journal which remains in the family's possession. He titled it a 'Memorandum or Journal on board the ship "Marco Polo" which left Liverpool on 7th June 1857'.[16] The small, leather-bound shipboard diary is one of few extant personal artefacts remaining from MacGregor's early life, giving us our first opportunity to meet the young man and glimpse his character. Keeping it became his regular disciplined activity for the first 27 days of his journey. For the educated passenger, journal writing was a common and popular practice. Some considered there would be an interest in a first-hand account of their journey and indeed many were later published in book form.

As well as Duncan's journal, two other diaries for the journey to Australia during May–September 1857 have been found. One is by a fellow passenger on the *Marco Polo*, the other is by a passenger on a rival ship, the *Hornet*.

James Cooper Stewart was the 21-year-old son of James Stewart, a master house-painter from Edinburgh.[17] The young gentleman travelled as a First Class passenger on the *Marco Polo* and wrote his diary in the form of a letter to his father.

The second diary is that of an English immigrant, Thomas Boyne Atkinson, formerly of the Great Seal Patent Office, London. He and his wife, two boys and an infant sailed on the *Hornet*, departing Southampton on 24 May 1857, two weeks before the *Marco Polo* left Liverpool. The Atkinson family were amongst 448 government-assisted emigrants on the *Hornet*. Thomas kept a lively, engaging and informative account of his journey to Melbourne. His record of the conditions he and his family experienced on board the *Hornet* provide an interesting point of comparison to MacGregor and Stewart's record of their trip on the *Marco Polo*.

MacGregor's diary sheds light on his personal beliefs and sketches the characteristics of the young man. He was a keen observer of the interactions between his fellow passengers and he committed to his journal all that he noticed of shipboard life. Keeping a journal may have also helped him adapt to cloistered shipboard life, quite unlike the outdoors life he had previously led. For a shepherd managing stock in all weathers to suddenly find himself confined to small spaces within a crowd of people he had never met must have been a confronting experience.

MacGregor's diary begins on 7 June 1857. Being a Sunday, before the ship departed, Captain Clarke held a divine service on board. From his very detailed record, we learn the lesson was 'taken from the eleventh chapter of Hebrews and mostly from the 8, 9 and 10 verses'. After the service, the clergyman returned to shore on the tugboat. Duncan took this opportunity to send some letters back from the boat before they set sail. Aware of the dangers of the sea voyage, he sent one to his father and some others 'in case any accident may happen before my arrival in Melbourne'. Duncan counted his fellow passengers: 'Scotch 180, English 110, Irish 105 and Germans 8', as well as a crew of about 80 men. The *Marco Polo* was tugged out of the Port of Liverpool in fine weather and 'after some cheers from the tug boat we fired a cannon as a farewell'. With the night coming on, our no-nonsense young man 'went to bed and slept sound till morning'.[18]

His compatriot, James Stewart, also recorded his impressions of the first night on board. He depicts his cabin-mate as a 'real Highlander from Ross Shire'. We instantly hope he shared his cabin with MacGregor, but as Stewart was travelling First Class, this could not have been the case. Stewart described his cabin-mate's physique as a 'dainty body', possibly indicating he was athletic or finely built.[19] This was not Duncan MacGregor who we see, from later photographs, was sturdily built, even as a young man.

When he came up onto the main deck the following morning, Duncan experienced the joy of a fresh breeze which continued all day, blowing the ship down the Irish Channel. In contrast to his own sense of wellbeing he noted 'most of the passengers unwell and in a miserable state'. Seasickness was common during the first weeks of sea journeys until passengers found their 'sea-legs'. James Stewart suffered sea-sickness for the first three days of his journey, then seemed to recover. Thomas Atkinson on the *Hornet* also wrote of 'Sickness and Misery!',[20] but it is clear from their diaries that neither he nor Thomas succumbed to seasickness.

Duncan quickly became friendly with two family groups, the Stewarts and the Campbells. The Stewarts were Mrs Mary Stewart, aged 31, and Mr Archie Stewart, 50, and the second family, the Campbell's, were John, 40, Isabella, 36, and their five children.[21] Duncan considered the remainder of his fellow passengers 'an uncomfortable and rotten heterogeneous mass' of people.[22]

The major and ongoing irritant for Duncan and his friends was the distribution of rations. He describes them as 'irregular' and blames the administration for this situation. Part of the cost of passage included weekly rations of food and water. In 1857 a typical ration for adults and children over 14 years of age included 56 ounces of biscuit, 6 ounces of beef, 18 ounces of pork, 24 ounces of preserved meat, 42 ounces of flour, 21 ounces of oatmeal, 8 ounces of raisins, 6 ounces of suet, three quarters of an ounce of peas, 8 ounces of rice, and 8 ounces of preserved potatoes.[23] By the end of the first week, when a full complement of rations was not forthcoming, Duncan and his circle of friends were aggrieved. Stewart also complained that the rations were 'very coarse' and that he could 'not manage any of them'.[24] Compared to the sturdy Duncan, James Stewart was a man of delicate sensibilities.

Duncan paints a bleak picture of life at sea. He wrote that 'The wind thundered today … and the sea is continually breaking over the bow of the ship'. He was 'everything but comfortable' and was having a miserable time. His physical discomfort was due to more than the weather. Hygiene on board sailing vessels was, at the best of times, poor. Most ships provided only basic toilet and bathing facilities and conditions were ideal for the spread of disease, not least because the air below decks was oppressive. Mattresses were made out of straw and attracted fleas and cockroaches; during stormy and wet weather, they were often soaked through.[25] Such a lack of hygiene made deaths at sea inevitable. Stewart notes that a death occurred on board during the voyage. On better-managed ships, such as the *Marco Polo*, the areas below decks were thoroughly cleaned every few days, and Duncan notes at least one occasion when the ship's officers 'exert themselves to cause the passengers to clean out their berths'.[26] Regardless of these efforts, Duncan's expected standards of cleanliness were not met.

Despite fine breezes and sails 'set to beam us along', Duncan struggled with the unfamiliar routines of communal life. However, he began to record particular highlights of his journey. Mrs Stewart bestowed many kindnesses on him and he described in detail the cakes and soups she shared with him and her inner circle of friends. However, the inconsistent rationing of food remained a daily problem. On a brighter note, when he found they were making 12 knots an hour, he considered this to be fine progress.[27] They were now over two thousand miles from Liverpool, the weather was 'favourable for expediting the passage' and the world looked a little brighter.[28]

How did Duncan occupy his time? It is easy to imagine him striding around the decks each day, checking the sails and the height of the sea. He had an enquiring mind, and frequently noted and clearly relished his regular estimates of both the ship's location and the speed with which they were travelling. He greatly regretted not having brought with him a good map or globe to be able to pinpoint his exact location. At the same time he confided to his journal that he saw very few passengers 'of any mind'. Those around him were not 'of the lowest grade' of people, but they did not 'come up to the middle class of my native land'.[29]

While the journey dragged on it is clear Duncan was unhappy. His true state of mind is revealed in the following entry: 'When at sea this evening the oaten cake I saw with some Irish sailors drew my attention very much for it took me in mind of the cubbits of cheese that I had been accustomed to see in my highland home.'[30] He was homesick. While the sea was dead calm and the ship could make no headway as they lay 'under a burning sun opposite Palmas [one of the Canaries]', the lack of movement caused discontent amongst the passengers. Fights broke out. But if Duncan was bored and homesick, he was not alone. To relieve the boredom and to improve their 'victualing', some of the passengers began fishing with a line off the top deck to catch their own dinner.[31] Duncan, however, does not report joining in the activity. In due course, the wind changed direction and the ship was again able to resume a steady pace, to the great relief of all on board.

Duncan's record of daily life at sea continued. One day he wrote that he saw some of his fellow passengers 'cursing and swearing and singing obscene songs with great mirth and glee'.[32] This was unpalatable to him, and it 'was akin to blasphemy to hear the name of my blessed saviour repeated in such vile and polluted lips'. James Stewart commented on the same day that his Highland mate 'solemnly remarked that God's vengeance will fall on us ere we complete our voyage.'[33]

Dozens of other vessels were sailing in the same direction as the *Marco Polo*. Duncan and James Stewart made notes of the different ships they passed. Duncan recorded:

> I see a ship to windward of us striving against a strong south-easterly wind. We are gliding onward beautifully, the wind right a stern of us. … This morning a fine steady breeze the ship making great headway and all seem so pleased. Many conjecture as to our position … One thing is that the weather is favourable and for my part I would not wish the wind to be any higher as by causing the vessel to lean more to leaward it would make the ship more uncomfortable.[34]

The shipping lanes on this route to and from Australia were busy. Passenger ships on the high seas in June and July 1857 included the *Hornet, Greyhound, White Star, Sardinian, Suffolk, Ursa Major, Pole Star, Commodore Perry* and *Ben Nevis*. Others *en route* to Melbourne during August 1857 included the *Hotspur, Donald McKay, Miles Barton, John Linn, Ellen Stuart* and *Melbourne*.[35]

Travelling in the opposite direction was the *Indomitable*, bound for London with emigrants from Melbourne. It came alongside the *Marco Polo* and the two captains exchanged news. As the two ships parted,

James Stewart wrote that 'the tears rolled uninterruptedly down our cheeks when our band played "Far Far Upon the Sea" and "Cheer Boys Cheer" as a parting salute'. He wrote: 'Home! What is it? An Emigrant only knows truly'.[36]

MacGregor's journal continues but as the wind picked up, the 'scale of victualing' declined. The biscuits were too hard and it was 'impossible any of us use them', the beef they were supplied was 'by no means good' and the sugar rendered 'such a noxious taste'.[37] That the crew chose to ignore his complaints made it worse: 'if a person chances to state his grievances he is insulted instead of getting any other redress'. He was 'very much annoyed' by this situation and declared he would not recommend any of his friends to try a similar passage. Most of all he missed his friends and 'some rational conversation and argument'. In short, life on board the *Marco Polo* remained 'very unpleasant'.[38]

On 3 July, without explanation, Duncan ceased writing his journal. What is known, through James Stewart's diary, is that a school of sharks hovered around the ship the very next day, fascinating and entertaining the passengers. Duncan did not record the social event of the voyage, the American Independence Day Ball on Saturday 4 July. This Ball was a 'cheering and happy sight' for Stewart who recorded that the Captain and all passengers appeared in 'full dress' while 'I was in my Tartans'.[39]

Time passed, the voyage slowly progressed, and on Tuesday 1 September 1857 the *Marco Polo* passed Cape Otway Lighthouse and 'A great many remained on deck to witness or rather watch for the happy land.' When James Stewart went up on deck he 'could distinctly see it – trees or scrub nicely pastured'. They were then picked up by a pilot boat and by 7.00 pm the *Marco Polo* had cast anchor in Hobson's Bay, 12 miles from their destination. On Wednesday 2 September they were towed to Sandridge (Port Melbourne) and the next day they were towed up the Yarra and landed on the wharf at Melbourne.[40]

Although it was not a record time for the *Marco Polo*, it was a swift voyage. The journey had taken 88 days from Liverpool to Melbourne, 12 days longer than the ship's record. The other emigrant ship, the *Hornet*, took 103 days and also arrived in Melbourne on 2 September. Thomas Atkinson recorded in his diary that on Thursday 3 September it was a 'Rough – Cold raining morning [and] ... the "Marco Polo" came to anchor alongside of us this morning'. The *Age* newspaper's 'Shipping Intelligence' reported the arrival:

> This favorite Black Ball liner still keeps up her reputation as one of the most regular traders we have to this port. On the present voyage she left Liverpool on the 7th of June, but owing to light winds and calms did not cross the equator before the 30th day, and the meridian of the Cape of Good Hope on the 63rd day out. Thus the passage was made from the Cape to this Port in 22 days. The passengers, 430 in number, have enjoyed excellent health, and all express themselves highly delighted with the passage, and as always is the case with those who have the pleasure of sailing with Capt. Clarke, speak in the highest terms of his unremitting attention towards them.[41]

This was a glowing report of the voyage and the Captain, although Duncan MacGregor certainly would not have agreed with it.

Duncan's account makes it clear he was disappointed in the long, arduous journey, but in all likelihood he was also excited and anxious about the adventures yet to come. What did he make of the bustling city still gripped by gold fever?

Arriving in the great 'Metropolis of the Southern Hemisphere'

The year 1857 was significant for the growing town of Melbourne; like Duncan MacGregor, the settlement was just 22 years old.

Although it was more than a decade before it styled itself the 'Metropolis of the Southern Hemisphere',[42] and two decades before George Augustus Sala dubbed it 'Marvellous Melbourne',[43] Melbourne in the mid- to late 1850s was a place of great expectation. The gold rushes, commencing in August 1851, propelled Melbourne and the colony of Victoria onto the world stage. In 1851 Melbourne's population was 77,345; in 1857, when Duncan arrived, it had increased to 410,766.[44] Gold had facilitated the extraordinary settlement of Melbourne and its hinterland.[45] The stream of people with 'gold fever' was constant and accommodation and facilities were stretched beyond capacity. Thousands were forced to live in a tent city on the south side of the Yarra at Emerald Hill.

The gold rushes provided opportunities for talented and ambitious young men and continued to be a 'pull' factor in migration to Australia.[46] As historian Don Garden notes, a high proportion of the unassisted migrants were unmarried young men from the artisan or middle classes of British society. Generally, they were educated, politically liberal and Protestant.

That these young men had joined the gold rushes was indicative of 'an adventurous streak in their character'.[47] In the years between 1852 and 1860, and largely in response to the discovery of gold, around 290,000 people migrated to Victoria from Britain and Ireland. Of these, 200,000 were unassisted by government.[48] In 1857 alone, 14,369 from the United Kingdom were, like Duncan MacGregor and James Stewart, unassisted, while Thomas Atkinson and his family, travelling on the *Hornet*, were amongst 28,304 that were government-assisted.[49] Duncan MacGregor was one of the '15,421 agricultural labourers shepherds and herdsmen' arriving in Victoria between 1851 and 1859.[50]

In 1857, as unsuccessful diggers left the gold fields and returned to Melbourne, and many immigrants arrived, Victoria began to experience a brief period of depression.[51] The culmination of a rapidly rising population on the one hand, and labour shortages because of desertion to the gold fields on the other, had led to rapid wage and price increases. The cost of food continued to rise. Soon after his arrival, Atkinson wrote home to his family in England: 'bread 10 pence/loaf; flour 3½ pence/lb; butter 3 shillings/lb; milk 1 shilling/quart; tea 2 shillings/lb; coffee 3 shillings/lb; beef 8 pence/lb and mutton 7 pence/lb'.[52] These prices were much higher than in England.

Despite the temporary economic hardship of the late 1850s, the colony of Victoria had achieved much in its short history. In 1854, only 20 years after official European settlement, the Melbourne and Hobson's Bay Railway Company opened its first line to Port Melbourne. In September 1857 trains began running to Williamstown.[53] With the arrival of the railways, Melbourne was as proudly modern as any British city.[54]

Happily for Duncan MacGregor and the other shepherds who arrived in 1857, pastoralism dominated the economy. A revival of confidence by British investors after the 1857 depression brought about changes in pastoral production, and pastoralists began purchasing and improving their properties by building homesteads, dams and fences. When Duncan arrived, nearly 41,500,000 acres of pastoral land was held under only 1,265 pastoral licences.[55] Shepherds and stock and station managers remained in high demand. Wool was one of the most important of Australia's primary exports. With an expansion in the pastured area available to woolgrowers, sheep numbers in Australia in the late 1850s continued to soar.[56] As economic historians B.R. Davidson and Boris Schedvin conclude, for a 'land-abundant, labour-scarce, isolated region dependent on long-distance transportation, wool was an ideal commodity' for Australian export. It had a high value-to-weight ratio and required little labour to produce.[57] Within five years of Duncan's arrival in Australia, wool, along with gold, was the dominant commodity on which Australia would soon depend. Australia, although it may not have been evident to Duncan MacGregor at the time, was soon to begin its 130-year ride on the sheep's back. And he was there for the ride.

Finding family and making friends

When he arrived in Melbourne and while looking for work, MacGregor stayed with his cousin Duncan Cameron, although it is unclear exactly where this was, or how long he remained with him.

It is clear from the extant collection of letters that Duncan wrote regularly to his family at home. Any young man or woman thousands of miles from home must have yearned for contact with their loved ones. The length of time it took to correspond must, however, have seemed interminable. The fastest postal service via ship from London, Southampton, Plymouth or Liverpool to Melbourne took a minimum of two and a half months, and a response to one of his letters was likely to take at least six months if not longer.

A letter from his father, John MacGregor, dated 5 January 1858, is clearly in response to an early, if not the first, letter Duncan sent home from Melbourne. His father comments on the economic collapse mentioned in the newspapers and that 'the colony was not in a good way', but his letter contained the welcome news that the whole MacGregor family were enjoying good health and he himself was in better health than he had been 'for the last fifteen years thank God'.[58] We imagine this was a relief for Duncan. The letter would not have arrived in Melbourne until at least April 1858, ten months after Duncan's departure from Scotland. When his 16-year-old sister Annie wrote to him in September 1858, a whole year after he arrived in Melbourne, she emphasised that it was 'a great comfort' that he was writing to his family "so regular"'.[59] Six months later, his sister Kate responded to one of his letters. Her main concern was whether he had taken his trunks from Melbourne to his current place of employment.[60] As we trace Duncan's early working life in Australia, it is clear that during his first years in the colony the family struggled to keep up with his whereabouts.

Sober and industrious, 1857–1867

Family stories recount Duncan's early working life in Australia. In 1937, Duncan's son, Donald, wrote in a letter that:

> When my father first came out he went to a Mr Campbell of Glengour [*sic*] Cattle Station on the Loddon River, in 1859 he went to Woorooma Station on the Edwards River, N.S.W. in 1868 he went to Mount Murchison Station on the River Darling N.S.W. In 1869 he married Margaret McRae of Calpalin [*sic*] Station of the Darling, after the marriage he took up an area of Cattle and Sheep Stations in Queensland.[61]

This letter has been scrutinised for its accuracy: the time Duncan worked for Donald Campbell and then at Woorooma Station, the years he worked at Mount Murchison Station, and the date of his marriage to Margaret McRae.

It is true that Duncan MacGregor worked for Donald Campbell, an Argyleshire man who had emigrated to Victoria in the 1830s. There appears to have been an understanding between the families that once he arrived in Australia, Duncan would seek out Donald Campbell for employment. This is borne out in the January 1858 letter from his father who wrote that he was 'well acquaint with his father and mother' and he believed Campbell was 'most likely … a man that has a good deal of influence in the colony'.[62] Campbell is described as a pastoral pioneer of Port Phillip, a Scot who was also an experienced stockman in Australia.[63] In the 1840s he had overlanded stock to the Murray and the Darling Rivers, the earliest days of exploration of those rivers.

Prior to purchasing Glengower in 1860, Campbell ran a pastoral property at Bullock Creek, not far from Harcourt in Central Victoria. Significantly it was *en route* to the goldfields at Bendigo. Diggers walked to the goldfields via Bulla, Lancefield, Carlsruhe, Harcourt and Bullock Creek. Campbell was a canny Scot who saw that he could make more money than the gold seekers by providing them with accommodation and necessary provisions. He consequently opened the Bullock Creek Inn and Camping Ground. When he purchased Glengower to settle there with his family it was a property of 16,000 acres.[64] Because contemporary references to Donald Campbell linked him to his highly successful Glengower property, Duncan's children have assumed that their father's first job in Victoria was working for Campbell at Glengower. Given that

Campbell did not purchase Glengower until 1860, when Duncan was already in New South Wales, it is more likely that he worked at Bullock Creek from late 1857 until some time in 1859.

Letters from Scotland in the years 1857 to 1860 provide evidence of Duncan's whereabouts as he gained experience working on holdings much larger than those he knew in Scotland. Several letters are addressed to him in New South Wales at Woorooma Station. Located on the Edward River, Woorooma Station was owned by another Scot, Lachlan McBean. Arriving in Victoria in 1839, McBean first worked with the stock and station agents Younghusband & Co. in Adelaide. He learned on the job and established his own pastoral company. In 1855 he purchased Woorooma Station for £12,000 with stock of 12,000 sheep. Woorooma was a well-watered property of approximately 60,000 acres. It was described as 'confined to the natural and original boundary of the run, bounded on the South by the Edward River, on the North and North West by the running water of the Billabong Creek to the confluence of the Edward River and that creek, on the East by the Murgah division boundary fence as originally owned by the Government'.[65] The homestead and station buildings were located on the banks of the Edward River; the woolshed was situated conveniently so that the bales of wool were loaded directly from it into the paddle steamers on the river. The following year McBean bought the adjoining Windouran Station, a property of 110,000 acres. The two properties included 130,000 acres of freehold land.[66] Working with McBean briefly in 1859 was MacGregor's next step on the path to Donald McRae's Caulpaulin Station.

While at Woorooma Station Duncan received a welcome letter from his school friend James McNee, who was then training to become a doctor. Posted from Edinburgh in November 1859, the letter would not have arrived before mid-January 1860. The letter describes McNee's latest vacation from his studies, the current news from 'Auld Reekie' (the historic name for Edinburgh), and news of Duncan's family. McNee's letter was friendly, chatty and informative, aiming to keep his friend up to date with the latest local gossip. It includes news of his two older sisters, who were working and living away from home, as well as a lively commentary on Duncan's friends and former neighbours. Reports on the weather as well as recent births, deaths, marriages and local scandals would have delighted and entertained young Duncan, who may have read them as he enjoyed the beautiful setting of the Edward River.[67]

Because he had moved from Melbourne to Bullock Creek in central Victoria in 1857 and then to Woorooma by 1859, Duncan did not receive all of the mail sent to him. The writers' frustration is made clear in several family letters. His sisters reproach him: 'I saw a letter from you to your sister Margaret saying you had gone across to Woorooma Station, and she tells me you were saying you had no word from me.' The letter had not caught up with him. In another letter his father writes: 'Margaret got your letter in July. She wrote and Janet wrote since, but likely you will not get them as you left the place.' The letter also highlights his father's ambitions for his son as well as his concerns about his son's remote location: 'Your Mother and Sisters is sorry you left the sheep way and went to cattle and living up so far among or near the natives as they must be dangerous and a man cannot have ease in his mind and even wild cattle must be dangerous. He continued: 'I hope you get a share of a run soon, as you cannot make much money with wages as everything is so high such as clothes & shoes unless you get to be a manager or something that you can be of your own.'[68] Having a run of his own was surely uppermost in Duncan's mind.

From Woorooma Station, in 1860, Duncan moved to John Baker's Menindee Station on the Darling River in New South Wales. Menindee later became part of the larger Kinchega Station. Once he began working at Menindee Station, Duncan kept a comprehensive notebook recording his work. It seems possible that the first entry, dated 15 April 1860, recorded his first day of work at the station. MacGregor's meticulous notes list the numbers of cattle, sheep and horses delivered, stock slaughtered each month, and the supplier of the animals. His notebook also confirms his movements during 1860.

John MacGregor's fear of his son's close proximity to 'the natives' was well founded. The Darling River settlement was less than ten years old, and as frontier country it was still dangerous for the white settler.[69] The original inhabitants rightly objected to the theft of their land and there were violent encounters. Yet, local Aborigines worked on the pastoral leases in New South Wales, and in years to come Duncan employed Aboriginal workers and recorded spending time travelling with them on various journeys through the outback.

Burke & Wills

In August 1860 the Victorian Exploring Expedition, instigated by The Royal Society of Victoria, travelled to Cooper's Creek in Queensland to explore the country south of the Gulf of Carpentaria. Robert O'Hara Burke, a Superintendent of Police at Castlemaine, led the expedition but was widely criticised because he had no experience as an explorer. Other key figures were William J. Wills (surveyor and astronomical observer), Dr Hermann Beckler (medical officer and geologist) and Dr Ludwig Becker (artist and naturalist). The Expedition was competing with John McDouall Stuart of Adelaide to become the first white men to cross the continent from south to north.

When they left Melbourne, the Expedition consisted of 15 men, 27 camels, 23 horses and 21 tons of equipment. They were the first explorers to use especially imported camels. Thousands of people farewelled the party from Royal Park, Melbourne on 20 August 1860 as they headed for Cooper Creek in Queensland.

Before reaching Menindee on the Darling River in New South Wales, Burke met William Wright who offered to assist the Expedition. Against the advice of the locals, because there was no 'dependable watering place … from Menindie to Duroadoo', Burke and his party set out on 19 October 1860 after dividing the group at Menindee. They reached Cooper's Creek on 11 November 1860 where Burke then left Brahe in charge. Burke, Wills, King and Gray then departed for the Gulf of Carpentaria. Although they did not reach the actual shore of the Gulf, it was close enough to declare that on 11 February 1861 the Australian continent had been crossed from south to north.

After more than four months away, Burke's party arrived back at Cooper Creek to find the supply party had left early that morning. Supplies and documents for Burke were buried under a tree marked 'Dig, 21st April 1861'. Instead of returning to Menindee, Burke, Wills and King, headed for Mount Hopeless where Burke incorrectly believed there was a cattle station. Burke and Wills perished on 28 June 1861. John King survived the ordeal and lived until September 1861 with an Aboriginal group until he was rescued and returned to Melbourne a hero.[*]

---

[*] Michael Cathcart, *Starvation in a Land of Plenty: Wills' Diary of the Fateful Burke and Wills Expedition*, p. 65–7; Alan Moorhead, *Cooper's Creek*, p. 21; Damien Cash, 'Robert O'Hara Burke (1821–61), *Oxford Companion to Australian History*, p. 97; William John Wills, *Successful Exploration Through the Interior of Australia from Melbourne to the Gulf of Carpentaria*; Dave Phoenix, *Following Burke and Wills Across Australia*; Sarah Murgatroyd, *The Dig Tree*; Tim Bonyhady, *Burke & Wills From Melbourne to Myth*, p. 132; Ian F. McLaren, 'The Victorian Exploring Expedition and Relieving Expeditions, 1860–61: The Burke and Wills Tragedy', *The Victorian Historical Magazine*, November 1959, p. 223–6.

Burke & Wills and a family story

The story of the fateful Burke and Wills expedition is one of the great accounts of European exploration of Australia. A family story connects Duncan MacGregor to the expedition and it has been quoted in numerous articles about Duncan to highlight his skills as a bushman.[70] It is based on the existence of a single undated, unsigned note held in the MacGregor Collection in the State Library of Victoria which states:

> Grandpa was managing when Burke & Wills went through. They stopped six weeks with him. He (Gpa) saw what became Broken Hill all the silver bearing stone lying about. He followed B & W out on to the Herbert River and took up Glengyle for the Donald McRae Estate having Alex Campbell manage in the name of Duncan Campbell then managing Mt Margaret. Burke & Wills found dead at Innaminka, King found on Durham Downs at lingum hole alive was with Durham D's black Taberea on Mt Howatt. Gray was found on the Georgina near Clunie Station with a sabre cut in skull.[71]

Recent investigation has revealed that the note was written by Duncan's granddaughter Margaret MacGregor (1914–75), the daughter of John (Jack) MacGregor (1872–1942), but the source of her information is quite unclear.

Duncan MacGregor was managing a pastoral run on the Darling River when Burke and Wills 'went through' the area in October 1860. The 'Grandpa' who later took up Glengyle for the Donald McRae Estate was Duncan MacGregor. Diary notes made by Herman Beckler and Ludwig Becker indicate that when the expedition reached the Darling River they first stopped at McPherson's run near Bilbarka.[72] From Bilbarka the expedition followed the east bank of the Darling upstream as far as Kinchega, where William Wright helped them cross to the west side of the river.[73]

MacGregor's Menindee notebooks commence on 15 April 1860. They continue with entries for 18, 21 and 28 April; 1 and 24 May; 27 August and 14 November. The gap in entries between the end of August and the middle of November may indicate MacGregor's absence from Menindee Station. Alternatively, it may mean that he was not in a position to write notes on cattle or other station matters. While it is clear from these dates that MacGregor and Wright worked for the same employer from April to October 1860, it cannot be assumed that both MacGregor and Wright left Menindee together in order to guide Burke and Wills out to Cooper Creek.

The recently published travelogue, *Following Burke and Wills Across Australia*, traces the expedition. There is no mention of MacGregor in David Phoenix's analysis of their journey between Bilbarka and Cooper Creek. As MacGregor was the 'Grandpa' mentioned in the note it is surprising that details are not contained in the files. Where did the story come from?

It is proposed by one family member that on his return from Torowoto and Cooper Creek, Wright spoke glowingly to MacGregor about the pastures beyond Menindee. Later reports may also have encouraged MacGregor to attempt to find land to lease in western Queensland. However, this does not account for the intriguing note and the long-held family belief. The Mount Margaret, Glengyle, Durham Downs and Clunie Stations are also mentioned in the note. Mount Margaret Station on the Wilson River in Queensland was purchased by Donald McRae; it was later managed by Duncan Campbell for the McRae Estate. Glengyle Station on the Herbert River (later renamed the Georgina River) was leased by MacGregor in 1874 for the McRae Estate. MacGregor, with two partners, leased Durham Downs, close to Mount Margaret, in 1874. These stations were the most well-known of MacGregor's properties.

There are two 'Clunie' Stations in this story: one was the McRae residence in Chintin, Victoria. Another 'Cluny' Station is located on the Georgina River, 200 km north of the South Australian border near Bedourie. It was not a MacGregor Station. Although a connection between Clunie/Cluny Station and MacGregor does not exist, MacGregor's Glengyle Station is immortalised in 'Bedourie Pub an Old Queensland Ballard' by Anon. This poem celebrates the isolation of the Bedourie Pub, its drovers and its camel teams camped on the Georgina River. Two lines in particular reference Glengyle Station and its Scottish owners.[74]

The final sentence of the mysterious note states that Gray was found with a sabre cut in his skull. While it is documented that Gray died on 17 April 1861, and it is thought partly through ill-treatment by Burke, it has not been proved conclusively. David Phoenix writes that Charles Gray died at Camp 58R when the party were just a few days away from reaching Cooper Creek. In October 1861 John McKinlay, leading the first rescue team, found a grave he considered to be of Charles Gray at a place called Lake Massacre, near Coongie Lake, not far from Innamincka.

McKinlay reported that he thought Gray's wound was a sabre cut on the skull he found in the grave; this gave rise to speculation that Burke had killed Gray.[75]

The Victorian Exploration Expedition to the Gulf of Carpentaria, and the expedition by the South Australian John McDouall Stuart to cross the continent from south to north, were the most well-publicised adventures to take place in eastern Australia in 1860–61. Newspaper articles kept the country informed of Burke and Wills' progress. Local newspapers carried stories of the expedition: pastoralists and their families and workers, and people in Menindee and Wilcannia, would have been very aware of their journey, especially as they spent time in the district.

With such a famous expedition in the locality, some of the locals may have been keen to ride out to the Darling to meet and converse with the explorers. It is possible that Duncan satisfied his curiosity in this way. However, research into the official papers of the expedition fails to mention MacGregor's name as a paid or voluntary participant in the expedition. It seems unlikely that Duncan MacGregor took part in any official or unofficial capacity in the Victorian Exploration Expedition.

Duncan MacGregor was, however, justifiably proud of his achievements as an explorer and pastoralist. It has been said of him that so great was his navigation skill, he could set out without a compass and walk one square mile and return to exactly the spot he departed.[76]

Although Duncan MacGregor was eventually known as a great explorer of south-west Queensland, it does not explain the small, undated family document. This document has been a trusted and vital piece of family history for decades. The story remains baffling.

Steady in his habits: working in outback New South Wales

A black-rimmed envelope from Scotland containing black-rimmed notepaper and the news of the death of his father on 29 April 1862 was addressed to Duncan at Menindee. In the middle of May, Duncan's sisters Annie and Maggie also wrote to him with the news. Both letters were lengthy and emotionally charged. Both sisters pleaded with Duncan to return home to Scotland to help them. Both letters illustrate the depth of love they felt for him and the esteem in which he was held. They are moving letters and the pain at the death of their father and the consequent pain at having to move from the family home is palpable.[77]

The family moved from Ewich to Portsonachan, where Duncan's mother ran a farm, a ferry service and a hotel successfully for many years. The death of his father was the first but not the last time his sisters begged him to return to Scotland, yet he showed no signs of wanting to leave his new life in Australia and his sisters' pleas were ignored. Some months later, in August 1862, his sister Maggie wrote once again to let him know that their mother's health was failing. We have no sense of the emotional strain Duncan may have felt.

Duncan's diary entries, quoting sermons and psalms, indicate he was a man with a strong religious faith. He took his Presbyterianism seriously. On the death of his father we imagine he took what solace he could from prayer. He may have sought comfort in letters from home. His family remained regular correspondents, although they frequently complained when he moved and did not send a forwarding address. One letter in particular, date-stamped 13 May 1862, was addressed to him at 'Menindee Station, Darling River, via Moorulan, Sydney, New South Wales, Australia'. This well-travelled letter was stamped in Edinburgh, London, Sydney, Gundagai, Tarcutta, Deniliquin, and at least five other places that cannot be deciphered. At the earliest, it would have reached him in late July 1862. We believe the letter followed him from Menindee Station to Mount Murchison Station.

Mount Murchison Station

Duncan MacGregor was ambitious and clever. He had progressed to becoming the manager of Mount Murchison Station after he left Menindee Station. He combined hard toil with a strong work ethic to achieve his goals and ultimate fortune.

Located on the upper Darling River, Mount Murchison Station was 100 miles north-east and upriver from Menindee and owned by Ross and William Reid.[78] Ross and William were the sons of John and Jane Reid of Newry, County Down, Ireland. John Reid had been involved in shipping in the British Isles. Once they emigrated to Australia, the family lived first in New South Wales and then in Van Diemen's Land. The brothers acquired first-hand knowledge of the pastoral industry in two colonies.

In October 1838, with his family and servants, John Reid sailed from Van Diemen's Land on the *Orleana* to South Australia. Keen to rebuild his depleted fortunes, he took up 4,000 acres of a Special Survey Grant, but by 1852 he had lost most of his money. His son Ross tried his luck on the Californian goldfields and then went on to the Victorian gold fields before travelling to the Darling River. While their father was not a natural farmer, his two sons were. In 1857 the Reid brothers took up the abandoned Mount Murchison Run, fenced the paddocks, built water tanks and wells and improved the existing hut before erecting a new homestead, more outbuildings and a woolshed.[79]

Because of their isolation and the prohibitive cost of transport, some leaseholders on the Darling River chose to go into the transport business themselves, purchasing river steamers for the purpose. This was their best option for transporting their wool to the markets and transhipment to the English woollen mills. The Reid3s business increased rapidly and when in the late 1860s they built a new woolshed, it comprised 52 shearing stands.[80] This was sheep shearing on an industrial scale. The Ross brothers employed dozens of men: it was a vast estate.

In 1865 while working at Mount Murchison, Duncan MacGregor met and befriended the Englishman, Frederic Bonney. The son of Thomas Bonney (1802–53) and Eliza Ellen née Smith (1815–95), the family were of Huguenot background, descendants of French Protestants who fled persecution in the 17th century. The seventh of eleven children and the youngest son, Frederic Bonney arrived in Melbourne in August 1865. An older brother, Edward Bonney, had arrived in Australia in 1859 and worked for Hugh and Bushby Jamieson, who leased a number of runs (the original Jamieson's Run) near the junction of the Darling and Paroo rivers.

In coming to Australia, Frederic and Edward were following in the footsteps of their uncle, Charles Bonney (1813–97). Charles had accompanied the pioneer explorer Joseph Hawdon and the two had opened up the overland stock route along the Murray from the eastern colonies to South Australia in 1838.[81] It is thought that Frederic travelled by riverboat down the Murray from Swan Hill to Wentworth, then up the Darling to Mount Murchison to join Edward, who was already established on the Paroo River at Momba Station. By that stage, Ross Reid was managing the various properties together as Mount Murchison Station.

Bonney was a keen photographer and was very likely the first Englishman to photograph local Aboriginal tribes in the Australian outback. His collection of photographs dates back to 1865, the year of his arrival. In particular the collection includes a photograph entitled

'Mount Murchison Station, River Darling', showing the homestead and a group of around twenty Aboriginal workers. Photography involved the use of glass plates. This must have presented great difficulties for a photographer in remote areas: the wet plate had to be prepared in the field and used within twenty minutes; it then had to be processed immediately in a portable dark tent. Bonney would have travelled with about 50 kg of equipment. His remarkable photographs document decades of the outback's pastoral history and its indigenous inhabitants.[82]

Bonney and MacGregor worked together at Mount Murchison from 1865. Their friendship continued until Bonney left Australia in 1881. From Bonney's account they shared valuable and memorable experiences and they enjoyed reminiscing about their time together. More than 33 years after he left Australia, Bonney was able to recollect, with help of his notebooks, the number of cattle on Mount Murchison station in 1879. He wrote:

> My dear Old Friend
>
> It was nice to receive your interesting letter in January recalling our association in the faraway bush, our experiences there, our many kind friends and fellowships so general, the hardships as well as fond times are *often* in my mind. Happily my recollection of trials and troubles there are less impressed on my mind now and I can greater enjoy the recollection of that period of my former life. Although I am in the 'Evening of my life' I do not feel so old … I am sorry that you cannot give a better report of the country in our old district … on 'Momba'; it is sad that it has so much depreciated … I have heard that the management has for some years been peculiar but from what you say I judge that the seasons have been bad – at the end of the '70s (1879) the stock on *Momba Mt Murchison* was:
>
> Sheep: 330,000   Cattle: 9,000
>
> These figures I have recorded on the first page of an album containing about 150 photographs (of my own taking) of Momba Station, creeks, and other scenes on the run also Aborigines. These pictures constantly uphold memory of scenes and bygone friends (whites and blacks). I want to get a map of the country as it now is. My survey I made in pegging out the lines for fencing paddocks was I thought fairly accurate. I made a careful plan of paddocks and features of the country. Ranges, creeks, lakes etc. The Surveyor General (Du Faur) had it lithographed in Sydney and sent me a print. I should like to see what changes have since been made on Momba & Mt Murchison …

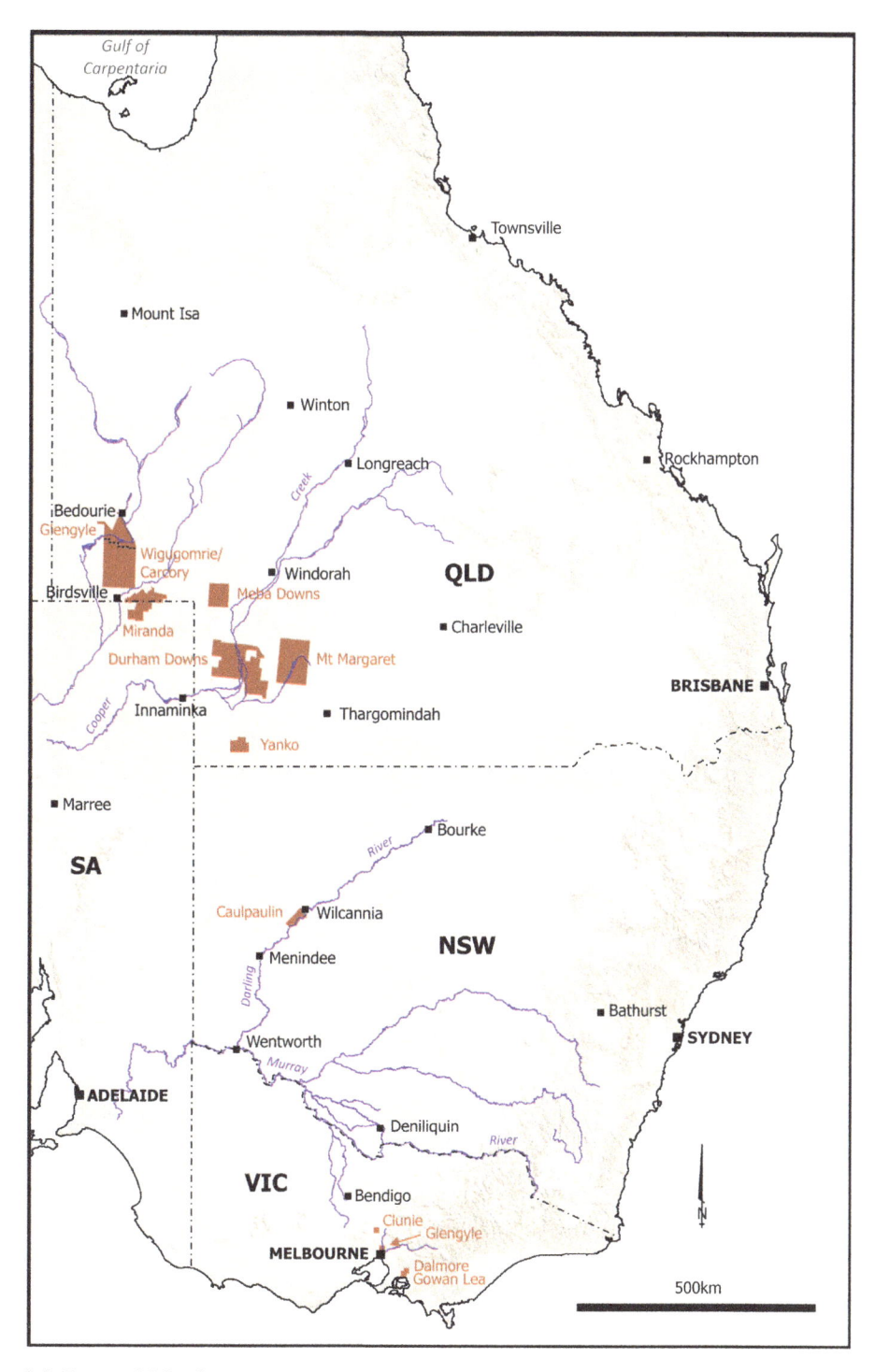

McRae and MacGregor properties in Queensland, New South Wales and Victoria, 1884

Map by Colin Pike, Magnetic North Design

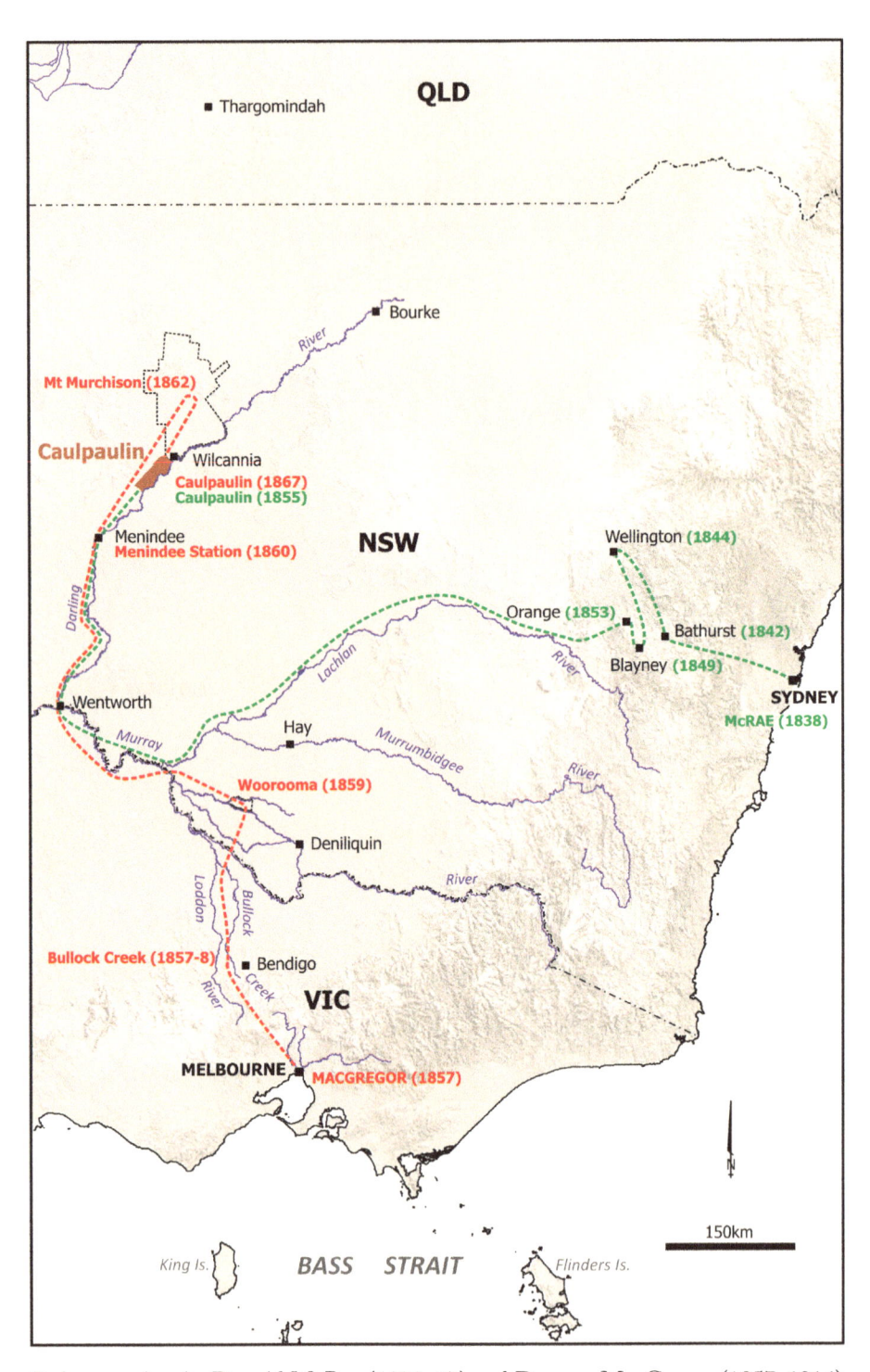

Pathways taken by Donald McRae (1838–67) and Duncan MacGregor (1857–1916)
Map by Colin Pike, Magnetic North Design

Bonney had retained his interest in the pastoral station and kept abreast of the Australian situation. When he wrote to MacGregor in 1914 he knew that there had been good rain over Queensland but not much had fallen in the Darling River side of New South Wales. He said 'tell your wife that I well remember my visits to Caulpaulin and the hospitable reception I *always* had from them all'.[83] MacGregor may have been pleased to read that the specimen of opal he gave Bonney when they parted in 1881 'still delights me and my friends with the beauty of their colours in such rarity'. The opal is now displayed at the Colton House Museum, Staffordshire, where Bonney lived. It also has displays of the artefacts he collected from Momba Station.[84]

While there is some reason to speculate on the timing of MacGregor's departure from Mount Murchison, it is clear he left that Station in 1867 not 1868 as previously believed. His letter of reference is dated 18 June 1867. Ross Reid writes:

> This is to certify that the Bearer Mr Duncan MacGregor has been well known to me for some time and that he has been on my Employment as manager of the 'Mount Murchison Station' for upwards of three years and I have much pleasure in certifying that during that time he has given me the highest satisfaction in his Management. Also that he is of sober and industrious habits and that he is now leaving my Employ, of his own free will, with a view to better his fortunes and it will be my greatest pleasure to hear of his success in all his future undertakings in whatever part of the World his lot may be cast.
>
> Prop. Ross Reid[85]

Reid's words echo those of Duncan's employer in Scotland, ten years earlier, and his desire to better his fortunes. It also emphasises his 'sober and industrious' habits. Did Reid know that MacGregor was going to Donald McRae's Caulpaulin Station, the neighbouring property, when he accepted his resignation? It seems likely.

Donald McRae and Caulpaulin Station – a brief family history

Donald McRae, the son of John and Isabella McRae of Lochalsh, Ross Shire, Scotland, was born 8 October 1816.[86] His father was a tenant farmer on the Balmacara Estate on the Kyle of Lochalsh.[87] Donald was the eldest of four sons and one daughter. When he left Scotland bound for Australia in 1838, he was 22 years old. His younger brothers Finlay, Farquhar and Duncan were 13, 10 and 6 respectively; his sister Margaret was just 2 years old. It was more than a decade before he saw his family on Australian soil.

When he decided to emigrate in 1838, Donald was amongst thousands of Highlanders doing so. Family folklore has it that he came to Australia by special invitation because of his experience in the handling of stock. It is also said that his employer helped him and other young men from Ross Shire to emigrate.[88] Details are lost to time, but his employer may have assisted by encouraging him to apply to one of the major merchants for a passage. Donald travelled to Australia as a bounty passenger on the *James Pattison;* it sailed from Plymouth on 29 August 1838.[89] The ship's register records that he was 'Imported' by the London merchant, John Marshall, for a bounty of £18. The *James Pattison* was an emigrant sailing ship of 573 tons, built in London in 1828. Her life was short but memorable. Amongst other journeys, she transported convicts to New South Wales between 1830 and 1840.[90]

The captain's log of the 1838 voyage describes the passengers as 'around 300 emigrants "of the usual description" who were in good health'. There were five births during the voyage and eleven deaths amongst the children. In the steerage class were 182 adults and 85 children. Amongst the steerage passengers, Donald was one of thirteen single men, including two other shepherds from Ross Shire, and eight single women. Crossing the sea was especially uncomfortable for those who travelled steerage, on the lowest deck and below the water line; it was usually the poorest, including bounty passengers, who travelled in this way.[91]

While a small number of diaries kept by educated migrants exist in archives across Australia, the illiterate could not commit their stories to paper. These stories have often survived as family folklore. One such family account concerns Donald's arrival on the *James Pattison* in Sydney on 11 December 1838.[92] A newspaper article about him, written decades later, has it that, when he landed in Sydney 'in his kilts', the sailors on the vessel presented him with his first pair of trousers.[93] Whether true or not, this evocative anecdote highlights the Scot's spirit as well as the camaraderie between passengers and crew.

Various bounty schemes to finance and encourage emigration were at their peak in the late 1830s. Between 1838 and 1842 a total of 3,416 Scots were brought out under these schemes.[94] The Bathurst pastoralist George Ranken was one of many Scots assisting single men and their families to come to Australia.[95] Ranken, who had come to New South Wales as a free settler in 1822, became very successful after taking out numerous pastoral leases. After disembarking in Sydney, Donald found work around Bathurst, the oldest inland settlement in Australia.[96] He would almost certainly have met Ranken and may have worked for him at some stage. In the nineteenth century wool was a significant part of Bathurst's rural economy and in 1838 when Donald arrived, shepherds like him were in great demand. The importation of Scottish Highlanders to the region greatly influenced Bathurst's culture, economically and socially.

Working and wedding in New South Wales, 1842

Donald McRae married Christina McKenzie at St Stephens Presbyterian Church, Bathurst, on 14 April 1842.[97]

Donald and Christina had much in common. Born on 27 March 1816, Christina was the eldest daughter of Roderick and Barbara McKenzie of Loch Broom, Ross Shire, Scotland. With her parents and siblings, she emigrated to Australia in 1838. They sailed on the *James Moran*, one of Reverend Lang's bounty ships, departing Loch Broom on 13 October 1838. Christina's father was a farmer aged 50; her mother was then aged 46. When she left Scotland Christina was, like Donald, 22; her sister Arrabella, 20; her two brothers, John and Kenneth, 18 and 14.[98]

Their journey on the *James Moran* was long and exhausting; after 122 days at sea they arrived at Port Jackson on 11 February 1839. On landing, Roderick McKenzie did not ingratiate himself: he was 'Expelled the Buildings for refusing 40 pounds per year'.[99] That is, when work was arranged for him at £40 per year with rations, he refused the offer. What did he envisage was the alternative? The family travelled to Bathurst, as Donald had done months before them. Once there, McKenzie found work and shelter.

Christina and Donald McRae probably met at the Presbyterian Church in Bathurst. After their marriage the couple did not stay in Bathurst but lived in Wellington, 97 miles away, where the twins Roderick and Mary were born on 1 November 1844. They were baptised on 20 May 1845 but died in infancy. Their third child, Isabella (Bell), was also born at

Wellington, on 17 March 1847, and baptised on 22 August. Margaret (Maggie) was born at Blayney, 37 miles south of Bathurst, on 20 June 1849, and baptised on 26 March 1850. Their last child, Anna (always known as Annie), was born at Orange, 34 miles west of Bathurst, on 27 March 1853 and baptised on 15 January 1854.[100]

Donald McRae quickly adopted the ways of the new country, including the customs of 'back country' cattle stations. While working for local pastoralists it is said he 'collected' stock of his own and put his own brand on them. Was there an element of the 'gully raker' in Donald McRae? Don Watson describes a 'gully raker' as someone who 'gathered stray cleanskin stock and put their own brand on them'. These men 'began their careers as a "gully rakers", and ended their lives much wealthier'![101] This was McRae's story. In due course, his employer expressed some astonishment at the number of stock bearing McRae's brand. Inevitably, he was ordered to muster his cattle and clear out! When he left the Bathurst region he took his own 700 head of mixed cattle down the Lachlan River before making his way up to the Darling River.[102]

The McRae family reunited, 1853

As Donald and Christina were raising a family and breeding cattle and sheep in the 1840s and 1850s in New South Wales, the plight of the Scottish farmer did not improve. For those who remained, the land clearances continued with devastating effects. In 1851, Sir Alexander Matheson purchased the feudal barony of Lochalsh, further reducing the land available for tenant farming in Ross Shire. Highland families were dependent on herring fishing, kelp collecting and their staple crops of potatoes, but in 1846 the potato blight struck, the kelp industry collapsed and herring fishing declined. Most Highlanders were faced with starvation and poverty. Emigration seemed the only answer for survival. Donald's success as a cattle farmer and breeder must surely have encouraged his parents and the rest of the family to join their son in Australia. They did this through the assistance of the Highland and Islands Emigration Society. Between 1852 and 1857 this particular society sent 4,910 men, women and children to Australia from the Western Isles and western Scotland.[103]

The McRae family group departed Liverpool on the *Arabian* on 26 October 1852 and arrived in Melbourne on 15 February 1853. Donald's father, John, was then aged 66, and his mother, Isabella, 62. John McRae was ready to embrace the opportunities his adopted country offered, and Donald's brothers Finlay, 28, Farquhar, 25, Duncan, 21, and sister Margaret, 17, could anticipate many years of fruitful work ahead. Most of the family remained in Victoria in preference to travelling north to join Donald in Bathurst. Duncan made his way up to Bathurst to work with his older brother and remained there for more than ten years. Donald's father survived only five years in Victoria. He fell ill a week before he died from 'natural decay' or pneumonia at Donnybrook, Victoria on 24 July 1858, aged 72 years. He was buried at Campbellfield Cemetery on 26 July 1858.[104]

A run of his own – Caulpaulin Station, 1855

After seventeen years of working for men like George Ranken in Bathurst and Joseph Smith at Georges Plains, a 39-year-old Donald McRae had proved himself to be a capable and successful manager and breeder of sheep and cattle. With new pasture land opening up on the Darling River, he decided to take a chance in this new region. Claiming rich pasture in the great expanse of Australia must have been every immigrant's dream. In June 1855, with 700 head, a resourceful nature and knowledge of stock, he decided to tender for the lease of three runs on the Darling River: Caulpaulin, Netallie and Bonley. Together they were known as Caulpaulin Station. Prior to the lease, he engaged Messrs Dalmahoy Campbell & Co. of Melbourne to assess the properties. The cost of assessing each run was £10; with a commission of 2%, the total cost amounted to £30/15/-.[105] This was a significant sum, given that the rental on each property was £75 per annum.

McRae's application for the lease of the three runs in the Albert District was successful. It was confirmed in the Supplement to the *New South Wales Government Gazette* of Tuesday 3 June 1856. Details of the runs were: No. 18 Bonley, 94½ square miles; No. 19 Netallie, 80 square miles; and No. 20 Culpaulin, 100 square miles – a total area of 274 square miles in the region south of today's Wilcannia township.[106] Each run had a capacity to graze 640 cattle.[107] An indication of the vastness of the properties is the fact that the land is described in square miles rather than acres.

It is hard to imagine the isolation felt by the early settlers on the Darling River in 1855 when Donald and Christina made their home there. Christina had three small girls to care for: Isabella, who was 8, Margaret, 6, and Annie, 2. Accommodation was basic. An undated drawing of the three runs shows a sparse property containing fencing and some buildings.[108] On the Netallie run, the drawing includes yards, hut and a house on the banks of the river. The Caulpaulin run has a house, horse shed, wool shed and yards on the banks of the river. The family would have lived in the largest house on Caulpaulin. It could not have had any of the comforts available in country towns such as Bathurst, Wellington or Blayney, yet it proved to have other benefits.

Historian Sandra Maiden investigates the rich history of the Darling River and Menindee, its first township. She writes about the pastoralists who first explored and occupied these vast pastures.[109] Her study describes the patterns of settlement and the churn of prospectors; it paints evocative portraits of the clever and the ambitious, those who made it, and those who were eventually forced to sell out through lack of experience or funds. It also documents the attacks on the Aborigines on the Darling from the 1850s onwards, something Donald McRae would have witnessed at first hand. It was a volatile time when the ownership of traditional Aboriginal land was still hotly contested.

Both the settlers and the local Aboriginal population of the Darling River region lived in fear of attack and the deaths of white settlers and Aboriginal men and women continued. It is illuminating to see that in 1863 Richard Gibson wrote to McRae asking him to 'send [Aboriginal] skulls, three or four if you can get them and state what tribe they belong to and any other particulars'. Gibson intended to send them to England to a doctor friend for examination and study. It seems likely that he satisfied Gibson's request.[110]

As an independent grazier, McRae needed to obtain the best price for his cattle and sheep. He also needed a good stock agent and a reliable stock route to Sydney, Adelaide and Melbourne. Correspondence between Richard Gibson and McRae indicates that he had a strong and friendly relationship with his Melbourne agent, Dalmahoy Campbell & Co.

The company's founder was Dalmahoy (Dal) Campbell (1811–67). The son of Campbell of Lochend, he was born in the Isle of Skye, Scotland. He arrived in New South Wales in 1821 and took up a station near Wellington. In 1838, with Evelyn Sturt, brother of the explorer Charles

Sturt, he overlanded stock to Adelaide.[111] He was married in Sydney in 1840, and was appointed general manager of all stations belonging to the Royal Bank in 1842. He arrived in Melbourne and in 1845 and entered into partnership, initially with William Morris Harper, as a stock and station agent. The company was styled Dalmahoy Campbell & Co., and he remained in business until his death in 1867.[112]

Richard Gibson was McRae's main contact at Dal Campbell & Co. They corresponded frequently. Gibson, born in 1831, was an Ayrshire man who had arrived in Port Phillip in 1852. He worked first in the office of Mickle and Bakewell, stock and station agents, but soon left to start an ironmongery business. After a short experiment with this type of work, he joined another stock agency, Kissock and Lyall, before being taken into partnership with Dal Campbell & Co. in 1858. He managed this business until 1872, when he began trading in his own right.[113]

Clever and talented though he was, our Scottish Highlander, Donald McRae, had to overcome one major difficulty in business: he could neither read nor write. However, he boasted that his eldest daughter, Isabella, took care of this side of the business and kept his books. She probably took dictation from her father or composed the letters herself and read incoming correspondence to him. He credited his great prosperity to Isabella, who took care of the clerical work of the station while he was out 'yackering' on the run.[114]

Letters from Gibson and others at Dal Campbell cover a range of topics from friendly discourse about his growing family to serious advice on the purchase of land and stock. While he may not have been able to read or write, to the frustration of his agents, he possessed the intelligence to make up his own mind, sometimes against the advice he was given. He clearly had his own ambitions yet at the same time realised his limitations. Settlement on the Darling River continued and McRae's business was making a profit. Queensland was being opened up in the late 1850s and McRae began to speculate. On the advice of Dal Campbell, he eventually acquired land in Queensland.

The colonies of New South Wales and Queensland separated in 1859. A Chief Commissioner of Crown Lands was appointed and local commissioners were made directly responsible to the Chief Commissioner instead of the Colonial Secretary. The question of who should occupy the land and whether it was to be used for pastoral or agricultural purposes became known as the 'land question' in Queensland in the late 1850s.[115]

At the time of separation Queensland's three and a half million sheep and half a million cattle occupied about a quarter of the new colony. Squatters contributed 70% of the revenue and 94% of the exports: pastoralism was Queensland's major income stream.[116]

In 1860 Queensland's premier, Sir Robert Herbert, introduced legislation aimed to attract ambitious squatters from the southern states. The terms of the 1860 Land Act were generous: anyone could apply for a one-year licence to occupy a run of one hundred square miles; and within nine months the occupier could apply for a 14-year lease on the condition of having stocked the run to one fourth of its assumed capacity of one hundred sheep or twenty head of cattle to the mile. Before 1860 the practice of registering runs without occupying or stocking them frustrated potential settlers, who were forced to look further afield. The new Act successfully stimulated the pastoral industry and brought a new wave of settlers from the southern colonies. As Fitzgerald writes, the two dominant features that characterised the men of the new pastoral frontier were 'restlessness and recklessness'.[117] The squatters were restless to acquire new land and often reckless with their money. Land was divided into pastoral districts, each controlled by a commissioner. Three new districts were 'thrown open' for settlement. They were Warrego, Kennedy and Mitchell. As one squatter's daughter commented years later: 'Nothing else was thought of or discussed. Everyone was infatuated with the desire to possess a run in Queensland.' The excitement was nearly equal to that of the gold rush seven or eight years earlier.[118] The land issue was all-consuming.

In 1864 Dal Campbell advised McRae to purchase some blocks of land in the 'back country' of Queensland. Gibson wrote: 'We enclose a sketch of some blocks that adjoins your country which is for sale in this place by Mr Brown, the price is £1,500 … even if they are no good they are well worth the money to you so as to improve the value of your property'. McRae expanded his holdings into Queensland in c.1865–6 when he leased six runs on the Wilson River in the South Gregory and Warrego Districts, over 370 miles (600 km) north of Caulpaulin. He named his new pastoral Station Mount Margaret. The first runs in Donald McRae's name were: Delga East, Delga West, Kowroungalla East, Kowroungalla West, Kalboora East and Kalboora West. In 1866–7 Dal Campbell encouraged him to take up additional runs: Boorarie South, Boorarie North, Ulloomunta, Aros, Cathoo and Cairn. They were taken up in his wife Christina McRae's name. She was possibly the only woman to have taken up runs in her own name. Other runs were subsequently added to the station in later years.

One letter to McRae from the Land Agent at Mount Murchison (the town not Reid's station) refers to land receipts from 'Mr Bryant for allotments purchased by you on the 26th September last'.[119] This letter is the only indication that Mount Margaret was first leased in 1866.

In February 1867, Dal Campbell corresponded with McRae about the properties on the Wilson River he had taken up: 'you should forward … [the documents] to McDonald so that he can produce them to the district commissioner and get the occupation licence after which we can apply for the leases, be sure and attend to this and see that it is not mismanaged.[120] The following month, in March 1867, McRae's station manager, Neil Macdonald, confirmed the acquisition of additional blocks of land. Although a lengthy letter, it is worth quoting in full:

> In reference to your letter of 21 Sept to Mr Macrae I beg to inform you that I have forwarded to your agent in Ipswich the necessary declarations of having stocked the Country, with applications for Occupation Licence signed by me before by Mr Chester Commissioner for the Unsettled District of Warrego under the impression that you had authorised him to act for Mr McRae.
>
> As the applications have to be made to the Chief Commissioner direct I think the quickest way is to send you back the scrips so that you can forward them to Mr Hendren with instructions to secure the six blocks of Country for Mr McRae as quick as possible as [the Wilson River is not in any proclaimed Unsettled District] the Government will not grant a Lease of any Country until it is proclaimed an Unsettled District so the Occupation License will have to be applied for every twelve months.
>
> If my letter to Mr Hendren has not miscarried he (which I think hardly possible) has all the information necessary to secure the Country.
>
> I remain Gentlemen, your obedient servant, N Macdonald.[121]

As McRae did not read or write, ensuring that someone who knew the routine and could fill in the paperwork was essential, hence Macdonald's letter advising that applications had to be made to the Chief Commissioner himself.

Education was as important to Christina and Donald as it was to many Scottish immigrants, but there were no schools on the Darling. A governess was engaged to educate the girls, though in such a remote location it was realised that she might not stay long. In March 1864, a letter from Gibson to McRae noted that 'we have had to give her £80 per year, but we think she is well worth the money.[122] In 1864 when the new governess arrived the girls were 17, 14 and 11 years of age.[123]

As well as welcoming the new governess, the McRae family, and especially Donald, welcomed the arrival of a new set of bagpipes ordered from Melbourne in 1864. A letter from Richard Gibson tells the story of his expedition with Mr Abercrombie and Mr McIntyre, 'a thorough judge of pipes'. Together they went along to William Glen's shop where they purchased a set of pipes for £14/10/-. William Henderson Glen was born in Edinburgh in 1825 and had arrived in Melbourne in 1853 'under engagement to the firm of Messrs Joseph Wilkie and Co.', the predecessors of Allan & Co. Five years later he began his own business as a music-seller in Bourke Street. His business was so successful he moved to larger premises.[124] The bagpipes were hand-delivered to Caulpaulin by Mr Abercrombie and the excitement at their arrival can be imagined.[125]

Much of the regular correspondence between McRae and Dal Campbell dealt with prices for cattle, sheep, freight, cartage and shipping expenses. Sometimes statements of account arrived, showing his balance or that of his brother Duncan's account. Duncan McRae appears to have begun working for his brother around 1860. McRae's cattle are sometimes referred to as the 'Menindee cattle', denoting the location. On one occasion they received a great compliment from a Melbourne newspaper: 'They were as a lot the finest draft of cattle we have seen for a long time from the North, being very prime as well as heavy weights'. They were walked from Caulpaulin via Deniliquin and Echuca before reaching the Melbourne market.

Clunie at Chintin, 1865

Donald McRae's friends James Tom and Ken McDonnell were pastoralists with stations on the Lachlan River.[126] In 1858 James Tom and his wife Marion bought the large property Chintin Grange at Chintin in the Shire of Romsey in central Victoria.[127] Around the same time Ken McDonnell bought a property near Chintin Grange and named it Glengarry. It was a clever strategic move for Tom and McDonnell to purchase land in this area. McRae and his fellow Scots knew their land and their stock and supported each other in their pastoral pursuits. Perhaps with their encouragement the brothers William and Thomas Wragge sold 910 acres to Donald McRae on 20 April 1865. It was Crown Allotments 51 and 52, Block A, Crown Portion 22 and Part Crown Portion 21 in the Parish of Chintin, County of Bourke.[128] Its boundaries were Government Road (now Romsey Road) to the north and the Deep Creek to the south.

This part of central Victoria was almost at the end of the southern stock route heading along the Deep Creek before cutting across to the Melbourne Road. The fertile hills of Chintin and Darraweit Guim offered abundant pasture for grazing cattle and sheep.[129]

When the Scots, Irish and English immigrant farmers at Darraweit Guim and Chintin settled in the area 50 miles north of Melbourne in the 1840s and 1850s, they grazed cattle and sheep and produced cereal crops and potatoes. They loaded their produce onto bullock wagons for Melbourne, or for the nearby Clarkefield Railway Station. Originally known as 'Lancefield Road', this station on the Sunbury–Woodend line opened in 1861; by 1864 the line had extended to Kyneton, Bendigo and Echuca on the Victorian–New South Wales border.[130] Chintin was therefore a significant location for McRae to transport stock between New South Wales and Victoria.

When he first purchased the land at Chintin, the property included an existing residence with commanding views of the surrounding landscape. McRae named the property Clunie; the origin of its name is unknown. A hand-drawn map forming part of the history of the Darraweit Guim School shows the close locations of Clunie, Chintin Grange and Glengarry, the homes owned by the McRae, Tom and McDonnell families.[131]

The original farmhouse at Chintin was probably constructed for the Wragge brothers. In early 1867, McRae commissioned the builder David Mitchell, father of Helen Porter Mitchell, later the famous opera singer Dame Nellie Melba, to construct a new homestead on the property. The house, which still stands, is a two-storey stuccoed stone villa with a slate roof.[132] When the property was put on the market for sale in 1923, it was described as having a 'typically spacious farm kitchen' with maid's quarters nearby, a large dining room, a billiard room and a lounge. It also boasted two bathrooms and a large cellar under the kitchen. This part of the house may well be a remnant of the original homestead. Upstairs there are four bedrooms reached by a staircase renowned for being made in England especially for Clunie, although this cannot be verified. The house is still set in a sheltered lawn and garden surrounded by giant pine trees. The property includes a three-bedroom manager's house and a solid three-stand shearing shed and wool press. Outbuildings to the rear of the main house, and visible today from the hill opposite, include a machinery shed, shearers' quarters, workshop, haysheds, silos, combined sheep and cattle yards and stables for four horses.[133] It was a fine Victorian villa, suitable for a man who could relax and enjoy the good fortune he had earned after a life of hard work.

Maggie McRae and Duncan MacGregor – an 1868 wedding

While working at Mount Murchison Station, Duncan MacGregor would have been well aware that the nearby Caulpaulin Station was owned by Donald and Christina McRae. The properties shared a common boundary. Despite the distances between properties, the Darling River pastoralists knew each other and were a community, largely of Scots.

Donald's younger brother, Duncan, worked at Caulpaulin and family history includes this story from him. He wrote that when he was out on a boundary one day at Caulpaulin a man rode up and asked for a job. Duncan 'sent him on to his brother Donald who took him on'. The rider was Duncan MacGregor.'[134]

As one family member asks, was Duncan keen to work at Caulpaulin because he knew that McRae had already taken up country in western Queensland? Was this a region MacGregor was keen to work in and saw opportunities for himself?

It may seem surprising that Duncan McRae was not appointed as manager of Caulpaulin instead of Duncan MacGregor. Duncan's appointment in 1867 may have been the beginning of a long-standing rivalry between Duncan McRae and Duncan MacGregor.

Duncan MacGregor would almost certainly have been considered an eligible bachelor. Long before he reached the Reid's station he had proved himself to be a prospective station manager; he was a personable young man whose good and sober habits were often noted. In agreeing to manage Caulpaulin or Mount Margaret on the Wilson River, did he also hope to marry one of McRae's daughters? Could he have been attracted to Isabella McRae or it possible that Duncan was already in love with Maggie McRae? Suitable women of marriageable age were in short supply in the bush. For young women, also, the bush offered only a small field of appropriate men.

Duncan's notebooks, written between 1860 and 1868, contain pages of love poetry and reveal a romantic sensibility. Some poems are in his own hand, some in another. Of the poems transcribed by him, some are authored, while others are untitled and conclude with the initials 'DM' or 'D McG'.

> *The Old Love*
> The roaming season comes and goes
> In each like flowers fresh passive blow
> They bud they blossom they decay
> And, from my heart they pass away
> But still the old love dieth not
> Soft passive tender warm and gay
> But transient as an April day
> Each in his short but potent reign
> Sweeps like a flood through heart and brain
> But that love it giveth not
> Listen ye breezes ye who decree
> Oer the black waves to sunny France
> I have a message ye must leave
> To some fain maid who dwelleth their
> Tell her the Old love dieth not
>
> By E.H. Pember[135]

In another flourish MacGregor wrote:

> A lovely bud, so soft and fair
> Called hence my early doom
> Its sent to show how sweet a flower
> In paradise would bloom
> D McG

And in this poem he is declaring his love for another:

> I said to my heart to my faithful heart
> I could not love but one
> So thou sweet dear my heart is sincere in loving thee alone
> And no other one my bosom shares, while ere in life am I
> But thou sweet maid I love so dear
> Shall be my guiding Sun
> So angle [*sic*] dear I do declare that no other one but you
> Can share my heart as all my love I have long given to you
> So thou alone just holds the seal that opens through my breast
> And hope secure may it be with you while I am on this earth
> As thou dear Maggie is my guide through life's long troubled year
> To share with me in sorrow likewise in all that is dear
> As Lilly June and guiding star my paths you will all true out
> And hope oh happy you may be with me
> Though in a humble country
>
> DM[136]

The pages of poetry are undated, but we may well assume that his 'dear Maggie' is Margaret McRae.

Death and disruption in the McRae family, 1867

In 1867 Donald McRae was eager to move into his new homestead at Chintin. He had taken the whole family to Victoria in February and then returned to settle up his affairs and to make sure the manager knew his instructions. However, in early April 1867 he received news that his eldest daughter, Isabella, was gravely ill. A young friend, John Barry, then staying in Wentworth, was charged with the task of delivering the news to McRae and assisting him to make his journey to Melbourne. Barry later included the details of his exciting 'long ride' as part of an Australian anthology of such rides. He wrote of the anguish McRae felt and their four-day journey on horseback together. After riding to Wentworth with Barry, McRae caught the train to Melbourne, where he was reunited with his family.

Isabella had been ill for over a month; the diagnosis of typhoid had been made around 27 March. She died on Thursday 2 May 1867, just 20 years old, and was buried near her grandfather, John McRae, at Campbellfield Cemetery on the following day.

A letter from Donald's brother Duncan, at Caulpaulin Station, is addressed to an unnamed recipient to give them the sad news. It is interesting that in it he writes of himself in the third person. He, like his brother may have been unable to read or write and may have engaged someone to write the letter for him. It reads:

> Dear Sir,
>
> I regret to inform you of the sudden death of Miss Isabella McRae which sad event took place at St Kilda near Melbourne last month. The first intimation we heard of her illness was by telegram to Wentworth and from thence by express here. Mr Duncan McRae was at the time and throughout her illness in constant attendance – as well as her bereaved father. Her illness which carried her off was Typhoid fever of the worst kind. … This of course has been a great blow to them all and I am afraid will take a considerable time for them to get over this.
>
> Mr McRae is still in Melbourne and will not likely be at the Wilson for some little time. He or some of the family would have been with you before this had not this sad event taken place.[137]

The remainder of his letter contained news of the property and the locality. Duncan conveyed the happier news that the River Darling was 'bank high' and it appeared likely there would be a flood; and that numerous steamers were going both up and down.

When he arrived in Victoria, Donald McRae was not a well man himself. He had had a hard, physical life, much of it outdoors as a shepherd or squatter tending his cattle and sheep. He had admitted to John Barry, on his last ride, that he was not as young as he once was. His death certificate indicates that from the middle of June McRae had been affected by a fever, possibly brought on by the exertions of his journey and the death of his eldest daughter. Complications set in and he was diagnosed with inflammation of the lungs. He died at Clunie on 17 July 1867, 51 years of age. On 21 July he too was buried at Campbellfield Cemetery, ten weeks after his daughter Isabella.

Seven months after Donald McRae's death in July 1867, Duncan MacGregor married Margaret McRae. The marriage was celebrated at

Clunie House, Chintin. Duncan married a day before his thirty-third birthday, on 25 February 1868; Maggie was 18. The marriage certificate records that the ceremony took place in the District of Lancefield and was No. 32 in the Marriage Register.[138] Because Maggie was not yet 21, the legal age of marriage, it took place with the written consent of her mother, Christina. It was solemnized according to the rites of the Presbyterian Church and witnessed by Duncan's friend, David Mailer, of whom we will learn more later. Family correspondence confirms that Duncan rode eight hundred miles from New South Wales to arrive in time for his wedding.[139]

Photographs of the couple on their wedding day in February 1868 have not been found. The local newspapers for Romsey, Kilmore and Wallan had either not begun publishing or the issues for 1868 are missing. Letters from Duncan's family acknowledging the marriage, if he received any, have not survived: this is somewhat surprising as the family closely followed his career from afar and admired his upward mobility.

One member of the family did not favour Duncan's union with Maggie. In April Duncan McRae wrote to a friend at Caulpaulin:

> McGregor is married to Maggie and I have got in the black books for opposing the marriage, in fact I very seldom hear from any of the mob. There is no Trustees appointed yet therefore nothing is properly settled. Mrs McRae administers to the property in Victoria and I have no doubt that she will do the same to the properties in New South Wales and the Wilson River.[140]

Duncan McRae was disappointed at this state of affairs. It was his ambition to manage or inherit his brother's Mount Margaret Station. He wrote: 'I am afraid my chance of the Wilson [River] Station is very little.' There were further issues Duncan was unhappy with. He was keen to change the name of the property from Mount Margaret to Mt Bell in memory of Isabella McRae. On 8 June 1868, he wrote to Neil Macdonald at Mount Margaret Station: 'I am thinking to leave them altogether about Christmas myself. I am getting sick of the whole concern'.[141]

Family relationships, and the way in which the fortunes of the McRae and MacGregor families were to be placed almost entirely in Duncan's hands, are explored in the next chapter.

Donald McRae, c.1850s
Leckie Archive

Donald McRae, c.1860s
Leckie Archive

Christina McRae, c.1860s
Leckie Archive

Portachullin, Scotland, home of Donald McRae's parents until they emigrated to Australia in 1853
Leckie Archive

Left
Isabella McRae, Melbourne, c.1866
Leckie Archive

Above
Annie McRae, Melbourne, c.1866
Leckie Archive

Left
Margaret McRae, Melbourne, c.1880s
Leckie Archive

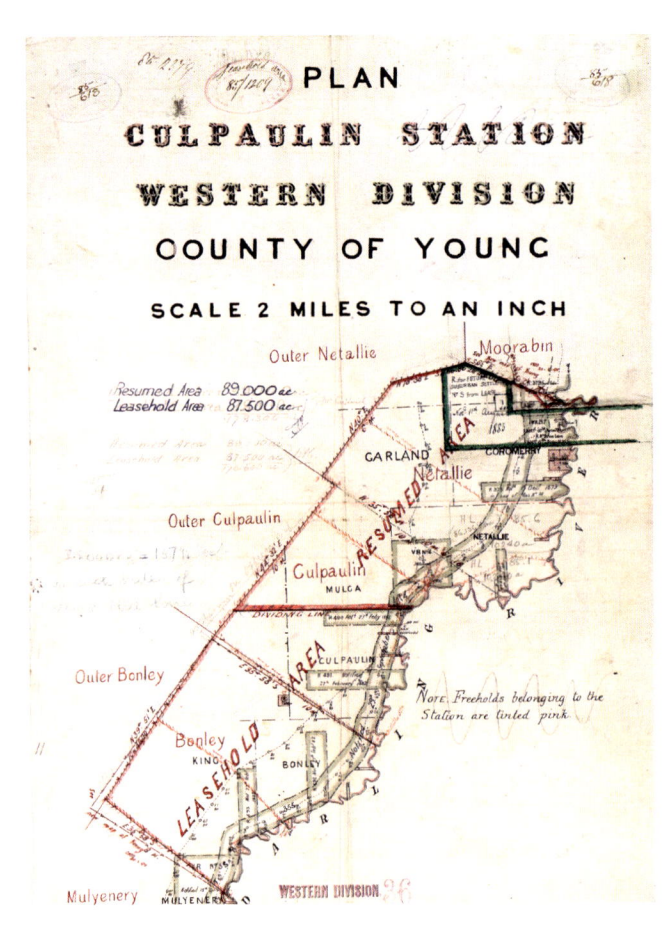

Caulpaulin Station, 1885
NSW Records Office

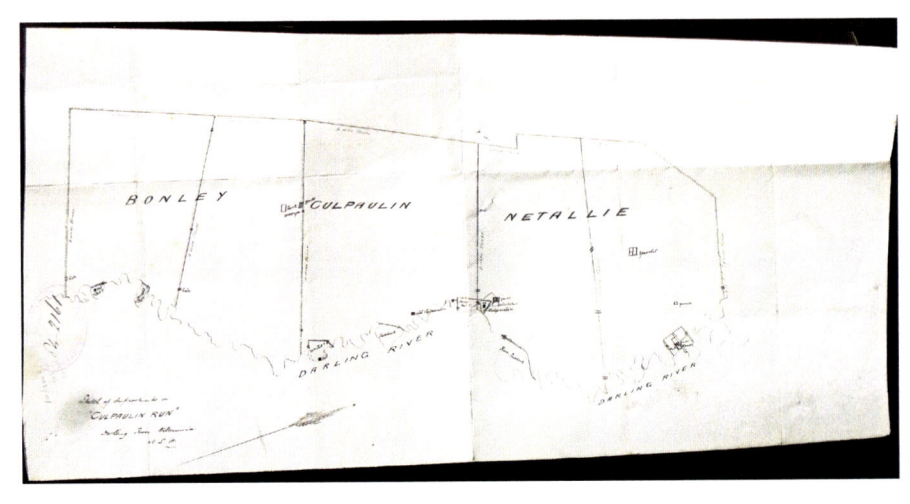

Caulpaulin Station original sketch, undated
NSW Records Office

The front of Clunie Homestead, c.1933
Leckie Archive

The rear of Clunie Homestead showing original buildings
Leckie Archive

View of the front of Clunie Homestead with child, undated
Leckie Archive

Duncan McRae, Donald's brother (1831–1904)
Leckie Archive

— 2 —
The Estate of the Late Donald McRae

Maggie McRae's marriage to Duncan MacGregor must have been a welcome family event for Christina McRae. MacGregor was a good catch. After eleven years in Australia and a good track record managing pastoral properties, MacGregor had proved that he was a good and trustworthy man. After McRae's death, Duncan quickly assumed the role of *de facto* manager of McRae's properties. He was the perfect candidate to manage the estate of the late Donald McRae.

Underpinning MacGregor's financial advancement and increased social status were the terms of his deceased father-in-law's will. Donald McRae's will was drawn up at Bathurst, New South Wales, and dated 24 June 1864. He appointed John Nepean McIntosh, solicitor of Bathurst, and Joseph Smith, sheep farmer of Georges Plains near Bathurst, his trustees and executors. Donald had retained strong connections with his friends and associates in Bathurst, especially his long-time friend Joseph Smith. The will was executed in Melbourne in the presence of McRae's friend Richard Gibson and his solicitor John Matthew Smith of Chancery Lane, Melbourne.[1] Donald McRae's will was clear. Although he appointed McIntosh and Smith trustees, he gave them the option to decline the commission; 'if the said Trustees … shall … be desirous of being discharged or refuse or become incapable to act … any other person or persons [may be appointed] to be a Trustee or Trustees in place of the [existing] Trustee'.[2] The two men resided in Bathurst yet McRae's estate was spread over three colonies and his widow lived near Melbourne. In these days before speedy mail services, this task was clearly too much for the two men to contemplate.

The original assets of the estate of Donald McRae in New South Wales,

Victoria and Queensland were valued for probate at £15,117-10-0. After deducting funeral expenses, costs of administration and legacies paid, the estate was valued at £11,817-10-0. As was customary, an application for letters of administration of the will was made to the Supreme Court; it was granted to Christina McRae, his widow, in September 1867. It was also proved that no caveat to McRae's will had been lodged. In August 1867, solicitor John Matthew Smith wrote to the two Bathurst gentlemen to confirm their agreement to act for the family as executors and trustees. On 13 October 1867 he signed an affidavit for John McIntosh and Joseph Smith. However, the two men sought release from their roles as executors and trustees. Had McRae anticipated this? A deed of renunciation by the two trustees dated 28 December 1867 followed. The deed stated that they were 'desirous … to renounce and wholly … disclaim all and every … right title or interest' in McRae's estate.[3] In his first response, McIntosh replied that although he was truly sorry to hear of the death of Donald McRae, and that he would be glad to help his widow and family in any way, he regretted that he was not at liberty to incur the responsibility of acting as a trustee. When John Matthew Smith wrote a second time to McIntosh requesting his agreement, he simply replied that it was 'quite impossible' for him to jointly administer the will. Joseph Smith also received two letters of request from Smith. He replied in detail:

> I find after mature consideration and also having been advised by a professional man that I must decline a second time having anything to do with the trusts under the late Mr McRae's Will. I should willing oblige Mrs McRae or family in any way that I could without incurring such a grave responsibility. You will please therefore inform Mrs D McRae of my intentions in order that she may apply at once to some party in Victoria and which I think will be better for all parties as they will be there on the spot.[4]

One of their reasons for declining the commission was the matter of distance. This made sense. A further affidavit made on 4 February 1868 reiterated McIntosh and Smith's earlier deed of renunciation.

Because of McIntosh and Smith's decision to decline the role of executors, Christina McRae had to find alternatives. But it was not a straightforward endeavour. In her affidavit dated 6 February 1868, she explained that she was 'almost a stranger' in the Colony of Victoria. She also stated that she had endeavoured but was unable to obtain two persons who were both able and willing to become sureties for the proper administration of the estate. Christina had to find two individuals with property worth £12,000 to assist her with the administration of the estate. Instead she found three willing participants to make up the £12,000. Her brother-in-law Duncan McRae and their friends Richard Gibson and Donald Ferguson committed to the surety required. Duncan McRae and Richard Gibson each declared they had property worth £3,000 and Donald Ferguson gave his surety of £6,000, achieving the amount required by the courts. The order of administration was granted to Christina McRae on 23 June 1868.

In writing his will, Donald McRae had his siblings uppermost in his mind. Before considering his wife and daughters, he bequeathed to his brothers Farquhar, Finlay and Duncan and to his cousin Donald McRae the sum of £500 each.[5] However, his cousin, the son of Alexander McRae of Kintail, Scotland, died at Caulpaulin on 25 September 1864. He was aged thirty-six. He was buried at Caulpaulin where his grave is still marked.[6] Next Donald McRae directed that an income of £1,000 per annum be paid to his 'dear wife' Christina during her life. The annuity was to be free of all deductions and paid by quarterly payments. The first annual annuity to his wife was paid on 7 July 1868. An annuity of £1,000 was to be shared between his three daughters and the interest on the annuity be paid to them. Because of Isabella's early death, on the death of their father Maggie and Annie McRae each had an independent income of £500 per annum once they married or reached 21 years. The £500 gratuities to Farquhar and Finlay were paid on 12 August 1868; Duncan McRae received his payment on 1 December 1868.

Christina McRae put her trust in her first son-in-law, Duncan MacGregor. Prior to the settlement of the administration of the will, in June 1868, just four months after his marriage to Maggie, Christina authorized him to travel to New South Wales 'with the view of effecting arrangements as to the administration of the Estate of my late husband Mr Donald McRae'.[7] Christina McRae made her mark on the letter carried by Duncan to New South Wales. This was Duncan's first official involvement in the estate of the late Donald McRae but was far from the last. His administration of the estate continued into the first decade of the twentieth century.

Maintaining Mount Margaret, Caulpaulin and Clunie

Immediately following McRae's death, on 18 July 1867, the family established a separate set of accounts for the estate. Duncan MacGregor's travel and other expenses, including legal fees, were entered into the appropriate ledger for each station.

Although a ledger for Caulpaulin Station has not survived, we can learn much from the extant ledgers for the other stations. For example, the men's wages on each station were calculated on a 'tab' basis. Against their credit or agreed daily or weekly rate of pay, the men were debited for expenses such as clothing, boots, tobacco and alcohol. Separate line entries accounted for the rations consumed on each station, amounts credited for the sale of sheep and cattle, and the stock on hand.

In 1868 an interesting note in the account indicates that Donald McRae's younger brother Duncan, who continued to work at Caulpaulin, was not charged with a great many items that he owed. Although it seems odd, his wages and expenses were treated differently to those of the other men. The accountant pointed this fact out in a separate account as he thought it should be acknowledged. Although no evidence has been found to support the idea, perhaps the brothers had a share arrangement in place? Caulpaulin Station, all 277 square miles of it, was a large run.

As well as running their own sheep, they also took sheep in to graze for neighbours.[8] Mount Margaret Station was acquired by McRae in 1866 and carried cattle. The first entry in the Mount Margaret Ledger indicates it was initially stocked with 699 heiffers and bulls.[9] Over the 15 years recorded in the ledger, the number steadily increased:

Year	Total	Branded	Slaughtered	Supposed Deaths	Sent to Market	Deaths on road	Bulls ex Melb.	Sent to Glengyle	Received ex Caulpaulin
1866	699		25						
1867	669	296							
1868	965	315	20						
1869	1260	696	10	50					
1870	1896	477	25						
1871	2348	768	18						
1872	3098	1071	25		270	9			
1873	3874	920	36	70	265	11			
1874	4423	1296	49	47	332		19		
1875	5310	1846	41	120	304	16			491

1876	7182	1324	70	125				991	
1877	7320	1525	78	100	786	73	13		
1878	7821	1471	83	205	945				
1879	8059	1370	52	50	609		8		
1880	8726	2154	70	50	776				
1881	9984								

Mount Margaret Station, Ledger 1866–1881

The table tells one story of Mount Margaret Station. It shows that it was not until 1872 that there were cattle available to be sent to market, a period of six years without income. The number of stock branded each year can be seen to slowly increase. The table also shows the movement of cattle between the properties, with bulls first sent from Melbourne in 1874, and stock sent to Glengyle or received from Caulpaulin, and also the number of deaths that occurred on the road. Mount Margaret and other stations also needed fresh meat for their stockmen. Cattle slaughtered in 1866 equalled about two per month and remained at roughly this number for ten years. However, in 1877 and 1878 the number was 78 and 83 respectively, or almost six cattle each month, reflecting the increased workforce on the station. It appears that it was through Duncan MacGregor's careful husbandry that increases in stock began to accelerate.

To manage the two stations and supervise the breeding of stock, Duncan had to travel frequently from Melbourne to Caulpaulin and Mount Margaret Stations. In 1868 and 1869, as a newlywed, he probably felt the separation from his wife and family in Chintin acutely. Duncan's notebooks are full of detail of the routes he took and the places he visited; on these occasions he does not record his feelings. Years later and in times of despair, however, he expressed his feelings through his poetry as he had in the period prior to his marriage. Sometimes his journeys were very lengthy, extending for between three and six months; at other times they were remarkably brief. The journey from Chintin in central Victoria to Caulpaulin took at least six weeks with stock and horse-drawn vehicles. As transport between the colonies improved, MacGregor also combined his travel modes – he rode his horse, took the train or Cobb & Co. coaches, and on one trip in the 1870s, boarded a ship from Melbourne to Brisbane, then hired a horse or took a coach to outback western Queensland.

Duncan's new lifestyle was established early in his marriage when he may have felt constrained by his residence in one place for months at a time. He had lived a somewhat nomadic life for more than a decade, moving from property to property. It is possible he yearned for the open spaces and the freedom to travel with his cattle. He probably took every opportunity to travel to New South Wales and Queensland and explore the countryside for new leasing opportunities. His reunions with Maggie were cherished events.

A man in a hurry – Inverauld at Riddells Creek, 1869

When this project began, the family were well aware of the McRae residence at Clunie in Victoria and the MacGregor properties in New South Wales and Queensland. Uncovering details of a previously unknown MacGregor property at Riddells Creek came, though, as a complete surprise. Ian Leckie, or Bernard MacGregor before him, had not heard of Inverauld, but when searching through the National Library's *Trove* database for the name 'Winter', his name was found as the manager of Inverauld at Riddells Creek, and from there the story began to unravel.

Ledgers and records for Inverauld have not been found amongst the records held in the State Library of Victoria. The property's name is found in a summary of losses that MacGregor drew up in 1902. Could the Inverauld ledgers, along with other papers, have been destroyed after MacGregor's death in 1916? It appears to be the case.

While the family were unaware of Inverauld, one house in Riddells Creek, Rannoch, was known to the family. This was a house that Duncan's daughter Jessie purchased in Riddells Creek in 1923, after the sale of Clunie. This house was occupied by the Winter family from 1923 to 1951 when it was sold. As a child in 1951 Ian Leckie recalls meeting an old man at Rannoch, thought to be James Winter's son, also referred to as Winter. James Winter Senior died in 1929. Winter grew vegetables at Rannoch and sent hampers down by rail to the family, including the Pestells and the Woods, living in Melbourne, an example of the strong relationship the family had with long-term employees.

To piece together the story, let us first reflect on Duncan MacGregor's situation in 1869, just one year after his marriage. In short, Duncan found himself in a very secure financial position. He and Maggie were living comfortably at Clunie, seven miles from Romsey. The 910-acre property was located in reasonable proximity to the Melbourne stock markets at Flemington. In addition to the location and good pasture, two well-known local cattle breeders, Robert Clarke and Robert McDougall, lived in the vicinity of Romsey and Darraweit Guim, as did other breeders of Shorthorn cattle, Leicester sheep and Clydesdale horses. It made sense to find a suitable portion of land in this area. It was Duncan's late father's ambition for his son, and Duncan's own ambition, to have a run of his own. With his own station he could devote himself to a breeding program. In 1869 MacGregor found a suitable property in Riddells Creek about 15 miles from Chintin. His decision to buy there appears to have been an inspired, well thought out plan.

The district of Riddells Creek is situated between Romsey and Gisborne in what is now the Macedon Ranges Shire. In the 1860s and 1870s the Great Dividing Range formed Riddells Creek northern boundary and William John Turner ('Big') Clarke's large estate formed the southern boundary.[10] Riddells Creek was first settled by two Scots: John Carre Riddell (1809–1879) of Roxburghshire,[11] and his cousin Thomas Ferrier Hamilton (1820–1905) of Cathlaw, Scotland.[12] They arrived in Sydney from England on the *Abberton* in 1839. Together they rode to Port Phillip where they worked briefly with Niel Black[13] before buying, in early 1840, the stock and depasturing licence of the Mount Macedon Run. By 1846 their run totalled thirty square miles.

In August 1850, under the special survey clause of the *Waste Lands Act*, William J.T. Clarke successfully claimed 31,375 acres at 20 shillings an acre near Sunbury, twenty-five miles from Melbourne. Under the order-in-council dated 1847, he then obtained the adjoining 31,000 acres. His single property therefore stretched from Sunbury to the Sydney Road in Coburg.[14] The Riddell area boasted good pasture and was much sought after. It was a good choice for MacGregor's first purchase of land. Other significant property owners in the vicinity of MacGregor's land included the Scottish-born builder and Melbourne city councillor Samuel Amess (1826–1898);[15] Thomas Sutherland; James Brock, whose brother also had property near Clunie at Chintin; and James Winter, MacGregor's manager at Clunie.

Memorials held at the lands registry confirm that MacGregor purchased lots 18, 42, 43 and 44 in the Parish of Kerrie, Riddells Creek. Rate books for the Gisborne Shire for the financial year 1869/70 confirm the purchase at 35 shillings per acre. The four allotments varied in size. The first, Allotment 44, contained 169 acres; Allotments 42 and 43 were each 98 acres; and Allotment 18 was 67 acres.[16] This was a total of 433 acres. The land was rated at £150 per annum. MacGregor purchased the land from a local farmer, Arthur Frost, who had acquired major portions of land in the Shire. The rate book for 1869 records that MacGregor's property included huts. From 1870 to 1882, improvements to the property noted in the annual rate book included offices and later a homestead. The acreage in the rate books varies yet MacGregor's records state that the property totalled 433 acres.[17]

The property name, Inverauld, is intriguing. The prefix 'Inver' comes from the Gaelic *inbhir*, meaning 'mouth of a river'. A name beginning with 'Inver' often ends with the name of the river, such as Inverness, which lies at the mouth of the River Ness. 'Inver' can also mean 'meeting of waters'. The second part of the name, 'Auld', is not Gaelic but Lowland Scot for 'old'.[18] A number of creeks run through the Parish of Kerrie. Two of these creeks – the Bolinda Creek and Main Creek – meet on the eastern boundary of Allotment 42, one of the two 98-acre blocks. MacGregor took poetic licence in naming his property, and its name reflects and emphasises his Scottish origins.

Gaps in the story of Inverauld and MacGregor's activities at Riddells Creek have been filled through newspaper reports from the 1870s onwards. Through them we also learn a great deal about breeding activity in the area. An article by the *Australasian*'s 'Travelling Reporter' in 1876 made farming at Riddells Creek its focus.[19] A similar report for Darraweit Guim appeared a couple of weeks later. According to the unnamed author 'the soil of the district is of a poor description, and, as a consequence, cultivation is only carried on to a limited extent, the bulk of the land being used for grazing purposes'. His tour of Riddells Creek provides first-hand descriptions of the region. It is an incisive report, noting amongst other interesting details the tenure of long-term property owners and the activities of the various farmers and their crops or stock. The roving reporter called first at the 800-acre property owned by Samuel Amess where a Mr Carnie tenanted the land and horses were the principal stock on the farm; amongst the 40 head of draught horses, some of them were 'very superior animals'. In particular they were stock by Marquis and Champion, imported from Tasmania. One, he wrote, was a particularly promising 3-year-old mare.[20]

MacGregor's Inverauld was the reporter's next stop. A lengthy description of the 'fine grazing farm of 435 acres, owned and occupied for the last seven years by Mr Duncan MacGregor'. The land, he wrote, 'is all used for grazing' with the exception of a few acres set aside for growing a little hay for the use of the stock in winter.[21] He observed that about half of MacGregor's land was sown with rye-grass and white clover; and that there were 50 head of cattle, mostly Shorthorns, 'a class that has received a considerable amount of attention from Mr MacGregor during the last few years'. Among the cattle he noticed in particular was a 'well-made young bull by Donald Caird, and two handsome cows bred by Mr Robertson of Woolling, that would be able to hold their own at any show'. He noted several other 'really good cows' in the herd, and a number of promising heifers, one and two years old. The author mentioned that MacGregor was the owner of 'a large grazing farm at Darraweit Guim, a few miles distant' and that he entrusted the management of Inverauld to James Winter, 'who himself possesses 60 acres of land adjoining'.[22]

An undated parish plan found at the Gisborne Historical Society confirms that Winter owned Allotment 47, opposite MacGregor's Allotment 43. MacGregor's neighbours included Arthur Frost, who kept 15 to 20 milking cows on his 250 acres; and Edward Baker, who kept a mixed herd of 40 cattle, mainly Herefords, which he was breeding in preference to the Shorthorn milkers. On Captain Gardiner's 1,000-acre property, he had 150 cattle of mixed stock but was also using his land 'chiefly as a breeding and weaning station' for thoroughbred horses. Nearby, Andrew Graham's 380-acre property was mainly under wheat but he also had a herd of 50 mixed cattle for the market, a few cows for milking and a large number of draught horses, including the mares by the imported sires Prince of Wales, Blackleg, Marquis and others. Of note were the fillies by Scottish Chief and Pride of Scotland. His 200 mostly cross-bred sheep included merino and Lincoln as well as a few pure-breds.[23] These men had all been in the area more than ten years. The brief survey of the stock kept by his neighbours shows that when Duncan chose to base part of his stockbreeding business in Riddells Creek, he was amongst like-minded men. MacGregor's program was based on the practice of breeding his stud Border and English Leicester sheep, Shorthorn cattle and Clydesdales at Inverauld. Selected bulls and rams would be sent north to improve the quality of the stock on the stations.

His Border Leicester and English Leicester flocks were eventually entered in the first volume of the British Breeds Flock Book.[24] By engaging his stock agent he could manage his own sales in Riddells Creek.

MacGregor boosted his Clydesdale stock when he first imported two pure-bred horses in 1876. A letter dated 21 June sets out the conditions of the agreement between Mr Duncan Sinclair, the agent; Aitken & Lilburn & Co., the owners of the vessel *Loch Ness*; and MacGregor. The agreement stipulated that Mr Sinclair guaranteed that one man would attend to the two horses and keep them clean during the voyage on the *Loch Ness* when it sailed from Glasgow on 3 July. The horses were to be carried on deck at the shipper's risk, their accommodation had to be of sufficient strength and properly secured. Mr Sinclair had to provide all necessary food for the horses, and the owners of the ship sufficient water for the horses for the voyage. The cost of freight and passage was £107 and this amount had to be paid before embarkation of the horses.[25] The captain would not be held responsible if the housing of the horses proved to be insufficient. The *Loch Ness* arrived at Port Phillip Heads on 21 September 1876.[26]

The first advertisements for MacGregor's sale of stock at Inverauld appeared in the *Australasian* on 6 and 13 April and 11 May 1878 for an auction to be held on 23 May. This was a full nine years after he purchased the property at Riddells Creek and two years after he imported the Clydesdales from Glasgow. At the auction MacGregor was offering 'two heavy Clydesdale mares'.[27] Over the next three decades' advertisements for the sale of Shorthorn cattle, Border Leicester sheep and Clydesdale horses from Inverauld frequently appeared.

Little more is known about the property except that the original homestead and offices have now been demolished. In 1882 the Riddells Creek district was excised from the Gisborne Shire and was included in the Romsey Shire. The rate books for this Shire from the 1880s to the early 1910s were not retained when the 1994–95 amalgamation of local shires took place. This is a major loss for the Macedon Ranges Shire, ratepayers and historians alike.

In his lengthy and enthusiastic analysis of MacGregor's life as a breeder of pure blood-stock, Harry H. Peck, the notable stock and station agent, acknowledged that it was in 1869 that MacGregor developed 'a small stud property … where he bred the nucleus or the stud portion of his Shorthorn herds'.[28]

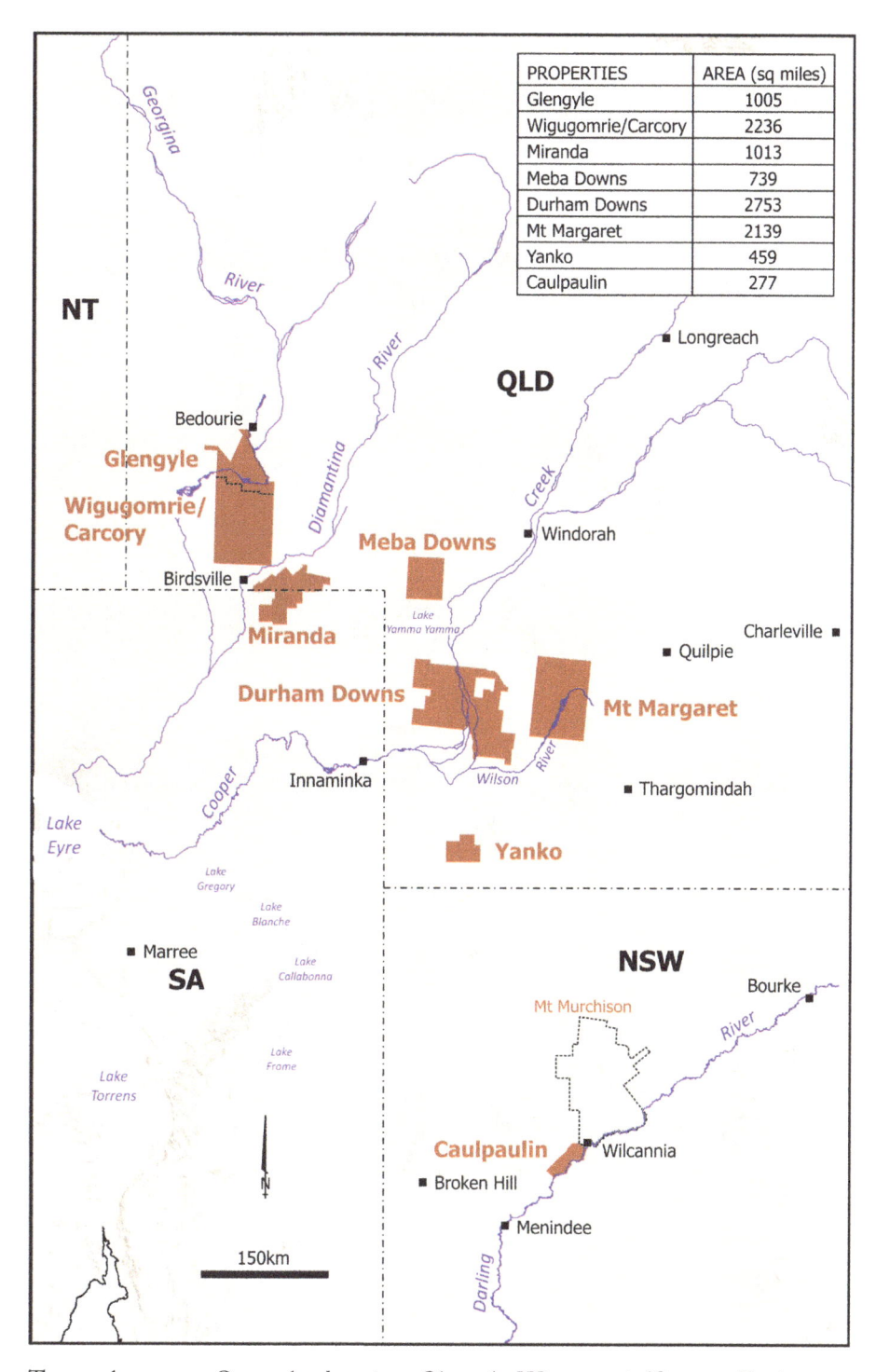

PROPERTIES	AREA (sq miles)
Glengyle	1005
Wigugomrie/Carcory	2236
Miranda	1013
Meba Downs	739
Durham Downs	2753
Mt Margaret	2139
Yanko	459
Caulpaulin	277

The south-western Queensland stations Glengyle, Wigugomrie/Carcory, Durham Downs, Miranda, Mt Margaret and Yanko and Caulpaulin in NSW, 1884

Map by Colin Pike, Magnetic North Design

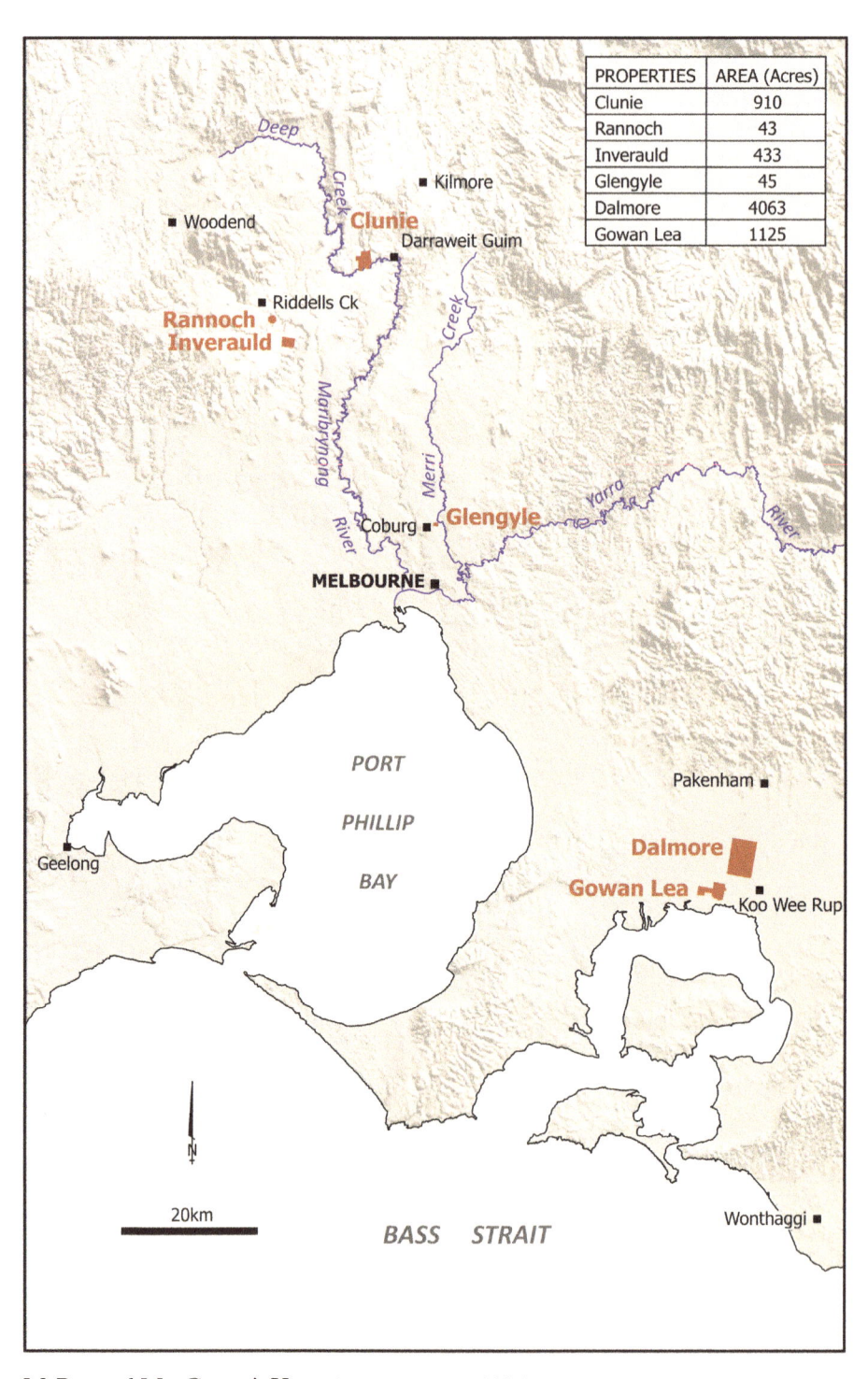

PROPERTIES	AREA (Acres)
Clunie	910
Rannoch	43
Inverauld	433
Glengyle	45
Dalmore	4063
Gowan Lea	1125

McRae and MacGregor's Victorian properties, 1884
Map by Colin Pike, Magnetic North Design

A new home for a growing family – Glengyle at Coburg, 1873

Maggie and Duncan's first child, Jessie, was born at Chintin on 16 December 1869. Nearly two years later, on 23 August 1870, their second daughter, Margaret (known as Goodie), was born. Their first son, John (always known as Jack), was born on 20 May 1872. The MacGregors now had a young family to accommodate and may have felt they had outgrown Clunie at Chintin. Although the house had four bedrooms, it was shared with Margaret's mother and sister, Annie.

There may have been more than one reason why the MacGregors chose to purchase the property in Coburg, now the City of Moreland. With a growing family the parents must have been looking ahead to their children's future. While it appears the children were all educated at home, a social life closer to Melbourne may have been considered preferable to remaining in country Victoria.

Located between the Moonee Ponds and Merri Creek valleys, Coburg was surveyed by Robert Hoddle in 1837. A village reserve was marked out and named Pentridge in 1840, it is thought after Pentridge in Dorset, England. Sydney Road, the main route from Melbourne to Sydney, was marked out along the western side of the village reserve and the Sydney Road Trust was formed in 1840.[29] The name Moreland has been associated with the municipality since 1839 when Scottish surgeon and speculator Dr Farquhar McCrae purchased over 600 acres of land on either side of present-day Moreland Road. Moreland was named after McCrae's grandfather's estate in Jamaica.[30] Along with Dr McCrae, the first purchasers included Melbourne 'founder' John Fawkner and Arundel Wrighte, squatter and speculator. Both McCrae and Fawkner, although antagonistic towards each other, were involved in the Sydney Road Trust. In 1859 the Pentridge District Road Board was formed, changing its name to Coburg in January 1869. Residents wanting to dissociate themselves and their suburb from the jail mooted the name change; Coburg was chosen because of the royal visit to Australia by Prince Alfred, Duke of Saxe Coburg, in 1867.[31] By 1870 Coburg boasted Catholic, Wesleyan and Anglican churches as well as a National School; there were 1,300 people living in the village. The prison held 645 prisoners. Warders and their families, farmers and market gardeners made up the remainder of the population. Coburg was proclaimed a Shire in 1874.[32]

David Mailer and MacGregor had been friends for many years; he was a witness at MacGregor's marriage in February 1868. David Mailer was born at Auchterarder, Perthshire, Scotland in 1824; his brother Robert was born in 1827. They were 28 and 24 years of age when the family emigrated to Australia in 1852. Enticed by the gold rush, Robert Mailer first went to the diggings at Forest Creek (now Castlemaine), but soon returned to Melbourne. Details of David's life have not been found, but Robert became a warehouseman before becoming the senior partner of the firm Mailer, McKersie and Love. Mailer was one of the petitioners who agitated to change the area's name from Pentridge to Coburg. In a short space of time, Robert Mailer's wealth enabled him to purchase land and construct his large home, Glencairn, in Craigrossie Avenue in Coburg.[33] It may have been through his association with the Mailer brothers, that Duncan became aware of the Coburg land being sold in 1873.

Originally Crown Portions 132 and 135, the 45-acre property had a frontage beyond Nicholson Street to Barrow Street; the northern boundary was the street later known as The Avenue; Merri Creek was the eastern frontage, and the southern boundary was Moreland Road. Originally owned by William Westgarth, it was purchased in 1871 by David Moore for £6,000. On part of the site he constructed a large bluestone house which he named Moorefield. In 1869 rate books described the house as a stuccoed stone house. Moore held the property until 1873 when he sold it to Duncan MacGregor. Conveniently close to Melbourne, it was also within a reasonable distance of Clunie. As historian Richard Broome writes, the MacGregor house was known in the area as: 'a large bluestone mansion of fourteen rooms, with bluestone servants' quarters, a coach-house and stables on forty acres of land by the Merri Creek between The Avenue and Moore Street … Even its servants' outbuildings were large two-storey bluestone structures.'[34] This prestigious location and impressive house indicated MacGregor's social status. The house was destroyed by fire in 1916.[35] The area now has 85 house blocks as well as a creek frontage.

When they bought the Moore Street property, Maggie MacGregor had been a wife and mother for five years. Her own mother had been responsible for the task of outfitting the new house at Chintin in 1867; with the purchase of the Coburg property it was time for Margaret to enjoy the task of setting up her own home. In August 1873, her Glengyle ledger reveals that a total of £880 was spent on household goods, furniture, saddlery, crockery, hardware, stationery and wages. Furniture purchased for a total of £435-2-2 included:

> 1 W Hutchison Colonial Oven, 2 feather pillows; French Bedsteads, 3 dressing tables; 1 set single toilet; 6 h c chairs; 1 gent chair; 1 ladies chair; Whitehead carving knife set; 1 dining room fender; 1 set fire irons; James McEwan & Co. 1 Kerosene lamp; 1 large wool rug – drawing room; 1 Japan coal vase; 1 set drawing room fender; 1 set steel fire irons; 1 pair glass lusters; 1 pair green vases; 1 pair bronze vases; James McEwan & Co. 1 weighing machine; 1 door foot scraper; Buckley & Nunn 84 yards carpet, making and laying; Law Brothers 1 hall table; 2 chairs; 1 walnut table; drawing room suite; 1 box ottoman ; 1 pair foot stools; 1 music stool; 4 small easy chairs; 2 level racks; 1 four poster bed; 1 hair mattress; 1 bolster; 2 feather pillows; 2 1/4 yards silks; 14 feet cornice; 4 ½ yards fringe; 8 yards silk; 8 ¼ yards lining; rings & wadding; cutting and making; 70 x 50 glass; 1 pair loop & wads, hooks; Law Brothers chimney glass; Law Brothers hall stand & expenses; Buckley & Nunn table cover.[36]

The task of selecting furnishings for the new home was substantial and it is imagined Margaret relished the challenge.

When they moved to Glengyle in Coburg in 1873, Maggie and Duncan had three children. Jessie was 4, Margaret 'Goodie' was 3, and John 'Jack' was 1. Four more children were born at Glengyle. Isabella, born on 11 May 1874, was named after Maggie's sister and grandmother Isabella McRae; she was always known as 'Tottie'. Annie was born on 7 June 1876 and was likely named after Maggie's younger sister Annie McRae. Annie MacGregor's childhood name was 'Cissie'. Christina, the youngest daughter, born on 28 April 1879 was named after her grandmother Christina McRae; she was the 'Pearl' of the family. The last child and second son, Donald McRae MacGregor, named after his grandfather, was born on 11 March 1882. His name was shortened to 'Don' by his mother. Throughout their lives the seven children retained their childhood names, and letters between family members were always signed this way.

Family life was focused on the Coburg area, social events in Melbourne and travelling to Chintin and later Gippsland. At the same time, Duncan continued travelling north to inspect and manage Caulpaulin and Mount

Margaret Stations. In September 1872, prior to his purchase of the Coburg property, he made a 'gentleman's agreement' with David and Robert Mailer. The three planned to go into partnership leasing property in Queensland with the intention of running cattle.

Duncan MacGregor's star was rising. He could sit back and survey the success he had made of his life as a Scottish immigrant. In 1873 he was 37, happily married with three children and living in a beautiful mansion. But he was a driven personality and his ambition to achieve great things meant he was constantly planning ahead. Everything was going well but he clearly wanted more. Whether or not he intended to, he was once again following in Donald McRae's footsteps. In 1855 after 17 years in Australia, Donald McRae leased his first station, Caulpaulin. In 1869 after 12 years in Australia, MacGregor purchased land at Riddells Creek for his breeding program. It is interesting to note that Inverauld was the only property MacGregor purchased in his own name.

When Queensland separated from New South Wales in 1869 and became a colony in its own right, various Land Acts opened up vast tracts of the country. The 1869 Land Act allowed applicants to apply for a licence for vacant Crown Land in the 'Unsettled Districts'; it was a licence to occupy the land for one year. The applicant must pay 5 shillings per square mile on the estimated area of the run, with a declaration that he had occupied the run with stock to the extent of one-fourth of the number of sheep or the equivalent number of cattle the Act deemed the run was capable of carrying. Each run would consist of not less than 25 and no more than 100 square miles with the external lines running east west and north south. The local commissioner of Crown Lands would compute the area of any run and could exclude any portion he deemed to be 'unavailable' for pastoral purposes. The maximum amount of land deemed unavailable could not exceed half the area within the external boundaries.

After a year, leases could be granted for a period of 21 years. Every run was deemed by the Act to capable of carrying at least 100 sheep and 25 horses or cattle. Licences could be transferred to another person upon application to the Commissioner of Crown Lands if it could be proved that the general conditions of the lease had not been met, such as stocking the run adequately or making improvements to the run.[37]

John MacGregor (1793–1862),
Duncan's father
Leckie Archive

Janet MacGregor (1816–1893),
Duncan's mother
Leckie Archive

Brooch belonging to Janet
MacGregor, Duncan's mother
Owned by Susan Vale, photographed by
the British Museum

Ewich Farm, Tyndrum, Scotland, Duncan MacGregor's home 1835–1857
Photographer: Janet Leckie, 2015

The *Marco Polo* 1858, painted by Thomas Robertson (1819–1873)
Accession no H306, State Library of Victoria

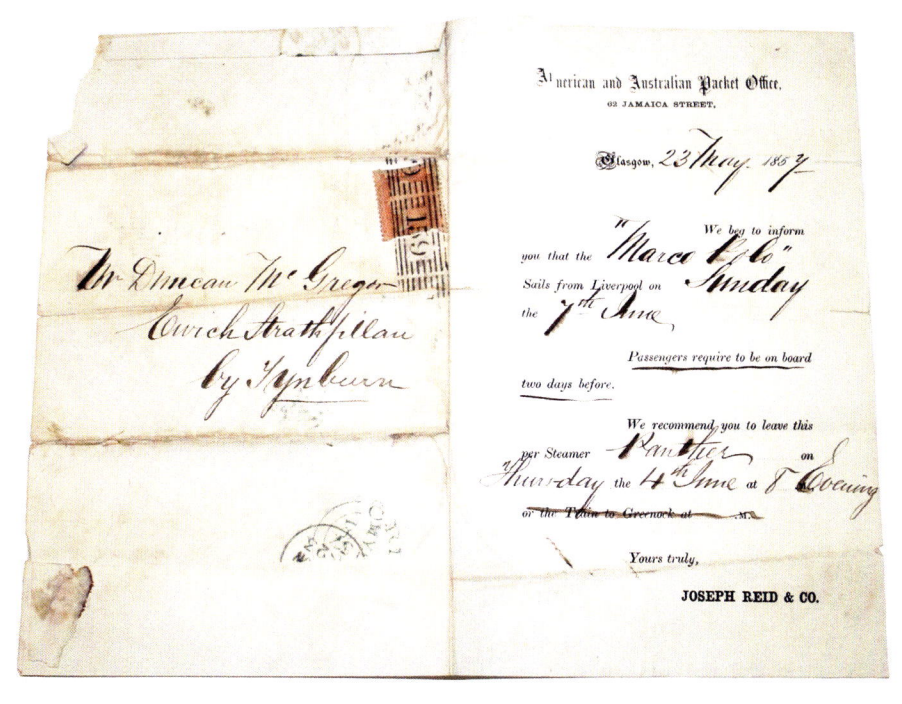

Letter from American and Australian Packet Office, London to Duncan MacGregor for his passage to Australia, dated 23 May 1857

MacGregor Collection, MS12914, State Library of Victoria

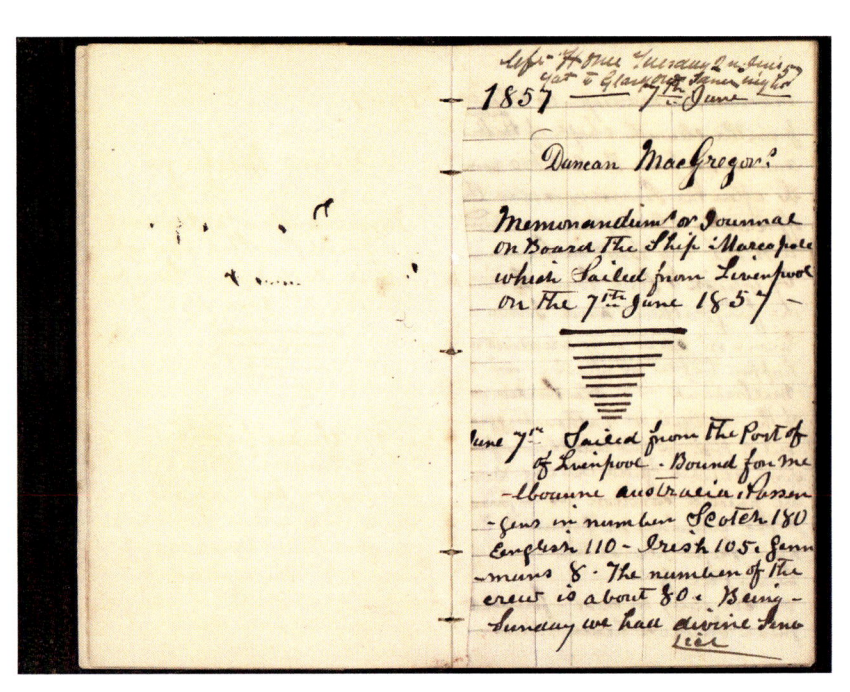

Memorandum or Journal on board the ship *Marco Polo* which sailed from Liverpool on the 7 June 1857

Leckie Archive

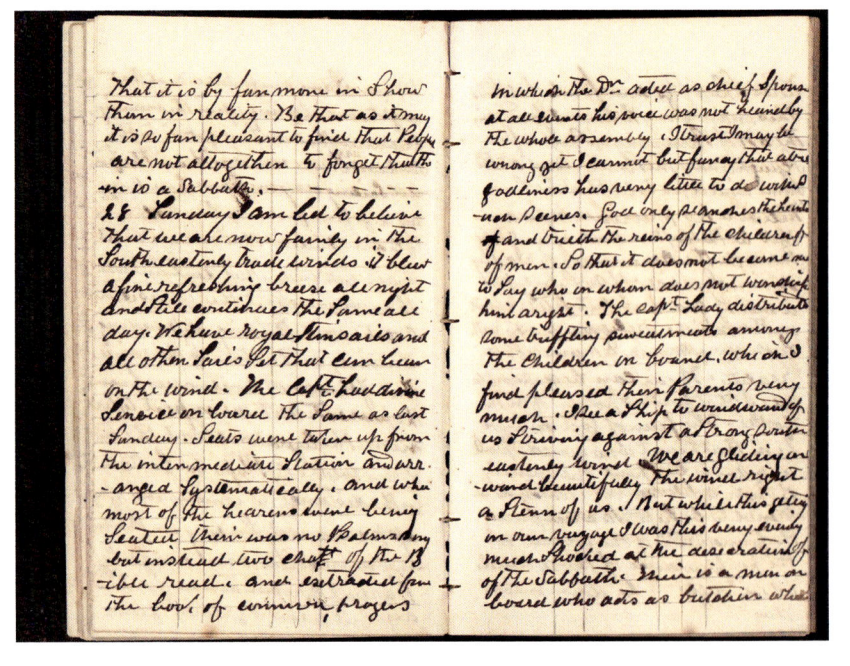

Two pages from MacGregor's 1857 shipboard journal

Leckie Archive

Portsonachan Hotel, farm and ferry. Home of Duncan MacGregor's family from 1862
Photograph c.1900, Portsonachan Hotel Archive

Portsonachan stables much as they would have been in the 1860s
Photographer: Janet Leckie, 2015

Port Gellibrand and Williamstown, *Victoria Illustrated*, Second Series, Sands & Kenny, Melbourne, 1862
Leckie Archive

Envelope addressed to Duncan MacGregor at Menindie Station, Darling River, 1862

Letters to Duncan Macgregor 1857–1915 in MacGregor Collection, MS12914, State Library of Victoria

Reverse of envelope showing numerous post-marks, 1862

Letters to Duncan Macgregor 1857–1915 in MacGregor Collection, MS12914, State Library of Victoria

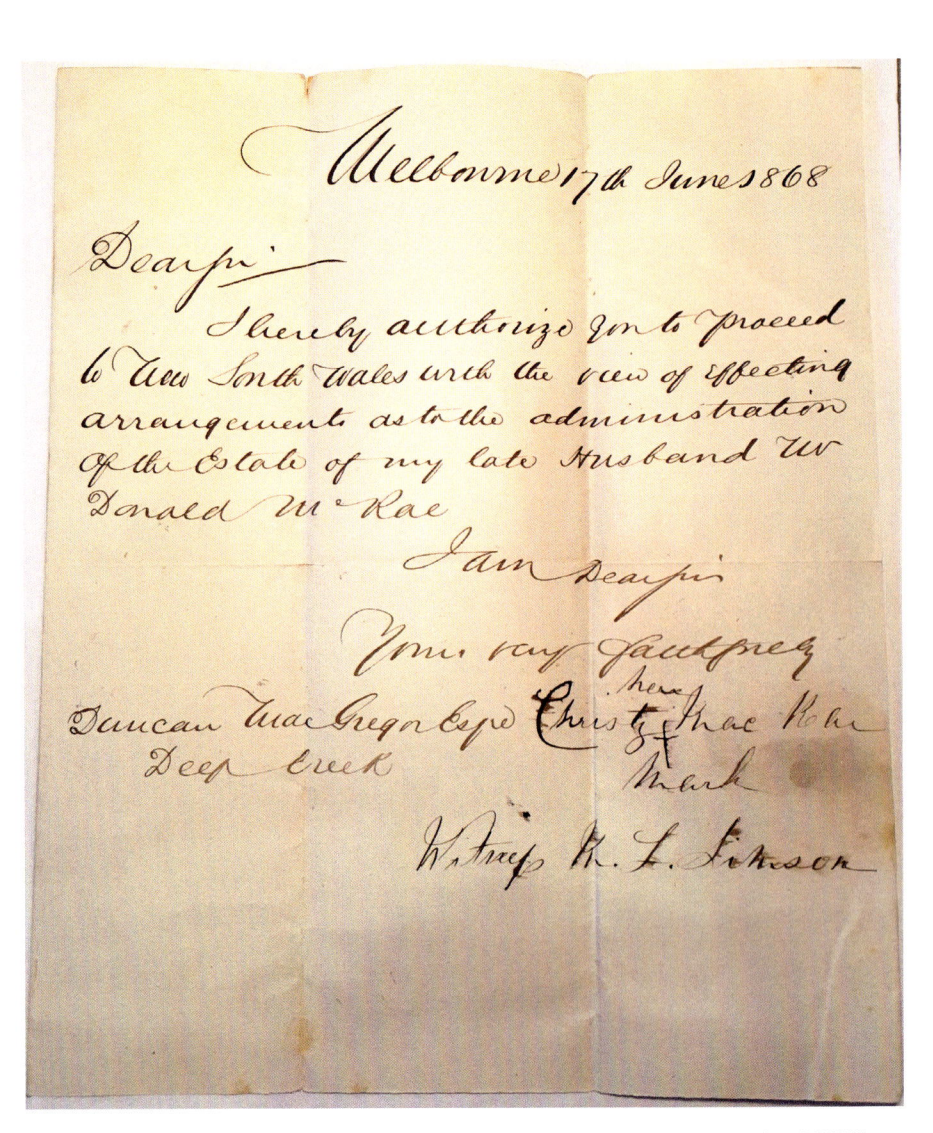

Letter from Christina McRae authorising Duncan MacGregor to travel to NSW
Letters to Duncan Macgregor 1857–1915 in MacGregor Collection, MS12914, State Library of Victoria

The Three Rivers

Cooper Creek was discovered by Charles Sturt in 1845 and named after Charles Cooper, the Chief Justice of South Australia. It is one of three major Queensland rivers that flow into the Lake Eyre basin; the others are the Diamantina and the Georgina. The Thomson and Barcoo tributaries are sometimes incorrectly referred to as the Cooper. Australian Aboriginals have inhabited the area for approximately 20,000 years, with over 25 tribal groups living in the Channel Country.

Cooper Creek is mostly a collection of dry beds or waterholes apart from in times of flood; it is clear Sturt first saw the Cooper while it was in flood; its flow depends on monsoonal rains falling months earlier in far distant northern Queensland. The Cooper is part of the Great Artesian Basin system and at 1,300 km in length is the second longest inland river system in Australia. The Murray River forms part of the 3,750 km combined Murray–Darling river system which drains most of inland Victoria, New South Wales and southern Queensland. Overall, the catchment area is one seventh of Australia's total land mass.

To the west of the Cooper, running parallel with it, are the Georgina and Diamantina Rivers.[38] MacGregor had properties on the three rivers – the Cooper, the Diamantina and the Georgina – 30 years before Sidney Kidman coined the term the 'Three Rivers' system. The rivers and their channels flow through a huge area of low-lying country. Ion Idriess in 1936 described the landscape:

> In a lot of places you can hardly trace a bank. The river-bed is indicated by wide flats, mostly lingnum bush, big old-man coolabahs, and big old gums in places … when rain falls … the Three Rivers flood and down they come. The banks can't hold then, and out the water spills, twenty, thirty miles to either side. When the waters of the Three Rivers meet, you can guess there are some sheets of water wherever the country is flat … and the flood waters gradually sink into the ground, and drain away as the rivers recede … The sun shines out and turns what were lakes of water into lakes of grass.[39]

The grasses growing throughout the Three River country are edible bushes such as saltbush, bluebush, cotton-bush, parakeelya, cane-grass, herbage, edible vines, creepers and other grasses. Many of them are drought-resistant and cattle thrive on them. MacGregor knew that this region was ideal for a large pastoral station. After more than 15 years in the Australian outback, he saw the potential for the development of this region for his own pastoral pursuits.

A partnership saga –
Macdonald, MacGregor & Mailer, 1872–1874

Unravelling the establishment of one of MacGregor's most well-known Queensland properties, Durham Downs, makes compelling reading. Durham Downs remains part of S. Kidman & Co.'s iconic cattle stations. The Durham Downs story commences in 1872 and involves MacGregor, David and Robert Mailer and one other party. The story also reveals two conflicting aspects of Duncan MacGregor's personality. It is clear that he was a tenacious and sometimes volatile character, but in this instance he also revealed a surprising level of vulnerability.

One letter in the files heralds the beginning of the long and complex saga. On 14 April 1872, Neil Macdonald, the manager of Mount Margaret Station, wrote to MacGregor enclosing a letter from Fenwick & Scott, solicitors in Brisbane. The subject was the leasing of land in Queensland. Macdonald emphasised to MacGregor that 'All country now must be taken up at Charleville [and] I must go there before the 1st of May to take up these outside blocks and not having heard anything from Fenwick about the Scrip, I shall have to give Cardew a cheque.'[40] The Crown Lands Office at Charleville dealt with applications for land in Gregory North, Gregory South and Warrego, the area MacGregor was interested in. Two weeks later, on 28 April, Macdonald wrote again: 'I told you in my last that all country is now taken up at Charleville. I have tendered for all the Blocks that we were speaking of and some more for my self. Not having heard from Fenwick I had to give cheques on Melbourne. When I get the Licences I will send them to you.'[41] There is more to this story than meets the eye.

When he replied on 16 July to MacGregor's 14 June letter, Macdonald first congratulated his boss on the addition to his family 'of a son and heir' and trusted that the newborn and Mrs MacGregor were well. John MacGregor was born on 20 May 1872 at Glengyle in Coburg. However, after a little station chit-chat, Macdonald's conversational tone changed. Was he simply frustrated and angry that

MacGregor disapproved of his previously discussed plan to walk cattle to Melbourne, or was there more to it? MacGregor, he understood, was dissatisfied 'if I am any judge from the way you underline that part of your letter'. He went on to protest that it was not for the pleasure of the trip he wished to go down to Melbourne, although he would enjoy himself when he got there. The fundamental issue appears to have been much deeper:

> I have now served Mrs McRae to the best of my ability for nearly six years for a miserable pittance. I waited all along until some one on her behalf saw the place, and as that does not appear to have had any effect upon the matter I think it is time that I looked out for myself. From your own expressed opinion I do not think you will find much fault with this. This is my sole reason for going with the Cattle, without which I would much rather stay and have the place put in a more comfortable and economical way than it is at present. (That is to finish the paddock and have a house built). I acknowledge that I take a pride in the Cattle and that alone is a great inducement. I will not start anything but what is good as the first mob will in a great measure secure a good sale for all succeeding mobs.

Although he was happy with the work, he was not happy with his pay and conditions. This may explain his actions. Macdonald had applied to lease some blocks on Cooper Creek for himself and was now informing MacGregor. Then in a somewhat spiteful tone, and to emphasise his forthcoming independence, he wrote that he had been appointed a justice of the peace for the district and had been approached by the postmaster general to deliver mail between Mount Margaret and Thargomindah for £100 per year.[42]

In his letter Macdonald reported to MacGregor that he had just returned from Cooper Creek and that the country was 'just what I had formerly described to you'. He added that the area had flooded and the sandhills were covered in an abundance of cotton bush, salt-bush and grasses of different description 'for about 4 miles when the stony ridges commence'. The frontage and flooded country had plenty of the white grass 'that the Blacks get the seed from … and plenty of pig grass and other herbage'. Importantly there was no doubt the water was permanent because one of the holes he saw was over four miles long and 150 yards wide; he could not get a pole long enough to find the bottom. He followed another hole over three miles and found that there was over 17 feet of water in some places. This was good news for the partnership who were planning to graze cattle in western Queensland.

A letter from Macdonald in January 1873 also informed Duncan that he was 'going to take up twenty miles' frontage by ten [miles] back on each side of the Coopers Creek'. He went on to say that the west side of the Creek 'would not feed a bandicoot' but he had marked on a map one permanent water hole on the Herbert Creek and several holes that would last six to nine months. He had also heard that there was a very high flood going down the Barcoo and Thomson Rivers and that more water was coming. This was good news because 'there has not been a flood on Coopers Creek for 12 months'.[43] Macdonald's letters to MacGregor written from Mount Margaret tell one side of the story. MacGregor's diaries and an undated legal statement tell another. In 1886 MacGregor documented the sequence of events and his part in the story because of legal action taken against him and the Mailers concerning Durham Downs. The true story begins to emerge after reading the two accounts and piecing together what really happened.

On 14 September 1872 Duncan MacGregor had left his Coburg home and travelled north, first to Caulpaulin Station and then to Mount Margaret. As it is clear from the correspondence, MacGregor intended to lease property on the Cooper and Macdonald was well aware of his intentions. Prior to his trip MacGregor had made the 'gentleman's agreement' with David Mailer to take up a large area of land in Queensland. He wrote that, after agreeing to take him into partnership, David Mailer:

> strongly urged upon me to take Robert his brother into the concern and time after time pledged his word of honor that he would see to Robert's good behaviour and that he would always guarantee that I would not be put to any annoyance or inconvenience or loss of any kind during the partnership. I then consented to allow Robert an interest, all this verbally.

Once agreement had been reached, Duncan MacGregor was keen to act quickly. He started his trip north immediately with the intention of proceeding to Queensland 'with the view of securing country and stocking same'.[44] After arriving at Caulpaulin and spending some time there, he met Neil Macdonald, who was on his way from Mount Margaret to Melbourne with a mob of fat cattle. This was the trip MacGregor was not keen for him to make. However, he told Macdonald of his intention of travelling to Mount Margaret to check the station 'before going on to Coopers Creek'. At this chance meeting MacGregor also told Macdonald that he had an agreement with David and Robert Mailer to 'have an interest' in the property. MacGregor emphasised that he 'would like to take up a larger area of country' providing he could get cattle handy for stocking purposes.

In his statement MacGregor wrote that 'when I told all this to Macdonald he said that before leaving Mount Margaret he [Macdonald] applied for four blocks and secured same' and that if MacGregor did not mind 'he would like to come to some arrangement with me' and that he, Macdonald would have an interest in the undertaking. Emphasising that 'as he had secured the four blocks already that he would put them into the concern with so many cattle and horses as well as his services for a given time under my directions'. With MacGregor's agreement, Macdonald returned at once to Mount Margaret. From there he would go to Cooper Creek to secure the country and then to buy cattle for the company at a cost not to exceed £5,000. Macdonald insisted that he would have one-fourth share in the concern 'the same as Messrs D. & Robert Mailer and self 1/4th to each', he said. Macdonald also stipulated that the country would have to be taken up in MacGregor's name or in the names of the four partners. This would indicate that MacGregor would be responsible for the land. Finally, Macdonald proposed he would 'superintend the station for a given time' but under MacGregor's guidance. Duncan MacGregor agreed to these terms. On the face of it, agreeing to Macdonald's proposal seems somewhat out of character for MacGregor, who liked to control any situation. Was he reflecting back to his own years of yearning for a station of his own and agreeing to Macdonald's wishes because he understood the young man's ambition and the position he was in? This may have been the case. Nevertheless, having devised their plan, MacGregor and Macdonald parted company; Macdonald to travel north to the Cooper and MacGregor to return to Melbourne. Once in Melbourne he explained all that he had done to the Mailers and they 'expressed themselves satisfied'.

In October 1872 Macdonald bought 2,088 head of cattle, drawing on the £5,000 advanced by MacGregor. The cattle were to be delivered in October 1873 to the blocks Macdonald had already secured on the Cooper. The reason for the delay in taking delivery of the cattle is unexplained. This was contrary to his earlier desire to take up land 'with as little delay as possible'.

The year 1873 progressed; MacGregor purchased a new residence, Glengyle, in Coburg. But business took him back to Queensland and he left Melbourne for Mount Margaret on 22 December 1873. This meant he was absent from home for Christmas. He reached Mount Margaret on 6 January 1874. His report, written in 1886 and more than one decade after the events, records that on 11 January 1874 he met Macdonald at 'Woodsville on the Queensland border ... on his return from the Crown Lands Office at Charleville'.[45] Woodsville, however, is in northern Queensland on the coast near Mackay, and this sentence appears to be a lapse of memory. The place they met may have been Birdsville, which is near the border of Queensland and South Australian. Nevertheless, the important aspect of this meeting was the news Macdonald delivered to MacGregor while they rode on toward Mount Margaret.

Macdonald informed MacGregor that he had secured all the country they had previously discussed. Duncan may have thought this was good until he learnt that Macdonald had secured it in his own name instead of MacGregor's name or in the name of the partnership. Macdonald had reneged on his agreement. It is hard to believe that, after he 'remonstrated with him ... as to his conduct', they continued to ride together to Mount Margaret and on to Cooper Creek. Was MacGregor formulating a plan during their ride? When they reached the Cooper Creek runs MacGregor inspected the cattle. He returned to Melbourne in the first week of March 1874 and explained to the Mailers what had happened. Were they outraged by the turn of events? How did they react to Macdonald deceiving them in taking the runs in his own name? Did they blame Duncan for the outcome? Would this hiccup in their new partnership lead to repercussions for future ventures? While the initial concern was over the rights to the land, the number and quality of cattle soon became a concern. Macdonald had purchased cattle with £5,000 advanced by MacGregor. Of the 2,088 cattle Macdonald was said to have purchased, only 1,250 were visible on Durham Downs Station. Some had been lost to disease; MacGregor wrote that he saw the remains of 103 head 'which had died of the pleuro'. Something had to be done.

The month of May 1874 was very busy for the MacGregor family at Glengyle. Duncan's younger sister, Annie, and her husband arrived from Scotland. Annie, born at Liaran on 9 May 1841, had married the Australian John Neilson Brown on 5 February 1873 at Portsonachan and the couple decided to make their life in Australia. They left Plymouth on 14 March 1874 on the steamship *Northumberland*. After dealing with strong head winds, the ship arrived in Port Phillip Heads on 6 May and berthed at Sandridge at 4 pm in the afternoon. Captain Skinner 'achieved another nautical triumph' for the P. & O. steamship; it was a 'run out' in 52 days. The achievement maintained the *Northumberland*'s record as one of the fastest ships of its day and upheld 'its reputation as being the quickest means of communication with England'. From the time it left Plymouth Sound until the sighting of Cape Otway on the morning of 4 May, the voyage had taken 51 days 18 hours. The ship had travelled a distance of 12,245 miles of which 4,543 were 'performed under canvas'.[46]

Only four days after Annie Brown's arrival, Margaret MacGregor gave birth to her and Duncan's third child, Isabella Barbara, on 11 May 1874. On the very same day, Duncan and Christina McRae had booked their passage, along with David Mailer, to travel by ship from Melbourne to Queensland to 'prosecute our claim against McDonald [sp.]' and to get an injunction against him. They had urgent work to do. Arriving in Brisbane on 19 May MacGregor immediately called on the Commissioner of Crown Lands' and ascertained the names of the runs 'already in N.H. Macdonald's name'.[47] After this meeting he met with his solicitor, Mr Peter McPherson. The following day he saw the Commissioner again, then McPherson 'who told us that we better make a written statement as thereby so doing would save time and expenses'. This was probably a Statutory Declaration setting out the facts. Once this was written he called once again at the Lands Office and bought a plan of Macdonald's runs and confirmed the date of licences.

Was Neil Macdonald being unreasonable in his demands for a share in the station? Details of the runs he had already applied for a licence for in 1873 were published in the *Queensland Government Gazette* in 1874. His applications to lease runs in the district of Gregory South were dated 29 January and 5 March 1874.[48] The following table lists the runs held in Neil Macdonald's name from 1873:

Register Folio	Lesee	Run	Rent
564	Macdonald, N.H.	Warlaby	£2-12-1
565		Durham Downs	£2-12-1
573		Larra	£3-12-1
616		Naccowlah	£3-3-4
685		Boorarie South	£6-5-0
686		Boorarie North	£6-5-0
687		Ulloomunta	£6-5-0
689		Aros	£6-5-0
709		Morinish East	£6-5-0
710		Morinish West	£6-5-0
711		Nilparoo East	£6-5-0
713		Stanley	£6-5-0
714		Turtulla	£12-10-0
715		Callilpie	£12-10-0
716		Dunoon	£6-5-0
717		Glasgow	£6-5-0
718		Greenock	£6-5-0
719		Edinburgh	£6-5-0

The Naccowlah run was transferred from Macdonald to William Shearer in July 1874. Durham Downs was a run of 50 square miles; it is evocatively described as:

> Commencing on the right bank of Cooper's Creek bounded on the south by a west line to a point eight miles sixty chains west of a koolabah tree, along the north boundary of the Warlaby Run and a prolongation thereof, in all seven miles and eight chains: thence on the west by a north line ten miles: thence on the north by an east line four miles sixteen chains south and about sixty chains east of a koolabah tree marked broad-arrow on the south side; and thence on the east by the right bank of that Creek downwards to the point of commencement.[49]

An accurate description of each run was vital; their significant features had to be comprehensively recorded in the Queensland *Gazette*. There could be no question of confusing the features and landmarks of the run the squatter intended to lease.

Continuing their quest to claim the leases in their own names, the partners complied with the requests of the Commissioner. After composing their statements, drafting a petition and submitting these documents to the Commissioner, their application was complete. Throughout this period, MacGregor had called on Mr McPherson eleven times in ten days. On one occasion he called on McPherson three times in the one day. Sadly the account for legal fees has not survived. On Monday 1 June 'after signing all the papers we attended court and got the injunction granted'. They then made arrangements to leave Brisbane.

On 2 June they left Brisbane for Dalby then to Charleville to visit the Lands Office there. On Friday 12 June MacGregor's notebook records: 'All day with Commission, 13 new runs' although the exact details of the runs secured cannot be confirmed. How did Christina McRae, at 58 years of age, cope with the physical exertions of the trip? Shipboard travel to Brisbane may have been pleasant, but a carriage journey would have been relatively uncomfortable and possibly tiring. Or did she, instead, relish the opportunity to travel to Queensland? Christina may have enjoyed time away from her home at Clunie. Returning to the outback to re-live her early experience as a young wife and mother would surely have been an attractive proposition. And this time, escorted by her son-in-law, her journey may have been much more comfortable.

Duncan MacGregor and Christina McRae applied on 12 and 13 June 1874, and on 27 August 1874, for a total of 25 leases in the Gregory South and Warrego districts. The leases were made in their own names but with funds from the Estate of the Late Donald McRae. Applications made by Christina McRae were for the following 18 Unwatered Runs a total of 1,088 square miles (696,320 acres). They were added to the existing McRae runs and were later consolidated as Mount Margaret Station:

12 June 1874	27 August 1874
No. 33 Moyo, 80 ½ sq. miles	No. 80 Ovens, 50 sq. miles
No. 34 Cromarty, 80 sq. miles	No. 81 Kenmore, 96 ½ sq. miles
No. 35 Dingwall, 100 sq. miles	No. 82 Killin, 34 ½ sq. miles
No. 36 Aberdeen, 100 sq. miles	No. 83 Clyde, 26 ½ sq. miles
No. 37 Forfar, 90 sq. miles	No. 84 Cairn, 37 ½ sq. miles
No. 38 Fife, 40 sq. miles	
No. 39 Clunie, 50 sq. miles	
No. 40 Romsey, 51 ½ sq. miles	
No. 41 Ann, 17 sq. miles	

No. 42 Havelock, 87 ½ sq. miles	
No. 43 Ness, 60 sq. miles	
No. 44 Chinton, 86 ½ sq. miles	

Duncan MacGregor applied for the following 8 runs on the Georgina River. The total leasehold was 505½ square miles (323,520 acres); they formed the basis of Glengyle Station:

13 June 1874	27 August 1874
No. 54 Glenlyon, 98 sq. miles	No. 85 Lock, 33 sq. miles
No. 55 Glengyle, 98 sq. miles	No. 86 Balloch, 58½ sq. miles
No. 56 Glenfall, 87½ sq. miles	No. 87 Taregowna, 44 sq. miles
	No. 88 Bowling, 45 sq. miles
	No. 89 Largs, 41½ sq. miles

Additional runs, including Ben Castle, Ben Doran, Ben Luigh, Ben Dheu and Ben Challum, were added to Glengyle Station, increasing the dimension to 1,004½ square miles. In 1883 when MacGregor, Ronald & Co. leased Wigugomrie and Carcory runs, they became part of Glengyle Station when it became a property of 3,240 square miles (2,073,600 acres). This station, now owned by S. Kidman & Co., remains one of their flagship pastoral properties measuring 5,540 square miles.[50]

The following runs, initially held in Neil Macdonald's name, were transferred into the partnership of MacGregor, Mailer and Mailer in July 1874. They were the basis of the consolidated Durham Downs Station:

Register Folio No.	Name	Square miles	Rent
564	Warlaby	50	£2-12-1
565	Durham Downs	50	£2-12-1
573	Larra	75	£3-3-4
714	Turtulla	100	£2-12-1
715	Callilpie	54	£2-12-1
716	Dunoon	50	£6-5-0
717	Glasgow	50	£6-5-0
718	Greenock	50	£6-5-0
719	Edinburgh	50	£6-5-0

The foundation runs totalled 529 square miles (338,560 acres). The total rent on the runs for 1874 was £38-13-0. These runs had a capacity to carry 13,225 cattle and/or horses or 52,900 sheep. The station eventually carried a combination of horses, cattle and sheep and was increased to 2,573 square miles.

When their applications were finalised, on 26 June 1874 the party of MacGregor, McRae and David Mailer proceeded to Cooper Creek to discuss the deficiency of the cattle numbers on Durham Downs with Alex Campbell. Robert Mailer seems to have made his way to Cooper Creek independently. After discussions at Mount Margaret the group travelled to Thargomindah and convinced Macdonald to sign the transfers for the blocks 'which he had wrongly taken up in his own name'. MacGregor notes with relief that on 9 July 1874 he 'parted with Mrs McRae this morning'.

Robert Mailer also returned to Melbourne on that day. Following their departure MacGregor continued to Mount Margaret alone, reaching the station on 22 July. On the day after he arrived at Mount Margaret he began the task of mustering. It must have come as a relief to change his daily routine from mental to physical activity.

How did the partnership deal with Macdonald's deceit and betrayal? Duncan was pragmatic. He realised they could not reconcile the lesser number of cattle delivered against what they had paid for. To simplify matters, he recommended that the discrepancy should be written off the books. This did not satisfy the Mailers or Alex Campbell who was managing Durham Downs Station.[51] In his legal statement MacGregor wrote that the Mailers thought it would be better to keep the original numbers 'as we could easily make a deduction after the cattle had increased and before the place would be sold'. Were the Mailers considering the purchase as a short-term venture? It appears so. Relationships had become strained and it is unclear at what stage the three resumed their former, trusted relationship. Nevertheless, they had achieved their journey's aim. Macdonald relinquished his claim to the various runs and they were transferred to the names of Duncan MacGregor, David Mailer and Robert Mailer.

After one year of holding the licence, the leases were officially taken up on 1 July 1875 and the newly acquired stations needed to be stocked. However, with Macdonald's departure, a new station manager was required at Mount Margaret. On 9 August 1875, Duncan Campbell wrote to Duncan MacGregor:

In a communication from my brother Alex he offered me, in your name, the situation of Manager of one of your Queensland Stations [Mount Margaret]. He has asked for a decided answer and at once as you wish to have the Manager on the Station by the 22nd September.

I will therefore say I am happy to accept and grateful for your consideration. As the terms have been arranged between you and my brother all that remains for me to add is that I will be on the Station by the time fixed. If you have any instructions to me before I leave Melbourne (address is care of Mr D. Mailer), I will be happy to follow them.

I am yours respectfully, Duncan Campbell

David Mailer features in the relationship between MacGregor and his new employee. Duncan Campbell arrived at the station on 20 September and began a regular correspondence with MacGregor. His first letters contained news of mustering and branding, the rations and stores required for the Station and news that the water was drying up in the back country. By the end of the year he was writing that the Mount Margaret cattle had brought a good price; that he had started breaking in some steers; and that he would be walking them to Wilcannia if he could get a good bullock driver. He was diligent in his reporting of station matters and alerting MacGregor to the continued dry period they were experiencing. In December 1875 he wrote that there had not been any rain but even if rain did fall in the coming months, Mount Margaret would still be very short of water. He estimated that 'Three months is about the period it will last. If you are not coming up soon I hope you will send instructions in case we have no rain till then.' In closing, he guessed that January would be the month 'we can expect rain'.[52] Duncan Campbell and his brother Alex proved to be reliable managers of MacGregor's Durham Downs and Mount Margaret stations.

By July 1875 MacGregor was responsible for considerable tracts of pastoral land in Victoria, New South Wales and Queensland. In his own name, MacGregor owned Inverauld, 433 acres at Riddells Creek. In June 1875 Christina McRae had added 1,088 square miles to the leasehold of Mount Margaret Station on the Wilson River in Queensland. MacGregor had leased 822 square miles on the Georgina River, which became the Glengyle Station. And the partnership of Duncan MacGregor, Robert Mailer and David Mailer had leased 529 square miles of pastoral land on the Cooper Creek, Durham Downs Station.

Did MacGregor sit back and reflect on his achievements? If he did, it may have been for a fleeting moment. It appears Duncan still dreamed of other ventures.

Dreaming of draining the Koo-wee-rup Swamp, 1875

In Victoria the succession of Selection Acts after 1862 involved a struggle to unlock the land and turn it into an idealised pattern of intensive agricultural settlements.[53] Detailed studies of the draining and development of the Koo-wee-rup Swamp have been made in the past fifty years. In particular, two academic theses have been drawn upon because of their examination of the role played by Duncan MacGregor.[54]

On 25 March 1875, the Victorian Government sold at auction 9,000 acres of marginal swampland in the Parishes of Western Koo-wee-rup and Southern Nar-Nar-Goon. The land was sold to seven buyers for a total of £11,968. The main purchaser was Duncan MacGregor who bought 4,063 acres for £5,085.[55] His first purchase was of Allotments 23, 24, 27, 28, 29, 30, 34, 35, 99, 100, 101 and 102. This purchase marked the beginning of his long association with the Koo-wee-rup Swamp. MacGregor's friend, David Mailer, also purchased 1,280 acres consisting of Allotments 18, 19, 21 and 22. Why did Duncan choose this part of Victoria to purchase land? Did he feel confident he could improve the land for agricultural or pastoral gain; or was he encouraged by his friend David Mailer to speculate on the newly opened up area? Could the fact that the Shorthorn breeder William Lyall had prospered in the region have persuaded him to buy into the swampland venture?

Apart from MacGregor and his friend Mailer, the other buyers were 'Mrs J. Bloomfield, 1,427 acres; C. Moody, 1,686 acres; F.W. Peers, 416 acres; Richards, 183 acres and Browning, 200 acres.'[56] An average price of 25/- [shillings] per acre was paid and an additional 5/- per acre was added as a drainage fee. At this price the land was expensive, perhaps indicating the confidence the buyers felt in its potential. To their regret the buyers found very quickly that the 5/- per acre drainage fee was completely inadequate.

A misunderstanding between the buyers and the Lands Department as to who was responsible for the drainage on the land had to be faced from the outset. The Lands Department failed to act so the buyers were forced to form the Koo-wee-rup Swamp Drainage Committee; this group undertook to build drains with the money levied. Based on his acreage, Duncan's levy to the committee alone amounted to over £1,000. The drainage process was long and tedious. The drains were dug by hand with contract labour at 8/- per day. Conditions were difficult for the men employed on the works. Although it is widely stated that 110 men worked on the committee-funded drains, in a fortnightly period, many of the men worked only one or two days, and only about half were employed for seven days or more.[57]

The committee constructed two main channels; the first was 10 feet wide at the top, 5 feet 2 inches at the bottom and 3 feet 6 inches deep. There was a good fall and the water flowed at a steady pace along it. On the right, or western side of this main channel, about a mile further down towards Westernport Bay, a smaller drain was cut close to the main channel. The earth was excavated from both, forming an embankment between the two.

Further down towards the Bay another drain, constructed by MacGregor, ran parallel with the committee's drain and about 3 chains away from it until Westernport Bay was reached.[58] MacGregor's private scheme of drains and embankments was a success, although, because of the lack of drainage in the surrounding area, his land was not immune from flooding. An important section of MacGregor's land was located on a sand ridge known as 'the peninsula' or island. It was about 15 feet above the water level and this became the site of his homestead.

MacGregor cleared this ridge first and named his estate and homestead Dalmore. When faced with the challenge of clearing the potentially rich swampland, he was perhaps more fortunate than his six colleagues because he had the capital to spend on the venture. From 1879 he records he spent £6,516 on his private drains to be able to cultivate his land. His levies to the Swamp Drainage Committee eventually amounted to £1,754. MacGregor employed more than 30 men on his private drainage works and is believed to have cut more than 30 miles of drains on his property. The work was done with shovels and wheelbarrows and he paid the men 7/- to 8/- per day. The swampland suffered through extremes in weather. It was 'a sea in winter and without a drop in summer'.[59] The working conditions were difficult. First the scrub cutters went into the swamp and slashed the ti-trees. Next went the diggers with their crescent-shaped spades to clear the path for the drains. John Dwyer, the overseer, wrote to MacGregor about the conditions: 'The men are most miserable with the wet and cold … being in the wet and sludge all day.'[60] Consequently the men petitioned MacGregor for extra money to compensate for the extra hour each day they spent trudging through the mud to get to their work. There is no evidence the men got their extra pay. Cunningham speculated: 'it could be expected that MacGregor, the true Scot, drove a hard bargain'.[61]

Despite the difficulties, MacGregor's land was eventually cleared and the cattle grazed, making deep paths through the mounds so that they could hardly be seen from the distance. One former worker, Mr Keith Larsen, who reminisced about his experience working for MacGregor, concluded that the clearing and cultivation on Dalmore was more efficient and successful than MacGregor's neighbours' efforts. The Dalmore soil had originally been peat, like the rest of the swamp, but the area had dried out somewhat allowing the formation of an organic black clay over the top of the original peat deposits.[62] The land supported MacGregor's bullock teams and further clearance could take place. His stock breeding experience in Australia, as well as the available capital to spend on his project, explains his success.

MacGregor purchased additional land in the area in 1888, F.W. Peers's 416 acres. This land was Crown Allotments 11, 11B, 11C, 12 and 13, Parish of Koo-wee-rup, County of Mornington. He named this property Gowan Lea and constructed a 9-roomed house, a fibro-cement lined 2-roomed work hut for the men; a large barn, a dairy, 2 storerooms, a 9-stall stable with a brick floor; a skillion harness room; a large feed bin, and blacksmith's shop and cow yards.[63] Further land was purchased and the total acreage was increased to 1,125 acres. It remained in the family until the 1930s.

A thorn in their side – Annie McRae, 1878

Annie McRae, the youngest daughter of Christina and Donald McRae, was born in Bathurst in 1853. She was 15 years old when her sister and father died in 1867, and 16 years old when her 18-year-old sister Maggie married 33-year-old Duncan MacGregor. Duncan was very much an older man in Annie's life. We don't know how well the two got on. Annie, Maggie and her mother had settled into Clunie in 1867 and, when Maggie and Duncan were married, Duncan also lived there. After the couple purchased the Coburg property in 1873 the family appear to have divided their time between the two houses.

While she remained at home with her mother, Annie had a governess or tutor as she was still of school age. Ledgers for the Clunie homestead chart the family's expenditure from 1867 onwards. While Christina McRae received a quarterly annuity of £250, cash payments for her allowance and expenses were also paid to Annie regularly. In 1868, 1869, 1870 and 1871 Annie's allowance was very generous. Items such as train fares, clothing and shoes were regularly noted. In 1872 her expenditure for the year totalled £87.[64] This was a substantial sum for a single young woman. Later episodes indicate she was a poor manager of money.

Other than records of her expenses, little is known of Annie's teenage years. However, a sense of her personality becomes clear when details of her life prior to her marriage emerge. In 1874, both Annie McRae and Maggie MacGregor gave birth to daughters. Maggie gave birth to her fourth child, Isabella 'Tottie', on 11 May. Annie's first child, Christina, was born out of wedlock and therefore illegitimate; Kenneth McKenzie was acknowledged as her father. Three years later, on 1 May 1877, possibly due to pressure from Maggie and Duncan, Kenneth and Annie were married according to the forms of the Presbyterian Church at 108 Albert Street, East Melbourne.[65] Kenneth was 33 and Annie was 23. Formerly of Clonbinane Station near Broadford, Kenneth was the son of Alexander McKenzie who had occupied the 25,600-acre property at Clonbinane since 1851. When they married Kenneth was working at Ensay Station in Gippsland.

Ensay Station was a major sheep farm taking up most of the region of East Gippsland. Angus McMillan, the notable Scott and Gippsland explorer, had taken up the land around Ensay in 1839 for his employer, yet another Scot, Lachlan Macalister. Ensay Station originally covered 38,400 acres – it was the largest and busiest sheep station and woolshed in the region. The original station covered most of the Ensay district down to Swifts Creek, where its boundary met the Tongio Station, held from 1845 by P.C. Buckley.[66] Kenneth McKenzie's occupation as 'station manager' is noted on the marriage certificate. Annie McRae's residence is also recorded as 'Gippsland' where she was undoubtedly co-habiting with Kenneth. Following their marriage, Kenneth, Annie and Christina moved to Clonbinane where four more children were born.

Donald McRae McKenzie was born in 1883; Margaret Flora was born in 1886; Colin Duncan in 1887, and Kenneth in 1891. Donald died at the age of 6 in a drowning accident at Clonbinane and is buried at Campbellfield Cemetery.

Under the terms of Donald McRae's Will, at the age of 21, Annie was entitled to claim her annuity of £500 per annum. This meant Annie McKenzie and Maggie MacGregor had substantial and independent incomes in their own right. Within a year of marriage in May 1877, Annie McKenzie made it clear that she and her husband wanted more than the annuity. In August 1878 they made a claim on the will and petitioned the Supreme Court of New South Wales. Under the terms of the will the trustees 'at their absolute discretion' had the power to postpone the sale of McRae's real and personal property. The rents and profits in the meantime were deemed to form part of the income of the estate and the trustees had carried on and managed the property. In the intervening ten years since McRae's death in 1867, some of the properties had been increased in size, area and stock. The question put before the Court was:

> whether the excess in the number of the stock at the time of the sale of Caulpaulin station … And the proceeds of the Glengyle station and stock wholly acquired since the testator's death, and in the increase in area, and in the number and value of the stock of Mount Margaret station, are respectively to be deemed part of the corpus of the testator's estate, or as income and profits, and divisible accordingly?[67]

After argument from both sides, His Honour, Mr Justice Hargrave, held that the increase of the sheep and cattle, and the increased area procured for depasturing them upon, formed part of the corpus of the estate, and was not income. While Annie and Kenneth's attempt to claim part of the increase in income from the estate failed, at the end of the day the costs came out of the estate, decreasing its value. This first incursion into the estate of her late father set the pattern for the remainder of the 'infamous' Annie's life.[68]

— 3 —

Eyes on the Prize: Cattle Breeding, 1878–1888

Duncan MacGregor was revered as a stockbreeder as well as a pioneer pastoralist. He believed that the essential for success in breeding animals was 'the gifted faculty that recognises the kind of animals that ought to be selected' and that the real fundamental principle of breeding was hereditary.[1]

MacGregor was an industrious man with a forthright manner; he was also a no-nonsense man who held firm convictions and acted on them. As we have seen in the last chapter, MacGregor planned and executed incursions into new territory in central Victoria at Riddells Creek, outback western Queensland and south Gippsland. In the early 1870s, the two properties – Caulpaulin and Mount Margaret – needed stock, as did the newly acquired pastoral runs making up Durham Downs and Glengyle Stations. Maintaining these properties was uppermost in his mind. He had to devise ways of building up his breeding stock in New South Wales and Queensland. After acquiring pure-bred cattle and sheep, he bred from them to improve his stock. Their offspring were nurtured to maturity.

When he arrived in Australia, Duncan was a shepherd; in 1860 his father was surprised that he had 'gone away from the sheep' and had begun to work with cattle. Living in the Scottish Highlands he would have been familiar with the various breeds of cattle such as the Highland and Shorthorn raised on the steep hills of his homeland. However, it is unclear how familiar he was with breeding them. Nonetheless, given his nature, we suspect once he became interested in a subject he would have researched it thoroughly. The files contain parcels of press clippings on a range of subjects including breeding information about sheep, cattle and horses.

Shorthorn cattle have existed in the Scottish Highlands for centuries. Perhaps encouraged by Robert McDougall, MacGregor made the Booth Shorthorn his major cattle-breeding stock. Inverauld and Dalmore were used to breed his stock. Breeding the Shorthorn, Border Leicester and Clydesdale Horse became his abiding passion. Breeding, showing and judging them may have been a salver to his spirit in his darkest moments during the late 1890s.

The Booth Shorthorn

In the Scottish Highlands, the local cattle grazing the steep slopes were typically the Ayrshire, Belted Galloway, Galloway and Highland breeds. Originating in the Scottish Highlands in the sixth century, Highland cattle were bred with long hair to suit their environment. The majestic, long-horned animals remain an icon of the Scottish Highlands. Scottish immigrants such as builder and later politician, Samuel Amess, first imported Highland cattle into Australia in the mid-nineteenth century and bred them at Churchill Island and possibly at Riddells Creek.

Beef cattle had, of course, been introduced into Australia in 1788 with the arrival of the First Fleet. The Afrikaner cattle 'had a strange hump between their shoulders … their tails were short and thin and their horns long and twisted'. Accounts vary, but the livestock purchased at Cape Town *en route* to Australia is believed to have included one or two Indian Zebu bulls, four or five cows and a heifer calf.[2] The cattle were brought to the new colony specifically for breeding purposes, not for consumption, but after months at sea they were thin and wasted.[3] Unfortunately the convicts and other members of the First Fleet knew nothing about cattle and the livestock escaped or perished.[4]

Other efforts were made to establish a herd for the colony. The Second Fleet arrived in 1791 with 11 cattle on board and more arrived in 1792. When the cattle from the First Fleet were rediscovered in 1795 in 'lush grazing country' nearly 40 miles from Sydney Cove, they had multiplied to 61. The wild cattle survived and bred in an area later named 'Cowpastures', now the city of Camden.[5] Once recaptured, they provided a source of meat as well as tallow and hides for the convict settlement. The next substantial shipment of 131 head of cattle arrived from India in 1795; they were followed by a further shipment of 296 cows from the Cape Settlement. Together, they became the basis for the government's first substantial herd.[6]

The origins of the Shorthorn breed can be traced back to the Tees River Valley in northern England, where the Teeswater breed evolved from a cross with a Dutch dairy type in the late eighteenth century. Teeswater cattle were big framed, heavy horned and attained great weight at five to six years. They were highly valued as beef cattle but were bred for both dairy and beef production. Certain bloodlines within the Shorthorn breed emphasised either one quality or the other. Using the selective breeding techniques they had learned from Robert Bakewell, who had used this technique on Longhorn cattle, the Collings brothers, Robert and Charles, started to improve the Durham cattle. At the same time Thomas Bates (1775–1849) of Northumberland and Thomas Booth (1755–1835) of Yorkshire were developing Teeswater cattle. The Bates cattle were developed for their milking qualities while the Booth cattle were developed for beef. Thomas Booth retired to his property 'Warlaby', in Hambleton, North Yorkshire, where he died aged 68 in 1835. This was the year Duncan MacGregor was born. Thomas Bates enjoyed robust health until 1849, when he died aged 74. These men are the acknowledged leaders in cattle breeding in nineteenth-century England.

The year 1825 is taken as the official date Shorthorns were imported into New South Wales by Potter McQueen of Scone. The following year the Australian Agricultural Company imported additional Shorthorns. The opening up of the Port Phillip District of New South Wales in 1835 created a new demand for cattle and a boom in the importation of pedigree bulls occurred between 1836 and 1840.[7] Scottish and English immigrants who had left their own country in order to prosper in the new colony were eager to establish good stocks and follow British trends.

Robert McDougall (1813–87), cattle breeder and agriculturalist, arrived in Port Phillip in 1841 or 1842. He was born at Fortingall, Perth Shire, Scotland in 1813. This was very close to Liaran where MacGregor was born, and this common bond may have forged their later friendship. Being twenty years older, McDougall might also have seen himself as a father figure or mentor to Duncan.

Prior to his arrival in Australia, McDougall spent three years in Canada trapping beaver before being attracted to the Port Phillip District, as it then was.[8] Initially he worked for Western District pastoralist, Thomas Learmonth, who led the pastoral settlement and wool production in Port Phillip.[9] After leaving Learmonth, McDougall explored the lower Loddon and middle Murray rivers. In 1848 he rented land (although it is unclear where) and, 'with sufficient capital to start in a small way himself', he bought stock and began to breed Shorthorn cattle, pigs and horses.[10] In the early 1850s he improved his Shorthorn herd by importing livestock from Tasmania; he rented property near Essendon to accommodate his growing breeding program. In 1856 he was elected to the Legislative Assembly for West Bourke but retired in 1857. In 1858 McDougall was appointed to a committee constituted to compile and edit a herd book for the colony. The committee included his contemporaries and rivals, the cattle breeders Niel Black of Mount Noorat and Jeremiah Ware of Minjah Homestead.[11] Personal animosities led to a dispute over the status of locally bred stud and McDougall was left to compile this book himself. The stock book was probably the first to be published in Australia.

In 1859 McDougall went to England to buy stud bulls, and in the 1860s expanded his stud and refined his breeding techniques. He is described as 'an excellent showman and constant prize-winner', active in the Port Phillip Farming Society, a trustee of the National Agricultural Society and strongly supported the creation of a Board of Agriculture.[12] In 1869–70 he visited England again and bought two prize-winning bulls, Field Marshall Booth and Major Booth, both bred at Warlaby.[13] In 1870 McDougall bought Arundel Farm at Keilor. Some time later he purchased 640 acres at Bulla Bulla and named the property 'Warlaby' after the home of Thomas Booth.[14]

Accounts of McDougall paint a picture of an irascible Scot who was 'respected but not popular'.[15] MacGregor's shared enthusiasm for the Booth Shorthorn accounts for the naming of one of his runs 'Warlaby', paying his respect to Thomas Booth's and Robert McDougall's properties of the same name. Robert McDougall's Arundel property at Keilor was just 26 miles from Inverauld and 34 miles from Clunie. MacGregor's personal association with McDougall probably dates from 1868 or 1869 when he first moved to Victoria. In his later years, McDougall treated MacGregor as a son, making him an executor of his will.

As well as Niel Black and Jeremiah Ware, McDougall's major rival in stock breeding was Robert Clarke of Bolinda Vale, Clarkefield. Born in Tasmania in 1841, but not related to the W.J.T. Clarke family, he began working for W.J.T. in 1851 as a 10-year-old boy. Robert crossed Bass Strait with Clarke when he first brought his sheep to Bolinda Vale in Victoria. Located close to Riddells Creek and Romsey, it lies in a protected valley south-east of the Macedon Ranges. At Bolinda Vale,

Robert Clarke grew into a 'sturdy young man of middle height … [with] the deliberate gait of the shepherd'. Early in life he developed a love of stock, and steadily acquired his knowledge of breeding. He became an acknowledged disciple of the 'illustrious English Shorthorn breeder, the immortal Bates' and adopted his teachings from the outset. He read every word that he could of anything associated with Bates; his ideals and practices were based on Bates' prototype.[16] Clarke's skill and reputation in the field were legendary. Robert Clarke and Duncan MacGregor held vehemently opposed views on their preferred stock. Publicly they argued loud and long about the advantages of the Booth over the Bates strain of Shorthorn. Given their individual dispositions, it is unlikely MacGregor visited him at Bolinda Vale.

The Morton brothers, Richard and Septimus, of Mount Derrimut were also revered breeders of pure Bates Shorthorns in Victoria.[17] Clarke greatly respected Richard Morton's methods and believed he 'did so much for Victorian-bred shorthorns'.[18] In 1871, on behalf of the Morton brothers, Dalmahoy Campbell sold by public auction 'four superior young bulls'. The prices paid were £173, 135 guineas, 155 guineas and 200 guineas, record amounts for the time. The animals were judged to be 'second to none ever offered in this colony, and met with unqualified admiration from every one'.[19] Jeremiah George Ware also favoured the Bates strain. He is described as 'one of the leading Shorthorn breeders. He made many notable importations of stud stock, including the Shorthorn sire Master Butterfly'.[20] These men made their mark on the Shorthorn industry in Australia.

Whether or not he agreed with their breeding practices, Clarke, McDougall, the Mortimer brothers, Niel Black and Jeremiah Ware must have influenced MacGregor's thinking.

Leicester and Border Leicester sheep

The sheep Duncan MacGregor tended in the Scottish Highlands would have included the Scottish Blackface, the Cheviot and the Leicester. The white Leicester and Border Leicester are large and coarse-boned, not easily fattened, with coarse, long wool; they are broad in the back with finely-arched ribs. Both sexes are hornless. They have been improved by crossing with Lincolnshire and Romney Marsh breed.[21]

Soon after his arrival in Melbourne in October 1857, an article highlighting the importance of the importation of suitable sheep appeared in the Melbourne *Argus*.[22] This was a topical issue and MacGregor may have read about it with great interest. The papers relished printing the ongoing debates between breeders arguing the merits of one breed over the other. Wool was an important topic and one of Australia's major exports at the time, bringing great prosperity to the country. From the newspapers we see sheep owners were importing Cotswolds, Leicester, South Downs and Merino sheep into Australia.[23] In 1858 William Lyall of Harewood at Westernport Bay entered the fray, declaring in a letter to the *Argus* that he preferred the Cotswold over the Leicester because 'he has more weight, better constitution, and more activity, with a great aptitude to fatten'. Unsurprisingly, he concluded that local sheep farmers would not be slow to 'adopt the system of breeding that will be most profitable to themselves'. The major pastoralist, W.J.T. Clarke at Bolinda Vale had his say on the issue of imported sheep. He wrote that over the 30 years he had bred sheep, he had crossed Cotswolds with Leicesters 'more than any other man in the colonies and I have never had occasion to regret it'. He also found that the cross-bred sheep thrived well on the poor arid land as much as on the rich lands.[24] Regular articles advising the best breeding methods were also reprinted from English papers and appeared in the *Farmer's Journal and Gardener's Chronicle* as well as in the *Argus* and the *Australasian*, while the debate over the most suitable sheep breed continued.[25]

Duncan MacGregor's breeding program at Inverauld began with Leicester sheep before adding the Border Leicesters. By 1876 he had a flock of about 900 'pure, seven eighths, or three-quarters bred Leicesters', and was introducing fresh blood every season. The sheep were attracting the highest prices in the Melbourne market.[26]

MacGregor held decisive opinions on the attributes required in the Border Leicester sheep he bred:

> Compactness, neatness of shape and beauty of form to harmonize, looking at the body and conformation of the animal as a whole, weight and quality is wanted, and you get it in proportion to the compactness of the form, and perfection of the beast is when the dead weight of all eatable parts approaches the nearest to the live weight of the living animal.[27]

As a judge of stock, his critique included the body shape – head, eyes, cheeks, neck back, chest, legs, knees as well as the quality of the wool. The attributes of the Border Leicester were vitally important. MacGregor was aware these animals had to be sturdy to survive the conditions in Queensland. His flock of Border Leicester sheep were included as No. 7 in the *Victorian Flock Book*, dated 17 December 1891. This stock was achieved through purchasing from Mr Robert Harper of Avondale, Sale, one ram together with ten imported ewes with nine lambs at foot. These purebred animals contributed to his famous stockbreeding program at Inverauld and Dalmore.

Clydesdale horses

The Clydesdale is a breed of horse derived from the farm horses of Clydesdale, Scotland, and named after the region. Originally used as warhorses in the seventeenth century, the Clydesdale has undergone many changes. With its history of over 300 years, the animal was first used as a draught horse on farms, pulling heavy loads. Generally bay in colour, it is a tall breed of over 18 hands, with white markings and extensive feathering at the ankles, making it easily recognizable. It is thought the feathering was developed during the first breeding between the Flemish and Scottish breeds around 1837. The feather, a thick mane and heavy coat helped the breed survive in the severe Scottish climate.

The first Clydesdales, Shire and other heavy breeds were imported into Australia in the 1820s but it was not until a century later that horse teams dominated haulage. Throughout the nineteenth century bullocks were cheaper and simpler to maintain.[28] Following the discovery of gold in New South Wales and Victoria in 1851, the best breeding stock of Scotland was imported into Australia and draught horse breeding began in earnest. The first breed registry was formed in Scotland in 1877 when thousands of Clydesdales were exported to Australia and New Zealand.[29]

MacGregor first imported pure Clydesdale stud stock from Glasgow in 1876. He enjoyed writing about the animals he bred, and his Clydesdales were no exception. He had exacting standards and wrote that attention had to be paid to the structure of the horse's legs. Defects, malformations and unsoundness should be noted and improved. Attention should be paid to the shape of the horse, particularly the placement of the legs. The bone structure, muscles, tendons and ligaments and their relationship to each other must be considered, and close attention must be paid to forearms, thighs and gaskins, he wrote.[30] MacGregor firmly believed that the pedigree of every horse and mare should be recorded because no scientific breeding could be undertaken unless the tendencies of animals to hereditary defects and unsoundness were well known and bred out.

In his pamphlet 'Particular Description of a Clydesdale Horse', he wrote of his ideal specimen:

> The Head on the small side, but masculine; not large, long or coarse; but full and wide between the eyes, slightly tapering to root of ears, which ought not to be too close at base, but active, inclining slightly forward and inward at points, and neither too long, thick and heavy, nor set too far back. The eyes should be full, but mild and placid, and not showing too much white. The jaws ought to be board, deep, and wide at gullet; the muzzle not too heavy, or too pointed; and the lips neither thick nor large. With nostrils full, and face even, a good head is assured.[31]

But the poet in the man needed an outlet for the passion he felt for his beloved Clydesdale. Combining his pride in his homeland and the horse, he wrote:

> O Scotland! That can justly claim
> The pride of place for Clydesdale fame,
> With feet and pasterns, arms, and thighs,
> And all good qualities besides;
> So loud thy praises sound afar
> Throughout all land where horses are.

Duncan MacGregor needed horses on the pastoral stations he managed and the ledgers reveal the numbers he bought and sold annually.

Working the stations

In August 1872, the two Duncans, as executors and trustees of McRae's New South Wales Estate, purchased 160 acres of land described as 'Unnamed at the head station Caulpaulin Run', in the Pastoral District of Albert in the County of Young. The land was Portion One and commenced on the right bank of the River Darling about three chains easterly from the eastern corner of the head station dwelling house on the Caulpaulin Run on the Darling River.[32] This appears to have been the only addition to McRae's existing property on the Darling River. Meanwhile, MacGregor was planning to expand his own land holdings, which he successfully achieved in the next two years.

The ledger books for the McRae and MacGregor pastoral stations make for interesting reading and give some indication of what life must have been like for the hundreds of labourers, shearers and cattlemen they employed. Where some of the details of leases have not been found, the ledger books appear to commence on the dates the Stations were acquired. The wages book for stockmen and shearers at Caulpaulin Station tells us only a little about the men and their various pay rates. In 1874 John Mansfield was head stockman at £100 per annum; James Shepherd was employed as a shepherd; Joseph Morris was employed for mustering and shearing; William McCarthy, Frank Worthane and J.R. Samuel were also engaged as shepherds at 25 shillings per week. In contrast, the same ledgers tell us that about his private life and his preference for clothing. In the year 1876–77, MacGregor paid for, through his private account, two silk dust-coats and one hat. Duncan MacGregor exhibiting sartorial splendour? On a more mundane level, Mount Margaret Station supplies included 'Flour, sugar, oats, tobacco, singlets, shirts, boots etc.'. The lease for Durham Downs was taken up on 1 July 1875. The following rations were delivered: 'Tea, sugar, tobacco, boots, apples, assessment, cartage, bottle brandy, Apples, boots, sugar and shirts.' They came to a total of £143/18/2.[33] Expenses for the year 1874–75 and 1875–76 were £9,949/11/3 and £10,517/15/3 respectively.[34]

The photographer Nile Godson shot a series of albumen silver photographs of Durham Downs Station in 1878. Workers resting while at the wool washing compound gaze at the camera as the photograph is taken; a second photograph captures the activities of the station hands with the wool drying in the background. Another photograph is taken from the distance and focuses on the accommodation where a few men stand under the verandahs shading from the sun. Durham Downs Station employed increasing numbers of Aboriginal workers. It is therefore of particular interest to see that the photograph of about 25 of these workers is remarkably similar in composition to that taken by Frederic Bonney at Mount Murchison Station on the River Darling in 1865. Bonney photographed the Aboriginal worker named Possum, also at Durham Downs. The series of four photographs discussed above are part of the MacGregor Collection at the State Library. They certainly enliven our perception of life on a remote cattle and sheep station during the nineteenth century.

Meanwhile, work continued on the Victorian properties of Clunie, Inverauld and Dalmore. Annual expenses at Clunie were recorded, and no doubt monitored, carefully. Expenses for Christina McRae at Clunie included railway fares to and from Melbourne, cab hire in Melbourne, doctors, rates, stationery and stamps, seeds and freight. Christina McRae regularly drew cash from the Estate and her quarterly annuity of £250 is also noted. Annie McRae's expenses, cash, sundries, clothing and shoes increase each year. Wages for Clunie remained constant at around £224 per annum. It appears that in 1879 Kenneth McKenzie was the manager of Clunie. In this instance it is unclear if McKenzie is Annie's husband Kenneth, or Christina's brother Kenneth. The confusion because of the duplication of family names, and of property names, is a constant theme of this story. It would have been surprising if Kenneth McKenzie, Annie's husband, was managing Clunie if they were living at Clonbinane. It is more likely Kenneth McKenzie was in fact Christina's brother managing it temporarily. He eventually settled in central Victoria.

In 1877, accounts for the partnership between MacGregor and Robert and David Mailer appear in the ledgers. In that year the group spent £190/4/3 on rations including flour, sugar, hemp, a butcher's knife, salt and oats. The following year the supplies included 6 wooden pipes, 1 quart billy, 8 pairs of boots, 20 pounds of tobacco. The account added up to £207/14/9. The accounts for 1878 and 1879 note movement of cattle between the stations in an account with two drovers 'travelling bulls from Caulpaulin to Durham Downs' and John McRae's 'returning with horses'. During a heatwave in New South Wales in 1878, a planned droving trip from Caulpaulin to Melbourne was abandoned. The head drover, Mr Battersby started out from Caulpaulin Station with 365 head of cattle for the Melbourne market. He got as far as Pooncarrie when he received a telegram to take the cattle back to the station owing to the 'bad state of the country on the lower Darling and upper Murray Rivers'. He passed Menindee bound for Caulpaulin on 16 February 1878 on his return journey. As the paper noted, this 'resulted in an unrewarded trip of over 310 miles (500 km).[35] Moving cattle from the Darling to Victoria was not without its difficulties. Losses due to unsuitable feed, the weather, or lack of water cost MacGregor dearly.

Reports of MacGregor's bulls being shown in various agricultural shows emphasised the presence MacGregor had in Queensland as well as Victoria where he concentrated on his breeding stock. The Queensland Exhibition was held in August 1878. There were 152 entries of horses, 118 of cattle and 58 sheep as well as pigs, poultry and dogs. MacGregor may have entered his Clydesdales and his sheep although they did not rank as winners. However, 'There was a splendid show of Durham's and MacGregor's roan Fandango was named the best bull in the show'.[36]

In Victoria, by 1878 Inverauld at Riddells Creek had become MacGregor's private saleyard and advertisements for the sale by auction of pure-bred Shorthorn Cattle, Clydesdale Mares and Leicester Sheep appeared in the *Australasian* and the *Argus*. The cattle were sold through the stock and station agents Peck, Hudson and Raynor. One advertisement reads:

> The cattle comprise bulls, heifers, and cows, all of which are only grass-fed, but notwithstanding will be found symmetrical in shape, thick and massive of flesh, and of sound and robust constitutions, with good colours, and equal as a lot of any ever offered to public competition in Victoria.[37]

MacGregor's role as a breeder was promoted, emphasising that he had carefully bred from 'Mr R. McDougall's bulls for years'. As a further enticement to attend the sale, MacGregor arranged for purchasers coming by train to be met at the Riddells Creek Station, then conveyed the two miles to the property in time for the sale. Luncheon was also provided. Regular advertisements for MacGregor's cattle sales continue until the late 1890s.

1881 was a good year in Queensland. The *Wilcannia Times* reported in June 1881 that in the history of the district since its settlement by speculating pastoralists, the area had never had a better season. Nearly two inches of rain had fallen in the past week and 'never was grass or water more usefully plentiful'. The rain was falling steadily and the paper congratulated 'our pastoral friends' on their good fortune.[38]

Leases of the Queensland stations Miranda and Meba Downs commenced in 1881 although an exact date has not been found. Miranda, a station of 1,013 square miles, consisted of runs totalling 457 square miles in Queensland and 556 in South Australia. Duncan Campbell secured the licences for Miranda from the Salmond Brothers for £1,500. Meba Downs, with runs totalling 739 square miles, was also acquired in 1881.

It is unclear when Yanko, another smaller station of 459 square miles, was acquired. The Wigugomrie Station was part of another partnership, this time between John Russell Ross and Robert Bruce Ronald. The deed of partnership was signed on 27 February 1883 and entered into for the purpose of purchasing '"Wigugomrie" … in the district of Gregory South in the Colony of Queensland' from Duncan Campbell, James Osborne the younger and Henry Houston Osborne. The Station consisted of 29 runs and was reported to consist of about 2,235 square miles, within 320 miles of the South Australian railways. It was purchased together with all improvements, 4,000 head of cattle and 50 horses and all plant, chattels furniture and effects for the sum of £22,500, with £8000 payable in cash 'and the balance by the Promissory Notes of the said parties and interest at the rate of five pounds per centum per annum by their Separate Promissory Notes'. Wigugomrie was secured by mortgage of the purchasers.[39] Two years later, the sale of 250 head of cattle from Wigugomrie was reported in the South Australian *Register*.[40]

One of MacGregor's oldest and long-standing workers, Farquhar McDonald, probably began working at Durham Downs in 1881. His role as stockman in charge of droving cattle to Melbourne or other southern markets was reported in various newspapers during the years 1881–85 in particular. In June 1881 he was not the only stockmen reported to be making the journey. The *Western Grazier*'s correspondent noted he was in charge of a mob of fat cattle passing through Kyabra in south-west Queensland on their way to the southern markets. Once again, in July 1883, McDonald was reported to be in charge of 315 fat cattle, of mixed sexes from Durham Downs, on his way to Melbourne. Good rain in the area was reported from the newspaper's correspondent on the Booligal Track. The rain was making the trip easier for stockmen and cattle.[41] The pastoral news and stock movements reported in 1885 also noted that Farquhar McDonald had left Durham Downs for Melbourne with a mob of fat cattle.[42] In 1881 Farquhar McDonald was 52. He was born in Kintail, Ross Shire, Scotland in 1829, the third of 8 children, 6 sons and 2 daughters. He came to Victoria as an assisted immigrant on the *Nelson* with his widowed father John and his seven siblings. He married Catherine McLennan in 1873 but it is thought she died young, possibly in childbirth. He remained with MacGregor and in later years helped train MacGregor's sons, John (Jack) and Donald once they were old enough to work on the Stations.

From drought to deluge – Koo-wee-rup, 1875

In contrast to the extreme drought MacGregor had to contend with in Queensland during the late 1870s and the 1880s, he encountered a very different landscape in Gippsland. The Pakenham Koo-wee-rup Swamp presented its own unique problems. Most parts of the swamp received about 34 inches of rain per year, with most occurring during the spring, thus while Queensland was in drought, the flood and damp of the Koo-wee-rup Swamp meant it was impossible to penetrate. Tales of the fabulous richness of the swamp soils attracted settlers, keen to sew crops and raise cattle.

MacGregor was persistent in his efforts to transform his swampland into viable grazing land. He was a most determined and vociferous member of the Koo-wee-rup Swamp Committee. He believed all members should share the expenses to gain from their joint drainage of the swamp. While he was able to spend large sums of money to achieve his dream of draining the swamp, his attitudes attracted controversy. Enterprising though MacGregor's drainage activities were, they caused two protracted legal cases, stimulating his love of litigation and incurring for him the temporary hostility of the Berwick and Cranbourne Shire Councils.

The first case occurred in 1880 when Robert and Edward Stanlake accused him of flooding their land. In this case he 'entered into the fray with some vigour'.[43] The Stanlake's complained to the Berwick Shire Council that MacGregor's drains and embankments were forcing the water back on to their property and damaging their crops.[44] The Shire engineer found that the embankment was causing the water to overflow onto Stanlake's property. MacGregor agreed to meet the council and discuss the matter. His arguments were persuasive as nothing was done about the matter. Stanlake complained again in March 1882. In May 1882, a group of 13 neighbours petitioned the Cranbourne Shire Council claiming that MacGregor was swamping them out. Their petition was referred to the Berwick Shire Council which at the same time received a counter-petition, stating that MacGregor's drains were providing a great benefit to them and the area. The council then received a second letter from the group who made the original complaint: they had changed their minds and no longer wished to complain about MacGregor's drainage works. The Berwick Council eventually resolved that, in their opinion,

MacGregor's private drain and the drain cut by the committee were a benefit to the district. They declined to interfere further in the matter![45] Duncan MacGregor triumphed at his win.

However, not everything in Gippsland was going well for Duncan MacGregor at this time. His sister Annie, who had immigrated to Australia in 1874 and settled in the nearby Shire of Drouin, became ill in 1880. She was just 40. She had been married for seven years and living in Australia for six, and was the mother of two sons, aged 5 and 2. In around May or June 1880 she was diagnosed with breast cancer. Her death certificate indicates that the doctor who saw her in July 1880 did not see her again before her death. Annie MacGregor Brown died on 21 October 1880. She was buried in the Drouin cemetery.[46]

The vast estate – a jigsaw puzzle of leases and partnerships

There is no indication in the files as to the reason, but on 22 August 1877 Duncan MacGregor and Duncan McRae, acting for the Estate of the Late Donald McRae in New South Wales, offered three properties for sale at the Menzies Hotel, Melbourne. They were Caulpaulin, Mount Margaret and Glengyle Stations.

Caulpaulin Station on the Darling River covered an estimated 177,000 acres (277 square miles) held under lease from the government, and 160 acres of freehold land. (The additional 160 acres had been purchased in 1872.) Caulpaulin carried the largest number of stock with 3,000 head of mixed cattle, 15,000 sheep and 35 horses. The improvements to Caulpaulin Station included a house, stockyards, horse paddock, and some fencing. The property was put up for sale in one lot at a lump sum. All calves and lambs under six months old were to be delivered at the time of sale. Caulpaulin was sold seven months after the auction, on 18 March 1878. Christina McRae may have felt saddened by the sale of Caulpaulin. She and Donald had risked their livelihood to lease the Caulpaulin property in 1855 when they were adventurous settlers on the then largely unexplored region of the Darling River. They had lived permanently in this remote location as a young family for twelve years, until moving to Melbourne, and Donald's sudden death, in 1867. The property had been in the family for a total of twenty-six years. Donald had bred his Shorthorns there and Duncan had carried on the practice, following in his footsteps.

Mount Margaret Station on the Wilson River, estimated at 1,368,960 acres (2,139 square miles) was held under promise of lease by the government of Queensland, together with 7,000 head of mixed cattle and 50 horses. The station had substantially increased in size since its initial purchase in 1866. The improvements to Mount Margaret Station consisted of a hut, stockyard, and horse paddock at the home station, and hut and stockyard at out-stations.

The final offering, Glengyle Station, was estimated to contain an area of 192,000 acres (300 square miles). The notice advised that a license for these blocks from the government of Queensland had been applied for, and the first year's rent, amounting to £46-10-0, had been paid. The station was to be sold together with 1,500 head of mixed cattle and 30 horses.

Although widely advertised in Victoria, New South Wales and Queensland, the sale of Mount Margaret and Glengyle was not successful. Mount Margaret was finally sold on 8 November 1881; it was purchased by William Moodie, John Donaldson and John Ord Inglis, trading as Moodie, Donaldson, Inglis & Co. When they took possession of the property in 1883, the McRae brand 'CM2' was also transferred to the purchasers.[47]

Taking risks with high finance

Duncan MacGregor began a long and complex series of investments and leases in partnership with many other individuals in the 1870s. With the wisdom of hindsight, he would have been wiser to stick to what he knew best: cattle, sheep and horse breeding.

The paper trail is long and wide yet largely incomprehensible. Much of the paperwork appears to be missing as many of the transactions, when viewed alone, are baffling. The ongoing relationship between David Mailer and Duncan MacGregor is the one constant in these arrangements. For example, on 8 November 1871 MacGregor paid £1,000 to David Mailer to be invested as Mailer saw fit: 'the profits arising therefrom to be equally divided between Mr D. McGregor and self'. Mailer agreed to pay all expenses and guaranteed MacGregor against all loss of capital or principal.[48] What was behind this agreement?

The Melbourne solicitors, Brahe & Gair, and his accountants, Rucker & McKenzie, acted for Duncan MacGregor and his family throughout

Duncan's professional life. As well as engaging them for their advice on numerous private legal and accounting matters, he also sought the services of Brahe & Gair when acting as the joint executor of a deceased estate. Seven years after his investment agreement with David Mailer, in September 1878, Brahe & Gair drew up a document for David Mailer giving MacGregor power of attorney over Mailer's affairs.[49] The reason for this remains a matter of speculation. Why did David Mailer give MacGregor power of attorney over his estate four years after he and his brother had entered into partnership? Together they had speculated on the numerous properties in Queensland, particularly Durham Downs. Yet the necessity to sue fellow speculators was raised in the document; its purpose was 'to take whatever steps my said Attorney may deem necessary for the purposes of protecting my [Mailer's] interest in the said Runs of Crown Land' and to begin or 'precede any action at law or suit in Equity or other legal proceeding in any court' in the Colony of Queensland. This determination indicates Mailer's steady resolve to win or retain whatever was at stake at all costs.

One further speculative transaction began on 27 February 1883 when MacGregor entered into a deed of partnership with John Russell Ross and Robert Bruce Ronald to purchase Wigugomrie for £22,500. The property abutted Glengyle Station. The scale of loans taken out by MacGregor is astounding: this was not the first loan arrangement MacGregor became embroiled in, and would not be the last.

While cattle and sheep breeding and sales continued in earnest at Inverauld, a decision was taken in 1884 to sell the nearby Clunie property at Chintin. Arranged by Messrs Peck, Hudson & Raynor in conjunction with Messrs King & Co., the sale was scheduled to take place at 3 pm on Tuesday 25 November 1884 at the Menzies' Hotel, Melbourne, a popular venue for sales of this kind. The property was to be sold in four lots, containing 230, 440, 92 and 136 acres respectively. Once again, the sale was not realised. At this point MacGregor's financial commitments were increasing.

When the Chintin property failed to sell, Christina and Duncan decided to lease the land instead. In May 1885 a lease agreement for Chintin was entered into with a Mr John Kerr of Glenallen in the County of Bourke. Christina McRae continued to live in the beautiful residence. Christina's brother Kenneth McKenzie was still managing Chintin at the time and signed the lease on their behalf. Leasing the property must have been a positive outcome for the family. The rental income would have eased their financial situation.

However, this issue must have paled somewhat when in 1886, twelve years after leasing Durham Downs with Robert and David Mailer, the partnership ran into trouble. The partners had to contend with a court case disputing cattle numbers. It was always going to end in the courts. Recalling the original arrangement between MacGregor and Neil Macdonald, the dispute over the original number of cattle purchased to stock the station had never been resolved. Whether this was an ongoing issue is hard to determine, yet we recall the Mailers were happy to leave the number of cattle actually purchased as understated because they expected to retain the property briefly. In 1886, when the property was mortgaged to Sir James McBain, Alexander MacEdward and John Bell, a dispute described as a 'squatting action of some magnitude' went before the Supreme Court of Victoria on 23 February 1886.[50]

When they mortgaged the station for £78,000, McBain et al were told the number of cattle on the station was 12,000, yet the number of cattle actually delivered was 9,689. McBain and partners sought to recover £21,000 from Mailer, Mailer and MacGregor for misrepresenting the number of cattle on Durham Downs Station.[51] A decision in the breach of contract case was reached on Friday 25 June 1886. The Court held that there was no evidence as to the fraudulent misrepresentation by Messrs Mailer and MacGregor; that there had been a difference of opinion among the defendants as to the number of cattle; and that the plaintiffs had been made aware of the difference of opinion.[52] All the questions were answered in favour of the defendants. MacGregor had a habit, or made it his business, to win any court case he engaged in.

In November 1887 Duncan MacGregor and William Walter Davis of Kerrie Station near Burke in New South Wales, together with the Australian Mortgage Land and Finance Company, advanced £50,000 to Daniel Hatten and Henry Dean of Yanda Station near Burke. The repayment of interest and charges would amount to £3,000, part of which MacGregor would earn for his efforts. This lease arrangement may have been a good idea in theory, but risky.

Only one year after the previous court case concerning himself and the Mailers, in 1887 MacGregor went into partnership with James MacBain, Alexander MacEdward and John Bell, as MacGregor & Co. This partnership then transferred Glengyle Station to Duncan MacGregor,

Alexander McEdward and James MacBain in 1891. The interest held by James MacBain, who died in 1892, then transferred to Simon Fraser, Alexander Morrison and Robert Whiting, executors of MacBain's Will. The mortgage was transferred to the London Chartered Bank on 20 June 1894.

The role of a trustee – a lesson in family arguments

MacGregor's mentor, the well-known cattle breeder Robert McDougall, died on 25 June 1887. His will, dated 6 April 1883, appointed his son Alexander McDougall and his son-in-law Alexander Smith as executors. Less than a year later, on 15 January 1884, he added a codicil appointing Duncan MacGregor as an additional executor. A second codicil, dated 18 June 1887 (just one week before his death), bequeathed to his son Alexander the sum of £3,000 in addition to his share of the proceeds of the sale of his assets.[53] At the time of his death, his estate, both real and personal, was valued at £51,872.[54] Probate was granted to A. McDougall, A. Smith and D. MacGregor on 22 September 1887.

It is interesting that McDougall chose MacGregor as an additional executor and trustee. The two men had a close relationship and McDougall knew that he was the executor of the McRae Estate. Did he feel he needed someone he trusted as an additional executor? Could McDougall have hoped MacGregor would act as the voice of reason between the son and son-in-law, who were falling out over the will?

McDougall's will appeared to be quite straightforward and according to his wishes his estate was sold. The cattle were put up for auction on Thursday 1 December 1887. From McDougall's estates Arundel and Warlaby his prize herds realized £40,000.[55] McDougall's estate included 13 mortgages to city properties. Did these property dealings whet MacGregor's appetite to dabble in property speculation as a fast money-making venture or was this simply the trend of the time?

The sale catalogue for the McDougall estate was extensive. It consisted of 175 pages of breeding details of his Pure Booth Shorthorn stud stock for sale. The pedigree of the sires and the dates of service were listed in the introduction, noting that the details would be made available on the day of the sale. McDougall had made his name in Australian pure stud stockbreeding and this was an important sale.[56]

It is no surprise that Duncan MacGregor, while an executor of the estate, was also a purchaser of a considerable number of McDougall's stud stock. Alexander Campbell of Glengyle Station's name is written on the auction catalogue against the cattle he purchased for MacGregor's Queensland properties. He secured seven yearling bulls, six bull calves, nine 2-year-old heifers, five yearling heifers, six heifer calves, sixteen cows and seven 3-year-old heifers. The prize specimens were, no doubt, carefully transported from Keilor to Inverauld or directly to Queensland.

Returning to McDougall's will. He bequeathed his wife Margaret the household furnishings and an annuity of £400 per year for her life. The executors set aside a sum of £9,000 for his widow's annuity. Realization of the estate through its sale in December 1887 and distribution of the proceeds to his beneficiaries, his son and five daughters, occurred simultaneously. A sum of £8,250 was distributed to each of his children.

In their role as trustees, MacGregor, Alexander McDougall and Alexander Smith acted in what they later declared was the best interests of the estate. They invested part of estate's capital in property. They were not alone when they misjudged the market. Their investment was made on the eve of the drastic economic Depression of the early 1890s. Their investment proved almost worthless; there was insufficient money in the estate to pay the annuities. In May 1899 J.R. Thompson, the solicitor acting for Mrs McDougall and her daughters, corresponded with Brahe & Gair, MacGregor's solicitors. He conveyed that his clients considered the management of the accounts for the estate to be unsatisfactory.[57]

Brahe & Gair responded that their clients strongly resented the letter's tone and that the executors had 'faithfully carried out the trust of the Will … exercised all caution that prudent men could do' and were in no way responsible for the depreciation in the value of the securities. They rejected the other allegations in the letter and did not like Mr Thompson's combative attitude. The trustees believed entering into litigation would seriously diminish the remaining assets of the estate.[58] Still completely dissatisfied with the dialogue between the two solicitors, in August 1899 the family then sought a legal opinion from Henry Bourne Higgins of 1 Selbourne Chambers, Melbourne. He presented it to them in March 1900. Higgins concluded that under the circumstances it would be possible to call upon the trustees to make good any loss, or to engage in litigation.[59] It was a volatile situation and at the end of the day the family chose to avoid litigation. Relationships on all sides were severely strained.

What lessons did MacGregor learn from his experience as an executor in this case? Could his experience with the McDougall family have influenced his decision not to make a will himself? If this was the case, it was a surprising choice for a man who prided himself on his business acumen.

The death of Christina McRae, 1887

The year 1887 was also marked by the most significant death in the MacGregor and McRae families since Donald McRae's death twenty years earlier. Christina McRae died at Glengyle, Coburg, on 9 December 1887 after suffering from chronic bronchitis and exhaustion for the previous ten days.[60] She was 71.

Christina McRae's last will and testament, dated 24 June 1879, contains one generous bequest and one surprising omission. Christina appointed her daughter Margaret MacGregor and her brother Kenneth McKenzie executors of her estate. At the time of her death Christina McRae's real estate was valued at £8,862 and personal property was calculated to be £5,849; a total of £14,111. Probate was granted to Margaret MacGregor and Kenneth McKenzie on 28 January 1888.[61]

She bequeathed her brother Kenneth the sum of £2,000 to be paid to him 12 months after her death. Waiting for 12 months before paying the bequest seems an unusual stipulation. Christina's real and personal estate, after the payment of her funeral expenses and debts, was to go to her daughter Margaret. The will also stipulated that the money would be 'for her separate use free from marital control'. No mention is made of her daughter Annie McKenzie. Christina's will contains a statement by the two witnesses that Christina McRae, 'being unable to write', they had subscribed their names to the document. The witnesses were the solicitors William Brahe and James Smith.

The administration of the Estate of the Late Donald McRae included a complex property portfolio instigated by his widow and executors. The properties were located in three legal jurisdictions – Victoria, New South Wales and Queensland. This was the primary reason McRae's chosen executors, John McIntosh and Joseph Smith, declined to act as trustees. Following Christina McRae's death, further problems arose. Her will was confined to her personal property, not the property she jointly purchased in Queensland with Duncan MacGregor through moneys belonging to the estate.[62] In January 1883, after the sale of Mount Margaret to Moodie, Donaldson & Inglis, Christina had transferred the runs that were in her name and those in Donald's name to the purchasers. On 29 March 1883, the Queensland solicitor Thomas Bunton was appointed as her Attorney 'under power to take out administration' of Donald McRae's estate in Queensland. To secure payment of the purchase money, Moodie, Donaldson and Inglis executed a mortgage dated 18 September 1883 to Christina McRae. She was acting as agent of her husband's estate, having 'no personal interest in the money further than what she acquired under the Will'. After her death in 1887, the mortgagees paid the money secured by the September 1883 mortgage.[63]

In September 1888, a further attempt was made to untangle the McRae affairs. Counsel opinion on the subject was sought: Henry Bourne Higgins deliberated on the situation. Higgins, successfully established at the Victorian Bar, became known more widely because of his 1907 'Harvester Judgement' allowing the concept of a living wage for a worker and his family.[64]

On the subject of unravelling the McRae estate, in particular the appointment of trustees, Higgins was precise. He presented the situation and offered a possible solution:

> The Victorian order makes Mr McGregor and Mr McKenzie trustees of the Will – for all the estate of which the testator died possessed within Victoria and I understand that the order of the New South Wales Court appointing Mr McGregor and McRae trustees was similarly limited to New South Wales property. Confusion has also been caused by Mrs McRae taking the mortgages and the bills for the Queensland properties in her own name. Mrs McRae has in effect taken it on herself to act as trustee of the proceeds of the Queensland property without being authorised to do so. Under the circumstances I am of opinion that the proper course is for the executors of Mr McRae when the bills mature to receive the proceeds and hand them over to the Victorian Trustees and also to transfer the mortgages now in Mrs McRae's name to the same Trustees. It will be noticed that the order appointing the Victorian trustees vests in them the right 'to see to recover and receive only those in action *subject to the trusts in the said will contained* or any interest in respect thereof'.
>
> There are no means that I can see of getting Mr McGregor appointed sole trustee of the proceeds of the Queensland property. If Mr

McKenzie retires some one else must be appointed in his place so as to keep up the number of two contemplated by the Will. But there is no need of any fresh administration being taken out *de bonis non administratis* of the testator the estate has been administered and is now to be held on the trusts of the Will.[65]

Higgins' suggestion of handing over the problem to the Victorian Trustees was sensible but was not embraced by MacGregor and the other Trustees for decades to come. It was clear that MacGregor could not have sole responsibility for the Queensland estate. What Higgins wanted was consistency: the trustees in Victoria, New South Wales and Queensland should be the same two people, that is Duncan MacGregor and either Kenneth McKenzie or Duncan McRae. Duncan MacGregor and Duncan McRae were brothers-in-law yet there are persistent hints of enmity between the two men. One had a large financial stake in the estate; the other had an emotional stake. The situation was some years away from being solved.

While the brothers-in-law were not necessarily on the best of terms, what was happening between the sisters, Maggie and Annie? What impact did it have on Annie to be excluded from her mother's will? When her mother died in 1887 Annie had been married to Kenneth McKenzie for ten years and had been supported financially since 1875 through her annuity. Annie received the first annuity from her father's estate on 11 January 1875. The sum of £5,345 was paid to her when she came of age. The payment was made in two parts: the first was the one-off payment of £5,000, the second was the annuity of £345. At the age of 23, Annie found herself in a very privileged position. She was an unmarried mother of considerable means. A Memorandum of Payments to Annie McKenzie 1875–1892 reveals that between 1875 and 1888 Annie had received from the estate the incredible sum of £41,602, an average of £3,200 per annum. This was a substantial sum of money. What did she spend her income on? Figures for the equivalent period detailing payments to Margaret have not been found. However, the document titled In the Estate of the late Donald McRae, 1886–1900 sheds light on Maggie's private income. Mrs MacGregor's half share of income was also significant. In 1886 her share was £3,235; in subsequent years it was £3,248 (1887), £3,605 (1888), £3,895 (1889) and £3,528 (1890).[66] Neither woman was dependant on their husband for income. This was an advantage as they were both retaining large households. They had an almost unknown level of independence at a time when the property of women usually transferred to their husbands immediately upon marriage. The two women held contrasting attitudes to their wealth.

While Duncan MacGregor decided to raise money by mortgaging his properties and the properties purchased or leased through the estate of Donald McRae, his wife and his sister-in-law had no such need for money. Duncan's father-in-law and mother-in-law's wills were progressive for the era, stipulating that the money belonged to the girls 'free from marital control'. But the issue is significant and would have an impact on the family fortunes of the two women. How would Annie and Maggie continue to manage their affairs? Managing money may not have been a problem for Maggie, but for Annie and her husband money became an ongoing bone of contention with tragic results.

Mount Murchison Homestead, River Darling, 12 December 1865, Pickering
PIC/8131/32 LOC Album 1026, National Library of Australia

Cooper Creek at Durham Downs
Photographer: Janet Leckie, 1999

Cooper Creek Country from Mount McGregor
Photographer: Janet Leckie, 1999

The desolate country around Cooper Creek
Photographer: Janet Leckie, 1999

Shearer's Hut Durham Downs, c.1878

Photographer: Nile Godson, H92.244/5, State Library of Victoria

Durham Downs Station, Cooper Creek, c.1878, Written in pencil on verso of H92.244/1: 'First hut built on Durham Downs Station by Angus Campbell manager for Duncan MacGregor … 120,000 sheep / 35,000 cattle.'

Photographer: Nile Godson, H92.244/1, State Library of Victoria

Washing Wool, Durham Downs Station. Men with forks in an outside work area, with a steam engine behind them, and paddocks in the background

Photographer: Nile Godson, H92.244/4, State Library of Victoria

Drying wool at Durham Downs Station. Men laying wool out on the ground, with a cart full of wool on the left and a small shed with bales on the right

Photographer: Nile Godson, H92.244/6, State Library of Victoria

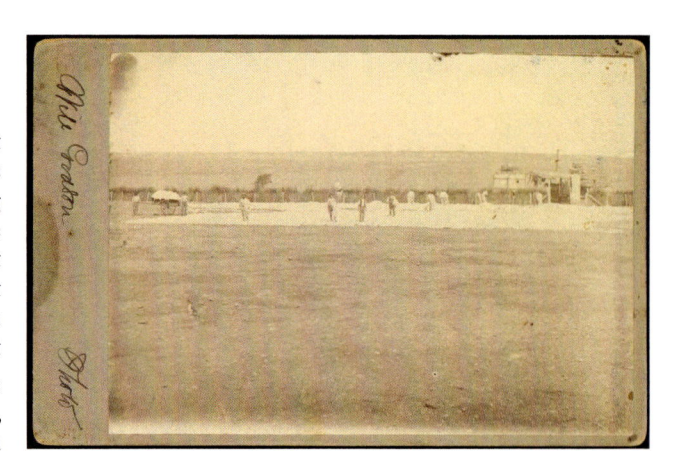

Aborigines employed on Durham Downs Station assembled in front of their huts, including a joey in the foreground, and with brick buildings in the background

Photographer: Nile Godson, H92.244/2, State Library of Victoria

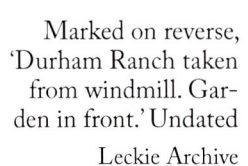

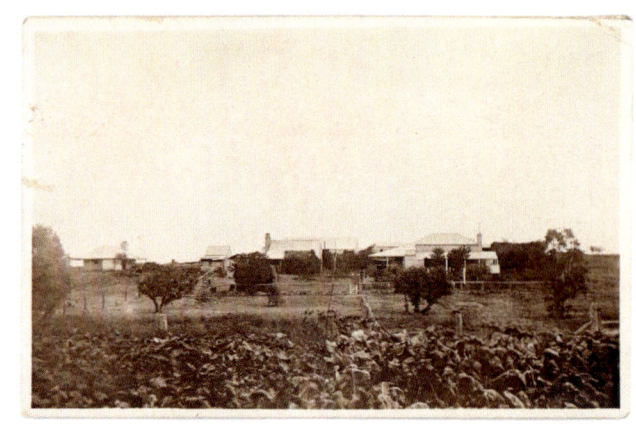

Marked on reverse, 'Durham Ranch taken from windmill. Garden in front.' Undated

Leckie Archive

Cattle branding, Queensland, c.1910
Leckie Archive

Bronchoing, Queensland, c.1910
Leckie Archive

'Possum' taken at Durham Downs, c.1878
Photographer: Frederic Bonney
Leckie Archive

Aboriginal axe and message stick believed to have come from Durham Downs
Leckie Archive

Marked on reverse: 'Tom Norman, looking round, acknowledged to be one of the smartest men on the Cooper today amongst stock and modest at that. Durham bred.'
Leckie Archive

Inverauld at Riddells Creek on sale day, 1880s
Leckie Archive

Annie McRae, Melbourne, c.1870
Leckie Archive

Duncan MacGregor with camel, Queensland, c.1880s, with the inscription on the reverse 'Yours truly taken by Afghan'
Photograph in possession of Scott MacGregor, England

Office of Peck, Hudson and Raynor, Bourke Street, Melbourne, 1884. Standing in front are from left: T.R. Raynor (of Peck Hudson and Raynor), James Hearn (of Wragge and Hearn), Duncan MacGregor (Great Western Queensland pioneer)

Harry H. Peck, *Memoirs of a Stockman*, Stock and Land Publishing, 1942

Margaret MacGregor with Donald, aged about one year, c.1884

Leckie Archive

Duncan's travelling album with images of his wife and seven children, undated
Leckie Archive

Glengyle Homestead, Coburg, c.1890s
Leckie Archive

MacGregor children, c.1888–90. Jack at rear, *L to R*: Tottie, Jessie, Goodie, Donald, Pearl, Cissie
Leckie Archive

The entrance to Glengyle with Miss Scott and two MacGregor girls, c.1880s
Leckie Archive

The gardens at Glengyle homestead with Miss Scott in foreground, Margaret MacGregor and three daughters, c.1890s
Leckie Archive

— 4 —
Of Droughts and Flooding Rains, 1888–1901

Since the beginning of European settlement of the Australian continent, major droughts have been recorded. The word 'drought' usually refers to an acute water shortage over a sustained period of time, most often due to low rainfall. However, the Australian Bureau of Meteorology highlights the fact that if it was simply low rainfall, much of inland Australia would be in almost perpetual drought, and that is not the case.[1] Today, on the basis of rainfall analysis, droughts are described as major, severe and/or widespread. A severe drought is defined as one in which ten or more rainfall districts are substantially affected by rainfall deficiencies for eight or ten months.[2] The rainfall districts can cross any Australian state and the dry spells can vary in length and overlap in time and space.[3]

The first recorded significant drought in Australia was 1864 to 1866.[4] Although there is little data available, indications are that the drought was severe in Victoria, South Australia, New South Wales, Queensland and Western Australia. In response to the two-year drought, in 1866 the Queensland government appointed a meteorologist, Clement Wragge. A colonial weather service was established and by 1901 there were 601 weather stations across Queensland, greatly assisting the recording of weather conditions.[5]

Duncan MacGregor was working on the Darling River at Mount Murchison during the 1864–66 drought, and like everyone else he was waiting for rain. John Cameron, his friend from Ross Shire and work mate at Mount Murchison, wrote to him in January 1866. While on holiday in Melbourne, he had met both Ross and William Reid, the owners of Mount Murchison. William Reid had just married, and Mrs Reid, he said, was 'a handsome young lady, and as far is my judgement, a very nice person extremely kind'. Cameron knew from reading the Melbourne papers that the country had no rain, and that the feed must be getting scarce 'all over the Darling'. He also conveyed to MacGregor that the papers were reporting that the Lachlan River had risen by five feet and he wondered whether Mount Murchison had 'got any of that rain'.[6] It did not appear so.

Donald McRae, at Caulpaulin, also experienced the drought. However, in time, he gained advantage from it. Though it is hard to understand how he did it during drought conditions, he managed his stock well enough to sustain them through the dry spell. Reports in the press in July 1866 indicate the high quality of cattle McRae was selling – bullocks were selling at £10 each. McRae had worked on the quality of his cattle for many years. Later in the year, the Melbourne *Argus* reported that, because of the drought, the demand for beef cattle continued. Dalmahoy Campbell, McRae's Melbourne agent, sold 808 head of cattle that proved 'quite equal to the requirements of butchers'. The greater proportion of cattle supplied consisted of prime quality, and one lot of 'DM brand' from Caulpaulin Station on the Darling bred by McRae 'arrived in prime order, and equal to any that passed through our market for years'.[7] The article elaborated on the Dalmahoy Campbell sale of McRae cattle. It showed considerable attention had been given to breeding, not only in the colour but also in evenness of condition, and the McRae beasts realised the top prices of the week. They wrote: 'We quote prime pens bullocks at from £9 to £11; second quality from £7 to £8; inferior from £4 to £6.' Altogether they sold 207 head of McRae cattle, the bullocks at from £8/10 to £11, averaging £9/18; the cows from £7/15 to £10/15, averaging £8/1/9.[8] This was a good year for McRae who managed to survive the drought by achieving high sale prices.

The year 1877 was a period of great expansion by MacGregor into both Queensland and Victoria. Because of the impact of prolonged drought, he engaged Peck, Hudson and Raynor to sell Caulpaulin Station on the public market, with 3,000 cattle and 15,000 sheep. At the same time, they attempted to sell Glengyle Station with 1,500 head of cattle. After both sales fell through, he chose an alternative – to build up his stock on these stations. Records show that on 28 August 1877, MacGregor purchased from Peck, Hudson and Raynor 1,331 head of cattle for the sum of £12,824 and 38 horses at £10 each, making a total purchase price of £13,204.[9]

As well as suffering drought, the year 1877 was also a year of a major flood on Cooper Creek. Alexander Campbell, Glengyle Station's manager, wrote to MacGregor on 16 February from Mount Margaret Station to keep him informed of his whereabouts. Campbell was expected back at Glengyle but was delayed because of floodwaters. He wrote:

> You will be surprised to see me writing from hear [sic] the worst of it is I cannot get home. Coopers Creek is flood all over the plain it come down very quick it is travelling from 20 to 30 miles per day. Ryan and I was mustering stragglers in the ridges for two or three days [and] when we got back the plains was one sheet of water … Being without rations I came hear [sic] …
>
> I finished mustering all but a few stragglers on this side that I could not get across – the cattle had a great spread on them when we started mustering. They are looking very fair excepting a few of the old bullocks which are showing symptoms of pluro. One or two of the bulls are ill. I branded close on 300 calves this muster. I would have had a few over 300 if I got all the stragglers home … The blacks tell me the Diamantina is flooded too, so is the Bulloo and the Paroo.[10]

When Charles Sturt saw the Cooper for the first time in 1845, he saw it while the country was in drought, he named it a creek, rather than a river. As historian H.M. Tolcher notes, the notion of the riverbed overflowing its banks to form a vast sheet of water must have seemed impossible to Sturt at the time.[11] It was not until 1877 that locals first saw the river's potential for disturbance. Campbell certainly experienced this major disruption to his work when the river flooded well beyond its banks, in places nearly one and a quarter miles wide. It was reported at the time that not even the Aborigines had seen floodwaters so high in living memory. John Conrick, one of the first settlers on the Cooper, commented:

> It is to be hoped that none of the white residents will ever see them higher, as the inconvenience that high floods are in these parts is beyond conception – there has been a complete stoppage put to getting supplies, which are now running short.[12]

The disruption they spoke of included the lack of supplies as well as mail deliveries from February until April 1877. However, the benefits of the flood outweighed any inconvenience for Mrs McRae and MacGregor: the flood plains grew fresh green pasture with lush herbage and new grass. Fields of 'sweet-smelling lilies appeared, purple-flowered verbine grew tall along the river bank and, when the water dried up, the beds of the shallow lakes were a carpet of yellow billy-buttons'. The pastoralists, such as MacGregor, were 'jubilant as the stock began to fatten almost as they watched'.[13] Becoming stranded for days because the rivers were impassable, as well as the other inconveniences, was quickly forgotten.

While George Augustus Sala was celebrating 'Marvellous Melbourne', a further devastating drought was affecting Queensland. Beginning in 1888, it was defined as severe because it affected ten rainfall districts across Queensland for more than eight months. The drought affected southern Queensland, but also most of New South Wales, Victoria and Tasmania.

Leading up to this drought, conditions in Queensland had been unusually bad in 1884 with summer temperatures reaching 130°F (today 54°C) in the shade. This was the worst season settlers had known and became the yardstick for any further drought events.[14] Rain coming at widely spaced intervals was an annual fact of life on the Cooper. In October 1888 the *Sydney Morning Herald* reported on the situation of the continuous drought in Queensland. The editor commented that there was 'no prospect of a change', the stock routes were 'terribly bare' and bush fires were raging in all directions. The weather all over the country was 'exceedingly hot'.[15] Duncan MacGregor, like many other pastoralists, suffered major losses of stock. The 1888 drought, which did not break until 1889, proved to be a troubling time for MacGregor, leading to severe consequences in later years for all the family.

The federation drought, 1895–1903 – compounding the problem

The drought that devastated eastern Australia from 1895 to 1903 is the most widely recognised in Australia's European history. As historian Don Garden points out, it is variously referred to as the Long Drought, the Great Drought and the Federation Drought because of the prolonged period of below-average rain in Queensland, New South Wales, Victoria, Tasmania and South Australia. Garden's ground-breaking research published in 2009 reveals that the rainfall deficit and its accompanying heatwaves, bushfires and dust storms were the result of three closely following El Niño events.[16] The first stage ran from 1895 to 1898 with the summer of 1897–98 suffering some of the most extreme recorded weather in Australia. The El Niño then subsided into a mild La Niña late in 1898 before another El Niño in 1899–1900. After a short break, a profound El Niño lasted from 1901–03 and brought the most severe period of drought to many regions in the country. One of the aspects most remembered of this time are the dust storms. [17]

Ferocious dust storms devastated the landscape and everyone within it. They destroyed the already struggling vegetation and 'permeated everything, including the wool clip whose value was thereby reduced'. One South Australian pastoralist wrote to the *Burra Record* in May 1898:

> While I am writing this the dust is blowing in clouds; no lambing for the last three years, and a bad prospect for one this year; high rents, and wild dogs galore; three parts of this country blown further east … It will take three good seasons for the country in question to be of [the] same value as it was before the drought set in.[18]

This was a bleak period in Australian history. The extended drought coincided with the 1890s Depression. The dust storms and the lack of food and water for the stock seriously affected every pastoral property and under severe stress, Duncan MacGregor experienced a debilitating physical and mental collapse.

The problems for pastoralists from 1895 were many. The land dried, vegetation disappeared and animals died of thirst or starvation.[19] Many bores had been sunk to provide watering points but when desperately thirsty animals congregated near them they ate all the surrounding feed. As Garden notes, 'many hundreds of thousands of stock were driven out to graze "the long paddock", the vegetation that grew along the roadsides and on Crown Land'.[20] Stock numbers had been in decline during the 1890s, but by the end of the drought the number of sheep in Australia had halved to about 54 million and cattle numbers had dropped by 40%. Consequently, wool clip earnings fell, to MacGregor's despair.

In the decade prior to the Great Depression, land companies could describe themselves as 'banks' and make loans to their directors. However, in London in November 1890 the money market learnt that defaults by several South American governments were jeopardising the survival of one of London's oldest banks, Baring Brothers. This news sparked a panic and in 1891 the governments of Victoria, South Australia and Queensland were 'unexpectedly rebuffed' when they tried to raise new loans. Soon after, wool prices slumped and British depositors began to withdraw funds from the colonial banks. Revelations of the lending practices of the 'land banks' were scandalous and the public voted with their feet. The sudden withdrawal of funds caused a run on the banks. In April and May 1893, 13 of the 16 banks suspended business, plunging commerce, industry and governments into chaos. Government outlays fell by almost 40% between 1891 and 1895 and gross domestic product fell by 30%. In Victoria, unemployment peaked at more than 28%.[21] In light of these circumstances, MacGregor's decision in the early to mid-1890s to mortgage many of his properties and become a moneylender may have been made in desperation.

Annie and Kenneth McKenzie, 1892

Kenneth McKenzie, Annie's husband of 15 years, committed suicide on 21 March 1892. Overwhelming debt and problems with Annie seems to have been the cause. Studies have shown that an increase in suicides in the 1890s was related to the collapse of the land boom, bank failure, periods of serious droughts and economic depression.[22]

The suicide note he wrote to his brother John and the evidence John gave at the Inquest reveal that Annie and Kenneth were estranged at the time of his death. Kenneth had left the family home at Clonbinane and been living for eight months with John in Devonshire Road, Elsternwick. This was an unusual act for a man in his position, possibly precipitated by the relationship Annie had formed with another man.

The note makes many requests of his brother and aims to explain his actions fully. First, he asks that 'the letters be put into Annie's own hands', because 'I really kill myself to induce Annie to pay the debts'. Kenneth could foresee the consequences of his actions and asked John to see that 'my character comes out as you really know it to be'.

Annie McKenzie was a wealthy woman: what did she spend her money on? How or why she had incurred considerable debt which she now could not or would not pay? McKenzie wrote 'I am confident she will do it when she finds what she has done.' He was blaming her extra-marital affair and her accumulated debts for his decision to end his life. While there is no record of her expenses, in the previous year Annie had received £4,483 from her father's estate. Evidence has not been found to shed light on the reason for her impecunious state.

Kenneth McKenzie's final letter indicated he could see no way out of his troubles. He went to the local chemist in St Kilda and bought an ounce of laudanum. When contemplating his death he discovered he 'had a horror of dying alone' and he took the laudanum early in the morning of 21 March in his room at his brother's house. Poignantly, he wrote that he exonerated John from all knowledge of his intentions, yet added 'you little thought when I joked and laughed with you last night what I meant to do before morning'. Suicide was a sin according to the Christian Church, yet he hoped that 'God may not be so hard on me'. The sadness and despair in his letter is palpable. 'Kiss the girls for me, I thought of giving them good bye'. He and Annie had four living children. Christina was 18; Margaret, 6; Colin, 3; and Kenneth only months old. Was the paternity of the youngest child in question? It may have been the cause of his departure from the marital home.

After the first two paragraphs, his writing becomes a little blurred as the laudanum was taking effect. In his final rambling words, when he writes that he is 'on the verge of eternity', he states that Phillip Forster was 'the greatest villain I have known' and to 'get the children away from him'. This was a vain hope. Phillip Forster was not going anywhere and was certainly not leaving Annie and the children.

At the Coroner's Inquest, John McKenzie recorded his brother's actions of the previous evening and the fact that he was in the habit of taking laudanum. At about 7.30 am John had gone into his brother's room and found that he was already unconscious; the letters on the desk made it clear that he intended to kill himself. He died at 1.30 in the afternoon. The doctor was called and he declared him dead. Kenneth McKenzie was 47.

Although it is unclear from the correspondence whether Maggie and Annie were on speaking terms, the tragic events in her sister's life must have affected Maggie, Duncan and their family. In the months following her husband's death, Annie caused further distress to the family. In October 1892, she married Phillip Forster, 15 years her junior. The children remained with her in what we now describe as a 'blended family'. Another two children followed, Arthur McRae (1894) and Henry Phillip (1895). Annie Forster became infamous for her continued and wilful refusal to pay her debts.

No doubt the suicide of his brother-in-law Kenneth McKenzie, followed by Annie's hasty marriage to Phillip Forster, caused Duncan a great deal of anxiety. But were these concerns by the way compared with his own precarious financial situation? As the country was suffering the effects of drought, his Queensland stations were suffering from lack of funding. In 1894, MacGregor took drastic steps to remedy this situation by mortgaging the leases he had in his own name for five major stations in Queensland: Durham Downs, Yanko, Glengyle, Miranda and Meba Downs. Stocks on these stations at the end of December 1895 were much lower than they had ever been: 130,850 sheep, 51,636 cattle and 825 horses. At Yanko, 32,074 sheep were shorn, making 445 bales; at Durham Downs, 98,776, making 1,042 bales.

Out into the world

Before Duncan took steps for financial survival, his son Jack began a transition of his own. In 1889, when he was 17, Jack travelled to Queensland to work for his father. This trip appears to have been a year of 'jackarooing', or the equivalent of the modern break between school and work. Part of the State Library of Victoria's MacGregor Collection contains a series of letters between Jack, his parents, his sisters and a close friend during the period 1889 to 1903. When read chronologically they weave together the family's intimate relationships and say much about the lives of the MacGregors. They also tell the story of Jack's enchantment with a young Tasmanian girl and their early courtship. Importantly, they reveal the impact of the drought on Duncan's pastoral business and on his personal emotional state and that of his family.

The series of letters begins with a letter from Maggie MacGregor to her son, written in September 1889. His first foray into the life as a pastoralist occurred during the heat wave Queenslanders were then suffering.[23] Jack's second stint began six years later when he was 24. During his time away he worked at Durham Downs, Glengyle, and Yanko before returning to Victoria, when he eventually worked at Dalmore.

In the interim, a major family event took place. Maggie and Duncan's daughter Jessie married the Reverend Donald Macrae Stewart on Wednesday 5 December 1894. Jessie was 25, Donald, 34, and the incumbent minister of the Ascot Vale Presbyterian Church. The ceremony took place in the Brunswick Presbyterian Church and was followed by a wedding breakfast at Glengyle in Coburg. The family photograph of the event shows a crowd of people in front of Glengyle; the bride and groom appear resplendent in bridal wear typical of the late Victorian period. A full report of the wedding was published in the *Australasian* three days later. The Reverend J.F. Mcrae of Toorak, uncle of the bridegroom, performed the ceremony. The service was 'quite choral in character' and the music was sung by the united choirs of the Brunswick and Ascot Vale churches. The church was decorated with pot plants, palms and choice ferns 'artistically arranged' by the bride's sisters and cousins. The bride was given away by her father and attended by six bridesmaids – her sisters Goodie, Tottie, Cissie and Pearl; Miss Ella Stewart, the sister of the groom, and Miss Ethel Macrae, cousin of the bridegroom. Mr Douglas Stewart, brother of the groom, was his best man. Jessie's wedding gown was made of ivory faille francaise, 'made very plainly, with a long Court train'. It is described further:

> The bodice was veiled with accordion-pleated silk-striped chiffon, with falling frill of the same and leg of mutton sleeves of the silk. Her plain veil was held in position by a pearl star, the gift of the bridegroom, and was worn over a wreath of small white roses and maidenhair. She wore a pearl heart pendent, the gift of her mother, and carried a large Princess May shower bouquet from Cheeseman's composed entirely of Niphetos roses and asparagus fern tied with broad white streamers.[24]

Details of the bride, bridesmaids and guests attire followed. A full guest list indicates that the MacGregor's of Glengyle entertained some notable Melbourne families, including the widow of Robert McDougall. Jessie and Donald Macrae Stewart moved into a small house in Ascot Vale, close to Donald's church, where they began their married life. They lived in Ascot Vale until Donald was promoted to the post of minister of the Presbyterian Church Malvern. Jessie's moves were the subject of many letters between the siblings while Jack was working in Queensland.

Jack's work experience is recorded through letters from all the family when they began in earnest to write from 3 September 1896. In her first letter of this series, Maggie chides her son that she had not heard from him the previous week, 'but' she wrote, 'I suppose you are kept so busy'. Included in her letter was the important news that Miss Alexina Scott from Tasmania was staying with the family in Coburg. Although she was called 'Alice' within the MacGregor family, it appears her name was shortened to Zena. It is unclear where or how they met, but Jack had taken a shine to her and was teased about this by his sisters. On this occasion his mother wrote 'She is such a nice girl, I like her so much'.[25] On the same day, his 20-year-old sister Cissie also wrote to say that Alice was staying with them. They clearly knew he was keen on her. To Cissie, not only was Miss Scott a nice girl, she was very pretty as well. Cissie also told Jack that their mother had not been well. Maggie MacGregor's headaches and sore throats persisted. On a brighter note, they were having splendid rain and the creek was high. She expected he was shearing and that he would 'be glad when it is over'; the family probably knew shearing was not Jack's favourite task.

The letters continue and are full of family stories, teasing and a great deal of love and affection. Two years later, Jack returned briefly to Victoria for the marriage of his sister Tottie in late November 1896. He remained with the family for their Christmas and New Year celebrations.

Tottie MacGregor was married to Mr William Pestell, son of the late Mr William Pestell of Williamstown, on Wednesday 25 November 1896. The bridegroom, the engineer William Pestell of Power Street, Hawthorn, was 28. Tottie was 22. The wedding ceremony took place in the drawing-room of Glengyle. The service was conducted by Tottie's brother-in-law, the Reverend Donald Macrae Stewart. The bride was given away by her father. She wore a 'handsome dress of ivory satin with a court train. The corsage had a full front of chiffon caught in by a wide corslet belt, and ruched sleeves of chiffon, with satin epaulets edged with chiffon'. Her tulle veil was arranged over a spray of lily of the valley, and was fastened by a pearl dagger, the gift of the bridegroom. She carried a posy of waterlilies, tied with ribbon streamers, with the bridegroom's initials in silver. Her sisters Cissie and Pearl were bridesmaids; they wore green silk with wide white satin sashes and neck frills of chiffon and carried posies and wore pearl swallow brooches. Also included in the wedding party was her niece, Christina McKenzie (Teena), Annie McRae's lovechild. The groomsmen were Mr George Wilkinson, Mr Norman Durham and the 14-year-old Donald MacGregor. After the ceremony the guests adjourned to the dining-room where a *recherché* wedding breakfast consisting of hors-d'ouvres, savouries, sandwiches and salads was served. After the usual toasts, the newlyweds departed for the Blue Mountains.[26]

As the year 1897 progressed, the ongoing theme of all the family letters was the impact of the drought. It was worrying the family, most especially Duncan, and his wife and daughters were very aware of his increasing anxiety. Early in 1897, when Maggie wrote to Jack at Glengyle in Queensland, she made it clear that 'poor Papa was dreadfully worried, there is no rain at Glengyle or Yanko, it really is very serious … I've heard not a drop of rain for some time, everything is burnt up. What must it be with you? I only trust [you] get a good downpour'.[28] Miss Flora Scott, who had come from Kyneton in 1886 as governess to the children, was now acting as a secretary for Duncan and a companion to Maggie. Her concern for Duncan was also mentioned in the family letters. It is unclear whether she was related to Zena Scott from Tasmania. Miss Scott remained with the family for 30 years. While Goodie and Cissie both expressed the desperate hope that Queensland would have good rain soon, at that stage the drought had been in progress for three long years; the summer of 1897 saw some of the most extreme weather in Australia recorded.[29]

Duncan MacGregor wrote frequently to his son. His businesslike approach was adhered to when he wrote with strict instructions for the many jobs he had to complete. To add to the pressure, his old friend and the manager of Durham Downs Station, Farquhar McDonald, also wrote regularly to Jack. The first letter in the file from Farquhar was written on 4 May 1897. The purpose of his letter was to let Jack know that he had written to the stock inspector on Jack's behalf, and that he would go and inspect the sheep, then send the permit on to the inspector. This type of correspondence and the filling in of the right forms was vitally important – sheep quotas had to be met as a condition of the lease. Despite his letter, it seems the stock inspector did not send the required forms after all.[30] McDonald's next letter was to advise that they had started scouring that day, something Jack would have needed to know.

These letters between work mates discuss the business of the station. But they were more than that. McDonald was a senior employee whose opinion was valued by father and son. It is interesting to see the extent to which McDonald takes a deferential attitude to MacGregor senior. When he wrote to Jack in 1898, Farquhar was 69. Not a young man himself, ironically he refers to MacGregor as 'the Old Gentleman'.[31] In another letter to Jack, Farquhar writes that the Old Gentleman 'mentions he is about letting the completion of the bore but says nothing about when he intends starting it up'.[32] Further correspondence fails to complete this story.

Letters from Duncan MacGregor to his family, while he was in Queensland, were in Cissie's words 'always so disheartening, poor Papa must be having a bad time, we wish he could come home'.[33] Margaret wrote that she was deeply grieved that they were still so badly off for rain: 'It really is dreadful, you can see by the papers the state of the country in New South Wales, it really could not be worse.'[34] On a more intimate note she continues:

> We are very lonely here at present, only Goodie, Cis and Pearl at home. Cissie was 21 last Monday. I cannot think how time goes so quickly. Pearl has left school [and] … is going to take painting lessons.[35]

Pearl was the MacGregor's much loved youngest daughter, and being the youngest girl she endured criticism from her older siblings; Goodie wrote of her as 'that brat of a Pearl'. Although they didn't write to Jack often, Cissie and Pearl's letters were always affectionate and informative. Donald was the youngest MacGregor child and was still at school; only a few letters from this period have survived.

Only a few weeks after her 27 January letter 1897, Maggie MacGregor was able to write positively about the weather, that 'rain has fallen in many parts of Queensland so I hope Yanko has had a good share'.[36] She was anxious to receive a letter from her son to see if they had, after all, had any rain. In her early August letter, she was happy to say that she had received his third letter 'enclosed with Papa's'; she was delighted to hear from her son and to know that he and Duncan were so well. Margaret could also report that Jack's older sister, Jessie, was currently staying with them. She had been very ill but was now getting better, but she concluded 'Papa will tell you how seriously ill she has been'.[37] Duncan was a complex character and this reveals a side of the man that is perhaps unexpected.

Duncan wrote almost every day to update his son and give him instructions. A typical letter directs his activities:

> My Dear Son
>
> Tassie O'May the shearer called here today and I am sending him down to Yanko so please give him a stand as he is one of the best shearers in the district and when done at Yanko … I am of opinion you had better put him on and get the wool well done. … The country about here is very dry and rain badly wanted … I am afraid of the dry weather … I will write you freely by next mail …
>
> I am yours affectionate, father, D MacGregor[38]

In a constant stream of instructions, the day after the letter quoted above Duncan directed Jack to 'put the shorter fleece in separate bales and brand differently, it might be advantageous'. Duncan wanted every attention paid to the wool. More instructions followed on how to conduct the shearing, baling and branding of bales. Duncan knew how the job was to be done and wanted to ensure that his son did exactly as he wished. On 16 June MacGregor wrote from Durham Downs in response to Jack's letter of 9 June, explaining his actions and making sure his advice was being followed. The letter sheds light on Duncan's own movements and highlights the amount he travelled and was away from home: 'Your letter of the 9th duly to hand by this mail but I have been out for a week mending lines and only got home late tonight to get the mail.' He hoped that one of his managers, Alex Campbell, had done a good job on whatever the task he had set him because as he wrote 'I do not believe in doing bad work of any kind'. MacGregor lived by this ethos and expected his sons and his staff to follow the same philosophy.

Duncan's letters to Jack in September and October 1897 cover both station and domestic life: 'Only a few minutes to say that I gather all safe at home', he wrote hurriedly. While also dwelling on the drought, he wrote that he was pleased to learn that they had rain in the weeks since he had left Queensland and was 'sure that same will do a great deal of good … 2½ inches at the home station but not so heavy out back' and of course, he contemplated that 'they ought to get the wool scoured now without any trouble'. By November he was pleased to learn that Jack was getting on with the shearing but he hoped that he would 'get a good many done while the feed was good'. Duncan was an old hand at shearing: after forty years in Australia he knew the seasons and the routines required to produce his high quality wool in Queensland, even while the country was in drought.

It is not difficult to see that, while allowing his oldest son to take on the management of one of his stations, Duncan MacGregor was closely supervising his apprenticeship. Duncan was a proud family man and no doubt expected that his two sons would take over his pastoral business in years to come. We can only guess how he really felt about this prospect in his heart. Did he have the same plan for his second son, Donald, who in 1897 was 15? It is surprising that Donald is not mentioned in family letters. Was it simply that Donald was out of sight and therefore out of mind? Unlike Duncan's own pressing reason to emigrate to Australia in

1857, at least the McRae/MacGregor empire had room enough for the two MacGregor sons to work different properties.

Did Jack really want to work on the family farm? Was Duncan relieved to hand over the property to his son or was he simply encouraging him to consider it at that stage? We can only guess. After nearly thirty years of continuous travel away from home, leaving his family in Victoria every few months, Duncan may have wanted to slow down, retire or give it up altogether. In 1897 Duncan was 62. In time, his burdens would affect his health and wellbeing.

Jack's older sister Margaret, always called Goodie, dashed off a letter in August 1897 to give him the news that 'everything was fine' at Clunie but mostly she wanted to know when their father was coming home. 'Give our best love to Papa, when does he think he will be coming home, tell us when you write next'. When she next wrote on 14 October, Duncan MacGregor was once again in the bosom of his family. Goodie's letter to Jack also sheds light on the activities at the Dalmore property. In contrast to the Queensland stations and the drought, 'Papa is so pleased with Dalmore, they have such a splendid crop and everything looks so well.'

Goodie also reported that their father had just voted in the Victorian electorate of East Bourke. She was fully informed and eager to pass on her father's activities in relation to the election. He had been around the local neighbourhood at Springfield and Wallan, near Clunie, campaigning with Mackay Gair of Brahe and Gair, his solicitors. Gair was standing against Robert Harper in the East Bourke electorate and won the seat.[40] Goodie clearly delighted in telling 'Jackie' as she called him, all about the election and the people he knew who were involved in it: 'Gair is opposing Harper for east Bourke. I hope he gets in and Berry and Hancock go out for Brunswick.'[41] James Newton Haxton Cook and David Methven were elected to represent the district in the Legislative Assembly.[42] Graham Berry and Frederick Hickford (not Hancock as Goodie had written) both contested the seat of Brunswick and lost. Goodie would have been happy but we do not know Duncan's response to the election result.

The following month when Cissie wrote to Jack, and although stating that she had no news, her letter is remarkably informative. The day she wrote it was very hot and her father and Goodie had gone to the Kilmore Show; Jessie had visited that morning and she was taking Goodie's letter to post. The family had just been to the Melbourne Cricket Ground to see the English playing cricket. She reported that 'The grandstand there is finished and looks splendid, in fact the whole ground is really perfect'.[43] In 1897 second-storey wings were added to the grandstand; this increased the capacity in the grounds to 9,000.

Jack in the meantime had moved from Glengyle back to Yanko and would later move back to Durham Downs. In an undated letter around November 1897, Goodie acknowledged these moves. Her letter illustrates her affection for her father and brother. At the time of her letter, Duncan MacGregor had not yet reached Yanko but had already written to say that the country was in 'a frightful condition'. She hoped that everything would look better after the 'weary trip our dear father has had'. Goodie urged Jack to write to let them know how their father looked because she had 'a box of powders' she had meant to give him before he left but had forgotten. Instead she decided to send them up by the man they had employed as a wool scourer.

From their letters it is clear that there is a lot of traffic between station workers and the houses at Clunie in Chintin and Glengyle in Coburg. Farquhar McDonald had frequent holidays at Clunie or Glengyle, and other workers spent time there as part of their annual leave. This also indicates the degree to which the staff were valued. One place or the other were perfect places to spend a week or two after droving cattle down to the Melbourne cattle market at Flemington. In Melbourne, Goodie also reported, 'there were prayers for rain in all the Churches and this afternoon it started to rain heavily'. While Victoria had been in drought, Goodie was conscious that rain was still needed urgently in Queensland and New South Wales as well. The significant underlying concern in all of the family letters was the effect the drought was having on their father.

Suddenly it was Christmas 1897 and Jack was not at home to celebrate the season. Goodie wrote to him:

> A Merry Xmas to you old boy and may you have a fine fat turkey well cooked. How we all wish you were home with us as you were last year but we can't get all we would like. Any way I hope you will have a real good downpour of rain on Xmas day which will continue until you have no more sign of drought left so you will be able to start 1898 really well. I do wish I could cook you a good dinner and send it to you and a lot of fruit but you will have to wait until you get back to Victoria.

News and gossip about the family and extended family and friends followed. It is clear Goodie missed her brother. Jessie, Jack's elder sister, wrote to him in January asking him about his Christmas and New Year because she also wished she could cook him 'a good dinner'.[44] Sadly he had to wait until he got back to Victoria for the pleasure. In January 1898 Pearl could report to Jack that she had used his Melbourne Cricket Club tickets. They were attending the second Test between England and Australia from New Year's Day to 5 January. Australia won by an innings and 55 runs. It is not surprising that Pearl reported that the matches 'were grand'.[45] In the meantime, the summer heat continued.

Bushfires in Victoria are usually precipitated by drought conditions, and the south-west of the state remains one of the most bushfire prone areas in Australia. In early 1898 fires burnt out over 1,000 square miles of bush and pasture in South Gippsland. Twelve people died and more than 2,000 buildings were destroyed.[46] The date, 1 February 1898, subsequently became known as 'Red Tuesday'. The bushfires raged through the villages of Warragul, Yallock, Korumburra and along McDonald's Track. The Strzelecki Ranges were burning out of control. Strong winds were pushing the fire along. It was 'the blackest Tuesday South Gippsland had known'. All the country south of Warragul was enveloped in thick smoke, and on the ranges at the back of Yarragon the fire burnt fiercely. The fires extended as far as Cranbourne, very close to Dalmore, and extensive damage was recorded. Newspapers reported that local municipal authorities were gathering together the dead cattle on the roads.[47] The landscape of South Gippsland was devastated.

The notable painter, John (later Sir John) Longstaff, captured on canvas the great Gippsland fires of February 1898. Longstaff had spent two years in London where he worked as a portraitist, but in 1895 he returned to Australia. In Melbourne during the Depression, he designed advertisements for a living until he established a portraiture practice. The National Gallery of Victoria purchased his painting of the 1898 bushfire. Three years after completing this painting he undertook a commission from the National Gallery of Victoria to depict the tragic death of the explorers Burke and Wills, a painting he did not complete until 1907.[48]

When Goodie complained to Jack on 10 February 1898 about a lack of letters from him, she wrote with mixed emotion: 'How we only wish it was through rain the letters were delayed but no such luck.' However, rain for Victoria must have been uppermost in her mind as she wondered: 'Do you think it will ever rain again here? The people are crying out dreadfully … here so many people have been burnt out. So far we have been fortunate enough no fires as yet, though they have been all round Dalmore … At Clunie they have been very much afraid of it as there is a great deal of grass there and so very dry.' As Goodie informed her brother, her mother and sisters were staying at Clunie, but because of the heatwave they were returning to Coburg the following day:

> It is so hot, but today is much better but we have had just awful weather, last week was just a cooker. I never felt anything like it.[49]

The ferocious heat continued. Pearl acknowledged this fact when she corresponded with Jack in April: 'We have had a very dry time here, never saw the horses and cows so poor, there has been a little rain and made the grass shoot a bit, but it has turned very cold. I think it will be a terrible winter. They have not had rain at Dalmore yet.'[50] On a happier note Pearl wrote proudly that she was going to 'put her hair up', at the end of the month, 'it is about time, as I shall be nineteen'. This gesture was a social rite of passage; it marked the time a girl became a young woman. A week later, Cissie wrote to let Jack know that Pearl and his mother were going to Dalmore the following day and she hoped the change would do her mother good.[51] At that stage Duncan was still in Brisbane and had written to say he couldn't come home before going 'outback' to check his roads after the rain. Goodie was enthusiastic about the state of the cattle on the station in her next letter: 'Your ever welcome letter I got last week and was so pleased to hear from you and you are at least having a good season. What a treat it must be for you to see the stock fat and have fat horses to ride. I only hope you will be able to say the same for many a day.'[52] However, the hot dry weather continued in Victoria, to the point where she told him that Victoria was having its share of the drought and that people were crying because in some parts of the state, things were so bad they were carting water many miles. She also mentioned that James Winter, their family friend and manager of the Riddells Creek property Inverauld, had written to say he was trucking water into that property but that 'everything was all right at Inverauld and Clunie'. Goodie and Pearl planned to ride up to Clunie as soon as they came back from Dalmore.[53] Pearl, Jessie and Goodie had another visit to Dalmore in September 1898 because of Jessie's state of health and because their mother was tired.

Jessie was unwell, tired and no doubt stressed by the events she had dealt with in the previous week. She and her husband, Donald Macrae

Stewart, had recently moved into a new home in Ascot Vale. She had had an 'awful fright on Monday' when their external wash house was burnt down. More frightening 'was a strong north wind blowing at the time, they were afraid it would cause a great deal more damage than it did'. Luckily, Goodie could report that the fire brigade soon stopped it once they got the water on from the plug in the street. However, 'the shock upset Jess a good deal and a few days away will do her good'. Goodie's letter was full of family news. She could report to Jack that they had finally managed to get 'Papa to go and see Dr about his nose. He went to Dr Moore who is dressing it with pure Carbolic Acid for 10 days and if it is not better he is to have it cut out'. Goodie seemed to be completely at ease with this description. She continued: 'but I feel sure it will be all right in a little if he is only patient enough but will keep washing it as it is very dirty'. But the news that Jack would have wanted to hear more than anything else was news of the stock. First it was the cattle sales and their father was very pleased with the price the cattle brought in Sydney. However, her explanation about the 'Glengyle' cattle in Adelaide is somewhat cryptic, only saying that they were hardly brought to market because of the 'wretches of drovers'. Further news concerned the horses: 'The two horses that came from England went away last week, one to Inverauld and the other to Dalmore.' These Clydesdale horses had been purchased in 1896 and were the subject of a special export agreement.

In her long letter, Goodie had a great deal to report on the activities at Dalmore, Clunie and Inverauld. It is easy to imagine Jack devouring the minute details she shared with him about the goings-on in Victoria. While she was sad to learn that Glengyle had not received rain, Yanko had received 2½ inches. 'Papa was sure when he came home you had got it', she wrote. Her disappointment at the lack of rain was evident; she could only conclude by saying 'we must only hope that you have had plenty rain long ere this reaches you'. In the meantime, Goodie assured him she would write to him from Dalmore.

The pattern of correspondence between Jack and the MacGregor family continues and these letters shed light on the ebb and flow of daily life in the family. In 1899 and 1900 the same questions about shearing, rainfall and the price for cattle are repeated; they are seasonal questions but the answers vary slightly as each year progresses. The names of the station workers in Queensland, New South Wales and Victoria become familiar to the reader as are the names and business of the extended family and intimate friends. Reports on Dalmore, Clunie and Inverauld are scattered throughout the correspondence. The plight of the Queensland properties is reported on, and it is possible to glean the state of health of Duncan, Margaret, Jessie, Goodie, Tottie, Cissie and Pearl.

It is imagined that one year after importing his two prized Clydesdale stallions Duncan took great pride in the spectre of advertising their services. An advertisement in the *Australasian* of 16 September 1899 announced that the 'Earl of Millfield' would 'Stand at "Inverauld" near Riddell's Creek'. The advertisement included an extract from the *Scottish Farmer* praising the animal:

> Earl of Millfield has much of Darnley in his breeding. He is a thick, powerfully built horse, with good bone, capital feet, plenty of hair and good action. His sire was Prince Millfield which won first prize at Glasgow when two years old … His dam was Princess Maud, a fine thick mare by Top Knot.[54]

His other prized stallion, 'Sir Murdo', was to stand at Dalmore. Written along similar lines, the advertisement emphasised certain facts about the pure Clydesdale stallion imported by MacGregor of Dalmore, Pakenham. A full physical description included detail such as the 'bay stripe on face, hind feet white' and that it was bred by Robert Watson, Esq., of Lanarkshire Scotland. The Stallion had foaled on 31 May 1896. These stallions were praised in the Adelaide newspaper, the *Critic*, five years later: 'Until the importation, some five years ago, of Earl of Millfield and Sir Murdo, there were few purebred stallions in the State'. Words MacGregor was surely pleased to hear as an endorsement of his skills and knowledge of purebred stock.

News in November 1899 from Farquhar McDonald at Durham Downs concerned the important subject of water and bores. Under Duncan's instruction, Farquhar and some of his men at Durham Downs had been charged with sinking a bore. Having a permanent bore would be a great benefit to the Station and ensure a permanent supply of water. This was now possible by tapping into The Great Artesian Basin. This aquifer is the largest underground fresh-water reservoir in the world, occupying over 1.7 million square kilometres beneath the arid and semi-arid parts of Queensland, New South Wales and South Australia. European settlers discovered the Basin in 1878 when a shallow bore was sunk near Bourke in New South Wales. The discovery and use of the underground water opened up thousands of square miles of country previously unavailable for pastoralists. To tap it, wells were drilled down to a suitable rock layer where the pressure of the water forced it up through casing, mostly without pumping.[55] Farquhar and his mate Martin were having an anxious time. He wrote and reported to Jack:

> Martin was in from the bore yesterday with the pleasing tidings that he had lost his sinker and jars in the bottom of the bore and has failed to get them out again owing he says to the hole caving in. While he is working to get them he did not get quite to the original bottom with the tools. He got down 2,900 feet. The depth should be 2,937 feet 9 inches. So that he was 37 feet short of the bottom. I truly hardly know what is to be done now. I am going over there today. … He has got a fair supply of water and I have every confidence in him getting a sufficient supply to water all the stock the country will carry. Tonga country is looking well but there is not nearly as much grass anywhere as last year. The frontage paddocks have improved.[56]

Farquhar McDonald and Martin were clearly struggling with their task. They had only a fair supply of water and must make a second or third attempt to sink the bore. Despite the frustration of not sinking the bore to MacGregor's instructions, Farquhar had time in his letter to tease Jack about the object of his love, Miss Zena Scott. Although he had previously been working at Glengyle, his letters from Miss Scott in Tasmania were being sent to Jack at Durham Downs. Farquhar insisted he had opened them and read them before sending them on. Jack, although initially worried, must have realised his friend was teasing him unmercifully.

The Boer War

Late in 1899, as well as keeping Jack up to date with his father's health, in particular that he was complaining of pains in his hands and feet, Goodie was keen to inform Jack of the most current household news. She and her cousin Mary had attended the Melbourne Cup the previous day. While at Flemington, they saw the New South Wales contingent of soldiers on display. These troops would soon be departing to South Africa to represent Australia in the Boer War. Goodie could report that the troops who marched around the course in a heavy downpour, 'got an awful ducking'.[57]

The first troops despatched from Australia in November were drawn from each of the Colonies' existing volunteer militia forces.[58] Goodie was excited by what she had seen the day before and this is obvious in her letter:

> They are a fine body of men, hard and wiry looking and walk much better than our men. Of course there are more going than from Victoria, 500 I think NSW men, not counting those there already of the NSW Lancers. Every one feels quite sure they won't disgrace their country if they only had more training and once they get in with the Imperial Troops [they] will have plenty to learn. Great excitement here over the War and the day the contingent left here was the biggest crowd I ever saw. So we must know a good few of the fellows who went, and you too.[59]

The overseas war was a welcome diversion from the drought and depression the country was still suffering through. The Boer War continued until 1902.

As the 1899 year continued and flowed into 1900, the usual family activities were reported to Jack in letters from his sisters. As late as October 1900 there was still no rain in Queensland while it is clear the Victorian properties had a sufficient supply of good feed. Letters from Goodie, Cissie, Jessie and Pearl reported that their mother was not well. Apart from this, the family appeared to begin the year of Federation positively.

Early in 1900, when Jack was staying at Clunie, Farquhar McDonald wrote to let him know that they had had some rain at Glengyle and that there was a good storm at Miranda. But the stock was 'falling away' and it was very dry. Although there had been no end of little showers of rain, there was not enough at one time to do any good, he wrote. Farquhar's concerns turned to his management of the stud sheep and whether he had taken the rams out yet because 'If they could hold their own in the paddocks it would be as well to leave them in till it rains.'[60]

In March 1900, Farquhar wrote from Durham Downs to Jack in Victoria to let him know that rain was reported from nearly all parts of New South Wales. It was 'light in some parts up to 8 inches in other parts. We have had a splendid rain in this Colony this last couple of days. Surely it will reach into Queensland?' He closed his letter commenting that he hoped the stud sheep would survive and that he was not surprised to hear that 'you have lost some of the horses and the losses in the cattle must be fearful heavy'. This was an understatement.

As summer rolled into autumn then winter, Farquhar continued to write from Victoria. He relished passing on the news of his adventures and family gossip. In the style of a war correspondent, or someone in the firing line, he wrote:

> Just a few lines from the front. I have not had any letter from you for a couple of mails but was glad to hear from your Papa that you had a little rain on portions of the Run. I hope sufficient to keep the stock out of danger for a while. I have been watching the weather reports but have not any news from Thargomindah district of rain all the reports of rain from various parts in Queensland and N S Wales there have been a good deal of rain in this colony where it is not wanted only to put out bush fires. It is a pity some of the Queensland stock was not here. Grass everywhere is knee deep yet but very dry and bush fires have done a lot of damage in some places. Half one of the paddocks here got burnt a little while ago and some of the fencing there is nice green feed on it now as there was a good thunderstorm soon after it got burnt. There has been great excitement about the war it is the only thing thought of.

Farquhar was out at the park on St Kilda Road when he saw the Army trying out the 3rd Contingent (Bushmen). Of their display of riding: 'I never seen such a poor exhibition of horsemanship' he wrote. Of the twenty he saw, he considered there were only four horsemen he believed would have passed the test. Because the horses were 'pretty fresh' several of them bucked their riders off. To Farquhar it was really amusing to see how some of them hung on: 'they were pluckey and gripped on to the front or back of the saddle or anywhere they could catch in sheer desperation'. A couple of them clung to their horses' necks; Farquhar assessed that they were principally 'town fellows' but they were game and he concluded that if they got 'a show' or a place in the unit, they would make riders. He would like to have seen a really good 'back country rider' because he believed riding was taken for granted by town people.

As far as family gossip was concerned, he wrote to Jack that 'you will get a good budget of news from the girls as they are writing. Your girl and Cis arrived in Tasmania I believe all safe'. Cissie and Zena Scott were holidaying with her family.

Farquhar had been in Victoria for two months at that stage and acknowledged that he was only just beginning to enjoy myself and did not know when he would make a start back to Queensland.[61]

A sudden death in the year of Federation

The year 1901 marked the Federation of the six British colonies of Australia. New South Wales, Victoria, Queensland, South Australia, Western Australia and Tasmania were united to form the Commonwealth of Australia. On 1 January 1901 the first federal parliament was formed. Before 1901 the six British colonies were partly self-governing under the law-making power of the British Parliament. The colonies each had their own government and laws, their own defence force, issued their own stamps and collected taxes on goods that crossed its borders. The colonies built railways using different gauges, permanently complicating the transport of goods across the continent. By the 1880s, the inefficiency of this system, a growing unity among colonists, and a belief that a national government was needed to deal with issues such as trade, defence and immigration, saw popular support for federation to grow. Australia's federation came about through a process of deliberation, consultation and debate. Federation went ahead after the approval of the people through a referendum.

By the middle of February 1901 there was still no rain on Meba Downs; the weather remained very hot. Farquhar wrote to Jack that it had been 'from 104 to 116 degrees in the shade' and they were still enduring dust storms and winds from the south.[62] The drought persisted, imposing hardship and financial strain on the family.

Jack continued to spend some time in Queensland but returned to Victoria to take up his role of manager of Dalmore by the middle of 1901. It is unclear when Duncan MacGregor transferred the property into the names of the seven children. However, on 25 September 1901, six of the seven MacGregor children signed an agreement to form a business, styled 'J. MacGregor & Co.'. The business was described as 'of Farmers and Graziers upon their Freehold Estate at Pakenham known as "Dalmore"' and was for the term of five years computed from 15 August 1901. It was made between 'John MacGregor of Moor's Road Coburg Esquire, Margaret (Goodie) MacGregor of the same place Spinster of the second part, Isabella (Tottie) Barbara Pestell of Hawthorn married woman of the third part, Annie (Cissie) MacGregor of Moor's Road Coburg Spinster of the fourth part Christina (Pearl) MacGregor of Moor's Road Spinster of the fifth part and Jessie Macrae Stewart of Ascot Vale married woman of the sixth part'.[63] Donald McRae MacGregor was unable to be part of this family venture because he was only 18 and could not take part in this legal agreement. His mother later compensated him for his lack of participation and subsequent income from the venture.

By 1901 Duncan was showing signs of severe mental and emotional strain. Added to this family anxiety was the news that Goodie, who had been ill for months, was diagnosed with Ovarian cancer. This news must have caused great distress to the MacGregor family. The truth of her condition was only found when her death certificate was obtained in 2016. The story handed down in the family was that she had died in a riding accident. The location varied in the telling, with two possibilities. The first was that she died at Glengyle in Coburg; the second, at Dandenong on her way to Dalmore. In many of Goodie's letters she writes about riding out with one person or teaching another. After suffering for almost one year, she died at Dr Fitzgerald's Private Hospital Melbourne on Thursday 28 November 1901. She was 31.

Soon after the death of her sister, Jessie wrote to Jack, who by then was working at Dalmore, giving him details of the funeral 'on Friday or Saturday' the following week, and the travel arrangements of members of the extended family. It is heartbreaking to read that 'Life seems to be full of sorrow and pain.' Pearl was away with family at Goldie; Cissie was in bed and had been there since Thursday, the day of Goodie's death. As Jessie wrote, 'Mother got her up for a short time yesterday afternoon. I did not see Pa as he was in town and I left before he returned'.[64] The family were plunged into a period of intense grief. It is unsurprising that further letters between Jack and his sisters cease; they recommence in May 1902. From that time, all family letters are written on black-rimmed letter paper and enclosed in black-rimmed envelopes. The MacGregor family were in deep mourning; this continued until 1903 when further disruptions to family life and financial hardship had to be dealt with.

Top:

Group photograph of attandees at Jessie MacGregor and Donald Macrae Stewart's wedding, outside Glengyle, Coburg, 5 December 1894

Leckie Archive

Middle:

Wedding party at Jessie MacGregor's marriage, 5 December 1894

Leckie Archive

Left:

Jessie and Donald Macrae Stewart, 1894

Leckie Archive

MacGregor children, possibly Christmas 1894. *Standing L to R*: Donald, Cissie, Jack. *Seated L to R*: Jessie, Pearl, Goodie, Tottie
Leckie Archive

MacGregor family, c.1895–97. Margaret, Goodie, Unknown male, Tottie (seated), Jessie and Duncan
Leckie Archive

Tottie MacGregor and her bridesmaids, Cissie, Pearl and Teenie McKenzie at her marriage to William Pestell, 25 November 1896
Leckie Archive

Jack MacGregor, c.1900
Leckie Archive

Donald MacGregor
aged 10, c.1892
Leckie Archive

Donald MacGregor
aged 18, c.1900
Leckie Archive

Goodie on left and another sister outside the stables at Glengyle, undated
Leckie Archive

Goodie MacGregor
(1870–1901)
Leckie Archive

Tottie Pestell with William MacGregor (Greg) Pestell, born October 1897
Leckie Archive

Tottie Pestell with Greg and Margaret Enid (Meg) Pestell, 1908
Leckie Archive

Cissie and Pearl MacGregor, c.1890
Leckie Archive

Pearl MacGregor on her 21st birthday, 28 April 1900
Leckie Archive

Christina McRae (1816–87) seated at writing desk
Leckie Archive

Miss Flora Scott, governess then companion to Margaret MacGregor, c.1900
Leckie Archive

Lieutenant William Pestell, 1915
Leckie Archive

Jessie Macrae Stewart, undated
Leckie Archive

Reverend Donald Macrae Stewart, undated
Leckie Archive

Christina, wife of
Donald MacGregor
with Bernard, 1910
Leckie Archive

Maud Hannam, Donald
MacGregor's second wife, c.1916
Susan Vale Archive

Case of surveying aneroid marked 'D.M. MacGregor, Durham Downs, 1897'

Surveying aneroid with case
In the possession of Tina Terry, Tasmania

— 5 —
'My Heart is Most Sad and Sore', 1902–1916

The Federation drought continued, with devastating effects on MacGregor's Queensland properties and on the household. On 30 April 1902, in what must have been a state of despair, Duncan MacGregor sat at his desk and made a series of notes. The figures he produced were his estimates of lost income and the actual losses incurred up to the year 1900.

The stations had been improved and built up through MacGregor's own hard work and that of his employees and his two sons. He had spent vast sums on his properties and he blamed the drought and what he described as the 'increasingly unrealistic' terms of, and amendments to, the 1869 Land Act for his current financial losses.[1] He set out the stark facts of his beloved Durham Downs, Yanko, Glengyle, Miranda and Meba Downs Stations as follows:

Name	State	Dimension
Durham Downs	Queensland	3,753 sq. m
Yanko	Queensland	459 sq. m
Glengyle	Queensland	1,004 sq. m
Miranda	South Australia	457 sq. m
	Queensland	556 sq. m
Meba Downs	Queensland	739 sq. m
Total		6,968 sq. m

Name and Dimension of Station

The 'Summary of Improvements' included items such as internal and boundary fencing, wells, bores and pipes, sheep and cattle yards, horse yards, houses, sheds, shearers huts, meat houses, engines, plant equipment and drays:

Durham Downs	£32,620
Yanko	£9,267
Glengyle	£2,830
Miranda	£4,220
Meba Downs	£3,680
Total	£52,617

Summary of Improvement to Stations to 1900

MacGregor's 'Summary of Actual Losses' specifies the number of branded sheep, cattle and horses lost on each station between 1894 and 1900:

Station	Branded cattle	Sheep	Horses	Total Value
Durham Downs	53,352 @ £4 £213,408	184,788 @ 10/- £92,394	569 @ £10 £5,690	£311,492
Yanko		52,229 @ 10/- £26,114		£26,114
Glengyle	23,006 @ £4 £92,024		100 @ £10 £1,000	£93,024
Miranda	8,611 @ £4 £34,444		103 @ £10 £1,030	£35,474
Meba Downs	8,995 @ £4 £35,980		274 @ £10 £2,740	£38,720
TOTAL STOCK	93,964	237,017	1,046	TOTAL £504,824

Actual Losses 1894 to 1900

In his table 'Loss of Natural Increase' MacGregor estimates the loss of anticipated income from cattle and sheep on each station over the same period had normal rates of breeding occurred:

	Cattle @ £4	Sheep @ 10/-	Value
Durham Downs	8,000	175,200	£119,600
Yanko		65,000	£32,500
Glengyle	7,500		£30,000
Miranda	4,900		£19,600
Meba Downs	3,000		£12,000
TOTAL STOCK	23,400	240,200	£213,700

Loss of Natural Increase

MacGregor included the residential property Glengyle in Coburg and

Inverauld in Riddells Creek in his final calculation of losses. Glengyle was valued at £5,500 and Inverauld at £3,000.

Adding the branded stock on each station, the loss of natural increase, residential properties, station improvements and stock lost to the Bank, MacGregor calculated his 'Summary of Actual Losses' for the years 1894 to 1900. The figure was £861,912. However, in a newspaper article revealing his 'Stupendous Losses', MacGregor included an additional loss of £162,000 for sheep and cattle for 1901 and 1902.[2] His losses for the period are therefore even greater:

Branded stock on Stations	£ 504,824
Loss of Natural Increase	£ 213,700
Glengyle and Inverauld	£ 8,500
Station Improvements	£52,617
Remaining stock lost to Bank	£ 82,271
TOTAL LOSSES TO 1900	£ 861,912
Unbranded stock 1901-2	£ 162,000
TOTAL LOSSES	£ 1,023,912

Summary of Actual Losses

The loss of £1,023,912 was staggering for 1903. In today's terms, the amount MacGregor lost would be $125,800,000.[3]

There are questions that have to be asked: How had the resourceful Duncan MacGregor allowed the situation to become so dire and the properties to slip through his fingers? Was it just the drought or was there something else at the heart of the matter?

To appreciate fully the situation Duncan faced, we turn from numbers to words on the page. The correspondence from Farquhar McDonald reveals the story more eloquently. By the middle of July 1901, some rain had fallen in Queensland, but the various stations were still in a dreadful state. He reported from Durham Downs that in the previous week the gauge registered 70 points but it was very patchy: 'It will not do much good. I don't expect any feed to grow as the weather is too cold.' The Yanko ewes were lambing but, he wrote, 'I am afraid we wont have as many lambs. They are miserable weady lambs and seem to die in spite of everything. Feed has got very dry and is getting pretty scarce'. The tale of woe continues and his sense of desperation permeates the lengthy letter.[4]

The situation became worse in 1902. Jack had moved back to Victoria permanently in 1901 and was now managing Dalmore at Pakenham and the 20-year-old Donald MacGregor was spending time with the old oracle, Farquhar McDonald, in Queensland. Their hard work and hopeful intentions are set out when Farquhar writes to Jack about the continuing drought. The conditions at Durham Downs were bleak:

> It is still drought here. Plenty parts of the run have not had a drop of rain since you were here. We are now putting the ewes on the Islay well, their being no feed in the front paddocks. There is plenty dry feed at Islay from the rain twelve months ago. We have not had any rain the last summer to make any feed. The Cooper has run through but only in the main channels. All stock are in fair condition but if rain don't come before long we will be as bad off as ever. I believe the drought is now being felt very severely up north in parts that were not effected before also in New South Wales there has not been any restocking in this district as yet and it is better it had not been done.
>
> I suppose you expect us to be down at any time but as far as I can see there is no telling how long we may be here yet. I wrote your Papa some time ago asking to be relieved but was willing to stay till it rained. As Donald and I had intended taking what few horses we have down with us but did not think rain was going to hold off so long and since we have to stay the summer through I am quite willing to stay the winter.[5]

The situation is clear. Though they regretted it, Farquhar and Donald were prepared to stay on the Station until the matter was resolved with the London Chartered Bank.

These were hard times for Farquhar McDonald who was a long-term employee of the MacGregors. Farquhar, the son of John and Annie (née McRae) McDonald, had arrived with his family in Port Phillip as an assisted immigrant in November 1848 when he was 19. While reported to be illiterate, it is clear from his correspondence to Jack that in his maturity he could certainly read and write. Although it is unclear when he began working for McRae and later MacGregor, the association probably commenced in Victoria either at Clunie or Inverauld in the 1860s.

Farquhar addressed a second and even more moving letter to Jack from Durham Downs, two months later. It evocatively illustrates the problems MacGregor faced:

> I scarcely need tell you that we have not had any rain yet. The last twelve months is the driest ever experienced here. You will think it could not be dryer than the last twelve months you were here. At the Station we have only registered 20 points for the 12 months. Of course there were a few thunderstorms on parts of the Run in February last but only on very small patches. The principal feed we have got is from the rain of last February 12 month and a little feed grain in the channels of the Cooper, after a fresh that came down last winter. So you can imagine what bit of feed there is very very dry. But so far most of the stock are in fair condition but if it don't rain before the summer I will be battling with them the same as before. But I suppose we will be relieved before then.
>
> We at first intended to stay till it rain but had no idea it would be as long without rain as it has been. And now it seems as if it is likely to go another twelve months but I will write and ask to be relieved before the summer comes on. Charlie Readford is likely to be back before the summer. And if they don't send some one I can leave him here till they send some one. We have not had a bad time although it has been so dry. There is so few stock there is not much to do although enough to always keep one going. … I would be very pleased to be going away from here any moment if the one who is entitled to the benefit was going to get it. But under present circumstances I must say I am loath to leave but my own sense seems to tell me there is no hope of recovery and holding on to it. Seems like a drowning man grasping at a straw. Of course the seasons will change and stock will increase as before but it will take almost a life time to build up again and perhaps at the end with the same result that everything would be lost.

Although not surprising, given Farquhar's longevity as an employee of the MacGregor family, it is touching to read his advice to Jack to value the love of his parents:

> … I am very pleased to know that you are established at Dalmore and I sincerely hope that you will have success and I hope and trust you will help your poor Papa in every way you possibly can. The knowledge of you and Donald being anxious to help him in his declining years will be very great support and comfort to him through his sad sad sorrow and trouble. I never will forget how anxious dearest Goodie was to help him. How cruel it does seem that she was taken from her loving parents. Yes, dear John, you have a great blessing in having

such generous and loving good parents, who will not be with you long and it is for all of you to try and make them happy.

You might think I am taking upon myself too much in writing you this but if I did not think of you as a brother and think of your parents as my parents I would not do so. It is only when one loses their parents that they feel what they should have done.

Trusting that you are quite well and with kindest wishes from Donald and self.

Yours sincerely, Farquhar[6]

Maintaining a stout heart

Duncan MacGregor responded in his own way to the drought: he expressed his feelings of desperation by writing poetry. The following untitled poem portrays the bitter story of his losses during the harsh Queensland drought:

> Where ere I now may wander
> My heart is most sad and sore
> With thoughts that constantly haunt me
> By day and night and morn
> Of those sad tales that I do know
> Of them that can repeat
> Of thousands upon thousands
> Of rotten bones in heaps
>
> The country that was fine to see
> When rain at time descend
> To moist the soil and grow the feed
> For horses sheep and rogue
> When each and all did drive about
> By streams and downs and plains
> With hearts so light to our delight
> And a full life to see
>
> But now its changed and sad our tales
> No rains for years around
> No floods to flow the feed to grow
> But clouds of dust over plains
> Like darkest nights they race along

> Before each wind and beast
> And what sad sad desolation
> To view the wreck when past
> The beasts that roamed these plains before
> And sheep and lambs and horse
> Are now all so haggard in every herd
> And dead along the flats
> No low of beast can now be heard
> Wherever one wanders forth
> But rotten bones deep buried and
> In mud and sand and dust
>
> The government is much to blame
> Tho had the drought may be
> No tenure to each they give for rain
> But high rents then dearer
> And those back rents did tell their tales
> When years of drought prevailed
> No sheep for sale or wool to shear
> Sad sad our tales indeed
>
> The many years of toil we spent
> In this most desert land
> And many thousand we have spent
> Which never can be regained
> And all we possess just now
> Are heading on the plains
> Now sad indeed for us in need
> But few to feel our pain

Writing from Dalmore in Gippsland, Duncan's emotions were raw:

> I see the gum trees by the stream
> With Gippsland scrubs entwined
> Their shadows deep in every place
> When sun above them shine
>
> The fragrant wattle on each hand
> The sunbeams of our clime
> With little songsters on each bush
> To sing so sweetly times
>
> My thoughts are fleeting sadly now
> To think of northern climes
> Among the dust and barren lands

That blows with every wind
Where not a blade of grass to see
But hides and bones and dust
And desolation everywhere
And nowhere feed but thirst

This is the land to break ones heart
Tho stout his lessons be
To see his studs and cattle prime
Without a blade of feed

And scattered round and everywhere
With eyes sunk deep in heads
And being mournful all around
To see their comrades dead

How many thousands starved to death
In this deserted land
How many wails and sighs and tears
From those that lost them all

Tis only these that suffered long
Can their sad tales repeat
Of thousands upon thousands of
Rotten bones in heaps

The woeful tales that can be told
Of what is gone or past
But no one can recall the bones
That is smouldering in the dust

I will now away to genial climes
Where floats the mist not dust
And see the green woods and the flowers
That grows among the scrubs

Amongst the green woods and the bush
Where rain does fall by times
And where your deepest thirst can reach
From springs and rivulets clear

To South Gippsland I resumed my way
And live amongst the ferns
With blue gums for my canopy
And scented flowers around

> I will soon wander north again
> Where dust and sands abounds
> And death and bones are everywhere
> Without rain to moist the ground
>
> The many years that we have toiled
> To earn but beef and bread
> But now it's gone and never return
> Most sad our life indeed
>
> Farewell for men and for age
> To such a cursed place
> I now shall live among the ferns
> Tho but a duty must[7]

As well as the poetry, Duncan made his feelings of frustration and despair known by writing to the *Brisbane Courier*. Two of his letters to the editor were published in 1901. Under the title 'Crisis in the Far West of Queensland', he spelt out the situation as he saw it. First he identified the 1869 Land Act as the main cause of concern: 'the Act was based on an absurdly exaggerated estimate of the carrying capacity of the country', he wrote, 'and the extent that could be stocked to that amount was very small indeed'. Next he pointed to actual stocking of the stations for the past 25 years: 'May I not say with truth that the actual numbers are just about a quarter of the numbers estimated?' This meant if only one quarter of the number of stock could be carried on any property, the costs would be greater than originally estimated and the profits lower. Added to the increase in costs of rent per square mile at the expiration of the first term of seven years of the lease and the seasonal droughts, it was clear the pastoralists would find themselves in financial difficulty. Put another way, MacGregor claimed that 'For the first seven years, according to the 1869 Act, the country was worth only 5 shillings per square mile' (not the amount he paid) which was 'more than a great part of it is worth today'.

MacGregor was a pioneer pastoralist of western and south-western Queensland. Of his years of experience he writes:

> As one who has known a great part of South-Western Queensland for many years, and who has spent much time, energy, and capital in the development of numerous costly improvements to the benefit of the colony – although, unfortunately, to my own loss – I can

> unhesitatingly assert that it is impossible for me to name a single station which is without a large tract of country unavailable for pasturage. I am confident that this statement will be borne out by every other man who has travelled the district of which I speak with observing eyes.[8]

It is clear that what galled MacGregor more than anything was the fact that the Commissioner of Crown Lands had recently toured the area. It was at a time when there was hardly a blade of grass to be found and there was nothing for the cattle to eat. The outlook was grim. As he pointed out: 'How anyone with eyes and a conscience, could come to the conclusion that he had ever seen a living beast eat gidya, turpentine bush … ti-tree that is found throughout the district, or any other shrub that even the rabbits would not eat' was a mystery to him and to the others who knew the country thoroughly. The issue here was the definition of 'available' and 'unavailable' country. Some of the land had previously been declared 'available' when, without inspection by the Commissioner as far back as 1869, should have been deemed 'unavailable'. If this land had been excised from their runs they would not have been required to pay rent and try to use them to run cattle or sheep.

While Duncan's own underlying problem requires further definition, the ongoing drought had exacerbated his plight. It was impossible to run cattle and sheep on unsuitable land and the requirement to improve the land was wasting MacGregor's resources. The ongoing drought worsened the situation. Additionally, the government was doing almost nothing to alleviate their position. While he believed the state's legislators had done their very best to remedy the existing critical condition by granting a concession of the postponement of rents due in September 1901, this was 'wholly insufficient'. He concluded: 'how anyone could view it in any other light is incomprehensible to me'.[9]

As the drought wore on, so did Duncan's arguments with the government. He wrote again to the *Brisbane Courier*, spelling out the reasons for the 'woeful wail from the sadly-depressed, heavily-burdened, and long-suffering unfortunates of the drought-stricken West'.

> The country that the Crown leases have undertaken to exploit is naturally dry and waterless. It is only at heavy personal expense that it has been made to yield any sort of return at all. There are a number of so-called rivers, such as the Paroo, Bulloo, Cooper, Diamantina, Eyre Creek, Mulligan, and their tributaries. These rivers drain an enormous

tract of country, and carry an immense quantity of water during flood times. In the rainy seasons they overflow the country adjacent to them … That is good, so far as it goes, but a little investigation will show that from all these so-called rivers only a few permanent waterholes are furnished.

MacGregor went on to explain that in the few months after the floods the rivers dried up and if they were not replenished they became chains of semi-permanent waterholes. Stock could get stuck in the mud and the waterholes become a death trap for cattle and sheep. Luxuriant herbage soon grew but it lasted only a few months before the ground dried out and cracked, making it impossible for the stock to travel. MacGregor's passionate letter spells out precisely the environmental problems faced by pastoralists:

> The land of the Far West is a land of drought, dry lakes, channels, and creeks, all filled up with drift and sand, and timber that is almost everywhere starved, stunted and crooked. Because these are the ordinary and natural conditions, the country is of no value to anyone until heavy expenditure has been put out upon it for the purposes of water conservation.

He offers the only practical strategy he believes would remedy the situation: amended legislation that would ensure that the leaseholds were converted into freehold land and provide certain tenure for the pastoralist. While good fortune and favourable seasons might repair some of the damage that the previous years had brought, MacGregor declared that his hope was that the crown lessees in the far west would not rest until 'new and equitable land laws' were written and 'placed on the country's Statute-book'. He concluded:

> No one who has any adequate knowledge of the facts can be found to assert that the vast pastoral possibilities of Western Queensland are being worked to the advantage either of the run-holders or of the State, under the existing land laws.[10]

Despite MacGregor maintaining his rage, the law was not altered. The drought continued. In October 1902 he wrote again to the *Brisbane Courier*, restating his case: that the only possible remedy to Western Queensland's pastoral problem was to grant tenure to the leaseholders. In the early years of the century, the bank foreclosed on his mortgages and he lost his Queensland properties. His state of mind is expressed in the following poem; he speaks of the many nights he spent:

>On this couch I lie me down
>With pains that rend my breast
>The lord above that only knows
>*Why I do suffer such*
>
>The allotted time that I am here
>May soon come to pass
>But God my guide that – on high
>*Will see me through the pass*
>
>My faith and trust is in the Lord
>That suffered on the cross
>To save our soles and live with God
>*When parting with this earth.*
>
>The many sins we do confess
>Before the Lord on high
>And ask our Saviour to forgive
>*Before the clouds draw nigh.*[11]

Deeply depressed and conscious of his mortality, Duncan MacGregor is fortified by his belief in God.

In Victoria, the situation was better than it was in Queensland, but also stressful. At Koo-wee-rup, a dispute with a neighbour came to a head. A Mr Vinnicombe accused MacGregor of flooding his land, finding fault in the drainage system MacGregor had designed. The matter went to the Supreme Court of Victoria. This was the second controversial legal battle over swampland in which MacGregor was involved.

The matter of Vinnicombe and MacGregor, dating from 1901, came before the Supreme Court for the final time in June 1903. The three judges decided against Vinnicombe in all matters.

After the result was announced, Keith Larsen, a long-term employee who had worked at Dalmore, Koo-wee-rup wrote to MacGregor to congratulate him on his success. He was adamant that 'the only conclusion I could come to when I heard the evidence … was that the trial was only started through spite and for the sake of extorting money'. He also believed that only 'a man with a stout heart' would have had the pluck to take on the job. Furthermore, he added: 'the Scotch people are noted all over the world for their pluck and perseverance, nothing ever discourages them'.[12] Larsen looked back on his time working for MacGregor with great fondness and stated that those years were some of the happiest of his life. He relished the memory of his own part in clearing and draining the swamp. He was proud of the fact that there were now more than 30 or 40 miles of drains and that the land was productive.

While MacGregor gloried in winning the case, it had been costly.

Relinquishing the McRae estate, 1904–1910

Messrs Brahe & Gair, solicitors, may have begun to doubt Duncan MacGregor's ability to maintain his role as executor of Donald McRae's estate some time before any action was taken to remove him from the role. He had been managing the estate since 1869.

From the mid-1890s, MacGregor invested heavily in mortgages and loans on behalf of the estate. The full extent of his mortgage activities still remains somewhat unclear. The files contain reams of documents detailing mortgages and investments, and it is apparent in the correspondence from the solicitors Brahe & Gair and Russell & Mears, and the accountants Rucker & McKenzie, that the complete picture was obscure even for these professional men.

In December 1907, Brahe & Gair wrote to MacGregor in most direct terms, advising him that:

> the Court has made an order for you to pass your accounts and on the application we applied for the assistance of an accountant in the preparation of the accounts. It was pointed out that there were accounts to the Estate but his Honour directed that an 'independent' accountant should be appointed'.

Brahe & Gair appointed the accountants Messrs Young & Outwaite and asked MacGregor to instruct Rucker and MacKenzie to give Young & Outwaite all the information they required and 'produce to them the books of the Estate and all vouchers, &c.'.[14]

Some years before this, MacGregor had written to his sister-in-law, Annie Forster, to solicit her views on the subject of his executorship. She was, after all, still receiving a substantial annual income from the estate. In March 1904, she responded. She wrote to assure him that she felt he was doing his best in administering the estate of her late father. But Annie's life was far from plain sailing. She was facing her own demons. Married to Phillip Forster, they had tried in different ways to sustain their lifestyle through her independent income, yet, it appears, with little success. She wrote:

> My Dear Mr MacGregor
>
> I received your letters also the enclosed. I write now to say that at all times I have been quite satisfied and am still so and it is not by any wish of mine that there was any thought of an other trustee being appointed. I do not wish it for I always have felt that you have done your best for myself and sister and it upset me very much that there was any upset and worry caused through me. I cannot express myself in writing but at any time you could meet me in town I will try and explain to you that it is not my wish to do any thing against you or my sister and I feel very much that you should have trouble and worry through me.
>
> I would like to meet you or Maggie … at any time or place you mention if you will let me … I know you will all be sorry to hear that Cecile came home from school very unwell today – I will be in town seeing the doctor with her on Friday next.
>
> I am yours sincerely
> Annie Forster[13]

The file contains no further correspondence from Annie. And while it is imagined Annie was sincere in her wish to assure her brother-in-law that she believed he was doing the best for the estate, at the same time she was attempting to secure additional money from it. Not long after this letter, the newspaper article accusing her of 'Impecuniosity' made it clear that she was once again in debt and before the courts to repay the money she owed. In 1900, after marrying her lover and having two more children, they bought Beachleigh, a large 20-acre property in Frankston, and lived there until they could no longer afford the luxury. She died in Sandringham in 1939.

In February 1908, details of the Donald McRae's estate were compiled and set out in a document.[15] In July 1867 the original assets, after deducting legacies and funeral expenses, amounted to £11,817.[16] In 1908, the corpus of the estate, including investments and mortgages of £83,055, amounted to £125,230. However, the mortgages taken out as investments by MacGregor could not be paid.

From January 1910, Rucker & MacKenzie attempted to establish the extent of the mortgages MacGregor had entered into. They wrote to

Brahe & Gair in confusion: 'There is a title to some land in Cunnamulla transferred by Mr MacGregor to the late W.J. Rucker. This deed was found at Messrs Williams & Matthews' office today. We do not know the nature of the transaction which brought about the transfer nor does Mr W.R. Rucker but we understand that Mr Rucker's executors will hand over this deed if Mr MacGregor can show he is entitled to it.' The land at Swan Hill was also mortgaged and, with a sense of exasperation, they wrote that it had 'never come under our notice in any way whatever'.[17] The papers were clearly in a mess.

It was March 1910 before MacGregor handed over the financial accounts for the estate to Rucker & MacKenzie, who then handed them to Young & Outhwaite. The inventory includes general ledgers, mortgage registers, cashbooks, journals, pass books and pay-in books. Passbooks for the London Chartered Bank covered 1870–83, 1893–95 and 1898–1908. Also included were vouchers, agreements, leases, licences, *Government Gazettes*, covenants, mortgages and copies of annuity payments. These papers represented 40 years of work on MacGregor's behalf.

On 19 May 1910, MacGregor signed a document transferring all of the mortgages he had taken out in the name of the estate to the Perpetual Executors and Trustees Association of Australia Limited.[18] Perpetual's Melbourne office took over the estate. MacGregor had been forced to give up the role he had carried out since 1869.

In the months following his relinquishment of the estate, Duncan MacGregor did not make life easy for Perpetual Trustees, the solicitors Brahe & Gair and Russell & Mears, or the accountants Rucker & MacKenzie and Young & Outhwaite. On 1 August, Young & Outhwaite wrote to him asking for his views on offering at auction some of the country properties. They were estimated to be valued at around £35,000. Two days later they were requesting again that MacGregor call on them 'within the next day or two'.[19] Refusing to address the question, on 6 August, MacGregor replied, stating that he would 'only be prepared to discuss the question of disputed accounts and Messrs Brahe & Gair's costs'.

Russell & Mears solicitors attempted to unravel the tangle of the Dalmore estate. The partnership of the six children created in 1901 was styled J. MacGregor & Co. In 1905 the survivors with an interest in the Dalmore partnership signed two mortgages to Duncan MacGregor for £5,300 and £16,260, a total of £21,500. The papers in 1910 showed that the amount owing was £18,719 and Russell & Mears had 'no definite information how these mortgages came to be, signed four years after the prior arrangement had been made'. Perpetual Trustee were calling for payment of interest under these mortgages and threatened to exercise their power of sale unless some arrangement could be made. The five remaining partners had signed an indemnity and took over the equity of Dalmore. In doing so they had acquired 'a very valuable asset' and the accountants believed it would repay them handsomely in the future. It was eventually agreed that a new partnership agreement be drawn up for Dalmore to enable them to improve the property and eventually sell it.

In the meantime, Duncan MacGregor remained belligerent in his opposition to Perpetual taking over the management of the estate. On 1 December 1910 Perpetual replied to a letter from him of 30 November relating to the sale of Gowan Lea. Arthur Outhwaite, Perpetual's Melbourne manager, began by stating that he did not 'propose to enter into acrimonious correspondence on the matters mentioned in your letter'. He had sought clarification of the stock register they had taken possession of in March 1910, pointing out:

> Have you forgotten that for months you refused without reason to sign the transfers, and never stated your willingness to do so upon receiving receipts until a Writ was actually about to be issued against you by a Solicitor employed by the Association?

Not only had MacGregor refused to sign the transfer, it appears he reverted to his default position: he sought counsel's opinion. When counsel's opinion was obtained, MacGregor 'still refused to sign'. In stating his case, Outhwaite wrote that Perpetual wanted to sell these properties 'as you were informed from the first', but they were unable to do so because 'you would not complete our Title'. Meanwhile, they could not obtain tenants for Gowan Lea and had no means of making the property productive or viable. Perpetual had applied to MacGregor and John MacGregor for assistance in establishing the level of stock held on Gowan Lea 'but were refused so consistently that we could only regard you as a coalition which has been at work against us all through'. A litany of accusations associated with his refusal to assist Perpetual in winding up the estate were listed. The three-page letter became more shrill. After making a final request to 'assist the truth to prevail by permitting us to interview you', the letter concludes with the frank statement that:

> From beginning to end consistent efforts have been made to make

our position difficult and untenable, and we beg you to take up a different attitude and set a different example.[20]

Reading the correspondence, MacGregor's actions appear to have been erratic. He seemed to have lost his grasp on the complex issues of the mortgages he had taken out and the money he owed. Some of the dealings remain unresolved. The solicitors and accountants began to write to Maggie MacGregor, indicating that she had taken control of the situation.

The Gowan Lea estate was transferred to Perpetual Trustees on 13 June 1910 with the expectation was that it would be sold as a going concern. It was offered for auction on 17 October 1910 with a reserve of £11 per acre but no reasonable bid was received. It was subsequently, transferred to Adolphe Seelenmeyer (24 March 1914), to the Victorian Railways (28 October 1914), to His Majesty King George V (27 March 1918) and to Donald McRae MacGregor (30 October 1930). On 15 November 1942 the mortgage was transferred to Mary Affleck Baillieu who sold it to the brothers Ian Marshall Baillieu and Richard Lawrence Baillieu in about 1950.

The Estate of the Late Donald McRae was handed over to the Perpetual Trustees as an ongoing entity, continuing to pay Margaret MacGregor and Annie Forster an annuity. Correspondence from Perpetual to MacGregor makes the point that the estate was to be retained as a whole. However, they were keen to sell such properties as Gowan Lea and Dalmore when appropriate. The large number of properties across Victoria were valued and a cash realisation was estimated so that some of the debts could be cleared.

When the management of Dalmore was transferred to the Perpetual Trustees in 1910, several problems in the management of Dalmore and the McRae estate were discovered. The Dalmore partners – John, Annie (Cissie) Hutchings, Isabella (Tottie), Jessie and the estate of the late Margaret (Goodie) MacGregor – were faced with a dilemma. Perpetual wanted to 'urge' them to 'consider the advisability of the sale ... of the whole or part of the Dalmore estate'.[21] But first the partners had to be convinced this was the right action to take. From 1901 to 1909 Duncan MacGregor had drawn interest on an amount of £7,049 from the estate for Margaret MacGregor. This amount of interest had been drawn 'with Mrs MacGregor's concurrence' and in such a manner as 'technically to constitute breaches of trust by Mr MacGregor for which he might be liable to the Estate'. This was a major sticking point for the solicitors. In order to settle the matter MacGregor had assigned certain stock to the Dalmore partnership in return for an indemnity against the £7,049. From 1901 there had been no profit paid to the Dalmore partnership. In 1905 the partnership had signed two mortgages to MacGregor totalling £21,560, which differed from the £18,749 shown on the books for the Dalmore. The solicitors had no information about the mortgages or the differences in the amounts concerned.

Russell & Mears put the argument to Duncan MacGregor that the property should be sold because 'No reasonable expectations of increased prices in the future' would compensate for the present losses they were suffering. Their next letter was addressed to 'Mrs MacGregor', again urging a decision which 'must be unanimous'.[22] The partnership agreed with the main framework for settlement: that all the net profits out of Dalmore be paid to Mrs MacGregor and that the partnership be extended to enable this to happen. An agreement was finally reached. The amount of £18,749 'be accepted as an advance by the Trustee … to her children (excepting Donald)' and that the Dalmore partnership and Donald pay Mrs MacGregor interest at 4 per cent during her lifetime'. It was agreed the mortgage be discharged and a new mortgage by the partnership be taken out to protect Mrs MacGregor against any claim for interest on the amount advanced to her children. The solicitors for John MacGregor pointed out that he had worked the property for 9 years but had not drawn his salary in full for years, 'if ever'.[23] Settlement was still being discussed.

Perpetual Trustees had a long way to go to fully comprehend the various mortgages taken out by MacGregor and to understand the financial situation. In 1911 they issued a balance sheet of the estate. Assets and liabilities amounted to £126,105-10-10. Losses on the realisation of securities and amounts written off were £27,428; mortgages foreclosed amounted to £57,194, and cash in the London Bank of Australia amounted to £3,685-15-8. Perpetual put the Dalmore property up for auction on 20 April 1912. It failed to sell. Two years later, on 17 April 1914, Tottie Pestell proposed that the partnership be dissolved. Russell & Mears recommended to John MacGregor that 'sooner than have a public application to the Court' that the land be put in the market at once which would satisfy Mrs Pestell.[24] It remains unclear exactly when Perpetual sold the Dalmore Estate.

Clydesdale champion, Earl of Millfield at Royal Melbourne Show, 1899
'The Royal Show', *Australasian*, 9 September 1899

Dalmore homestead, Kooweerup, undated
Leckie Archive

Kooweerup drainiage equipment, undated
Leckie Archive

Collection of photographs of Gowan Lea, c.1933
Susan Vale

Gowan Lea homestead
Photographer: Tina Terry, c.1980's

Dalmore Well, 2016
Photographer: Ian Leckie

Farquhar McDonald (1829–1913)
Leckie Archive

Miss Scott with Tottie later in life, undated
Leckie Archive

All four oil paintings by Frederick W. Woodhouse (UK b.1820, arrived Australia 1858, d.1909) were purchased from the Bridget McDonnell Gallery, Carlton by the Art Gallery of Ballarat with funds from the Joe White Bequest, 2016. Provenance: Estate of Duncan MacGregor; then by descent; private collection, Melbourne.

Breeding details included in *Herd book, Stock pedigrees 1874–1920*, Duncan MacGregor papers, Manuscripts, SLV

[Roan Shorthorn Bull, probably 'Duke of Coburg'], 1878.
The 'Duke of Coburg' was calved 1 October 1875, bred by R. McDougall

Galgacus Booth, 1879.
Inscribed on the frame 'Galgacus Booth (325) roan, calved 1st February, 1874. Bred by R. McDougall Esq. Property of D. Macgregor Esq.'

Desdemon, 1881.
Inscribed on the frame 'Bred by and the property of D. MacGregor Esq.'
Calved 7 March 1879

[Red Shorthorn Bull, probably 'Royal Ruby'], 1900.
'Royal Ruby' was calved 6 June 1895. Sire Duke of Albermarle. Dam Laurestina.
Royal Ruby won first prize in 1901 at the Royal Agricultural Show for Shorthorn Bulls, Four Years or Over. He had won second prize the previous year

Glengyle Station, 2016
Photographer: Glenn Campbell

During the years 1900 to 1916, Duncan MacGregor resided in various Melbourne suburbs including Kew, Malvern and Caulfield. Many of the properties were mortgaged in his name; it is assumed he decided to utilize them as residences. At this time Maggie was clearly still living at Clunie and it seems she was holding the family together. The children were spread across the Melbourne suburbs and country Victoria. Jessie and Donald Macrae Stewart were settled in Caulfield; Jack and Zena had moved from Dalmore at Pakenham to a new property called Dalmore at Baringhup. Tottie and William Pestell built a house in Hawthorn Grove in 1898 and were firmly ensconced there. Cissie and Frederick Hutchings were farming in Bairnsdale at the property suitably named 'The Farm Bairnsdale'. In 1916 Pearl was still a spinster; she married Ernest Wood in 1921; Donald and Christina were still living at Gowan Lea, Koo-wee-rup.

Religious references in MacGregor's poetry written in the early 1900s indicate a strong faith and had been the central focus of the young Duncan MacGregor when he left Scotland in 1857. In his later years he remained devout.

Duncan MacGregor died of asthenia and facial carcinoma (which he had had for 2 years) at Clunie on Friday 28 January 1916 and was buried at the Melbourne General Cemetery. He was 81. By many accounts he was a 'dour' Scot, yet the many sides of his character were appreciated by a range of commentators. Harry H. Peck referred to him as:

> Strongly and squarely built, wide and deep in shoulders and chest, of medium height, with a short iron grey beard and a piercing penetrating eye. Duncan MacGregor in appearance would fill the bill as Sherlock Holmes who weighed and took everyone and everything at a glance. Yet he was slow, careful and meditative and rather dour of speech, with a decided Scotch accent.[25]

Peck emphasised MacGregor's skill and expertise as a breeder of Shorthorn herds, Border Leicester and English Leicester flocks and as a pioneer in the swampland at Koo-wee-rup. However, it was 'as a pioneer of western Queensland' that Peck praised MacGregor's 'pluck and judgement, for which posterity should remember him'. He 'formed and stocked…many of the best stations in western Queensland'.[26] MacGregor was also described as 'another of those big Highlanders who 'seemed to have been born to an inheritance of cattle knowledge and country'. It was said, wrote one author in 1932, that 'you could put him down upon any point from the Diamantina to Culpaulin, near Wilcannia and night and day, without a compass', and he would take a 'beeline through that maze, rarely bringing up father than a mile from his objective on the Darling'. Furthermore, Duncan MacGregor 'was next to Robert McDougall', the greatest admirer of the Booth strain of Shorthorn.

Newspaper reports of his death also celebrated him as a 'noted breeder of Shorthorn cattle, Clydesdales, and Border Leicester sheep ... he was a recognised judge of classes of stock'.[27] Also acknowledged were his decades of service to the Clydesdale and various cattle associations. He believed that 'the essential for success in breeding animals is the gifted faculty that recognises the kind of animals that ought to be selected ... the real fundamental principle of breeding is hereditary'.[28] Other notices for MacGregor in Melbourne and country papers spoke of him as a well-known station owner and breeder of horses and cattle. They retold his history as a colonist for 59 years and that he was closely identified with the pastoral industry. The *Kilmore Advertiser* reminded readers that he was for many years a judge of stock at the Kilmore Show.[29] An entry in the *Australian Dictionary of Biography* described him as 'Dour and sturdily built' and repeated Peck's assessment that 'he was remembered as an intrepid explorer, bushman, conqueror of swamp land and judge of stud stock.'[30]

MacGregor's grandson Bernard Donald MacGregor, the son of Donald MacGregor (1882–1950), undertook considerable research into his grandfather's life. In 1969, in his speech to the Australian Book Collectors' Society, he retold some of the stories he had heard from his childhood about MacGregor.[31] As he was only 6 years old when MacGregor died, his memories and his oral history must be treated with some scepticism. Yet the stories he told evoke a sense of the man. Bernard MacGregor remembered hearing family stories that MacGregor insisted on his porridge being made in the true Scots manner, kept on the window sill to cool for a certain time. He remembered being told that he kept a moderate cellar and always carried brandy but 'he was never known to have taken a strong drink in his life'. This was a slightly contrary view to the general opinion and the opinion of some family members. Donald MacGregor and his son Bernard may have seen their father and grandfather through rose-coloured glasses.

The possibility that Duncan MacGregor chose to leave no will is as perplexing to the family as it is to the biographer. Searches through the vaults of Brahe & Gair (now Garland, Hawthorn, Brahe), MacGregor's solicitors, as well as wills & probates at the Public Record Office, have failed to produce a copy of his will. Although it is considered he was in a fragile mental state for the last decade of his life, why would he have chosen this path? However, Duncan would have known that even if he chose not to make a will his estate would go to his widow. His grandson Bernard addressed the issue in his speech. He explained that any gaps in the account were due to 'repeated acts of vandalism', explaining that 'On Grandpa's death his Trustee burnt most of his papers'. Could this be the truth of the matter, or was this another handed down family story? It is clear that parts of the story are missing, and this is not unusual.

Maggie MacGregor survived her husband by six years. She lived at Clunie until her death of heart failure on 25 March 1922. In her will, dated 12 October 1921, she made four bequests. To her son Donald she gave £1,500, to her daughter Christina (Pearl) she gave £1,000 and to her companion, Miss Flora Scott, she gave £500, amounting in total to £3,000 from her estate. Her estate was valued at £11,465-3-7, with real estate at £8,208 (the property Clunie at Chintin) and personal property at £3,257.

Fifteen months after the death of their mother, the six surviving MacGregor children received a distribution from her estate. John (Jack), Jessie, Isabella (Tottie), Annie (Cissie), Christina (Pearl) and Donald each received a cash payment of £1,100. The distribution of this money appears to be in addition to the money bequeathed to Donald and Pearl.[32] Because of his age, Donald had not been part of the 1901 Dalmore venture with Jack and his five sisters, but his mother had compensated him for his loss of income. Maggie's gift to Pearl after her marriage in 1921 may also have had personal significance.

As with many families, the six siblings found themselves in dispute over her will and possessions. Clunie at Chintin was sold soon after her death. Donald challenged his brother John (Jack) over the removal of papers, books and furniture from the house. The property, the house and 910 acres of land, were sold at auction and purchased by Mr Bryant who bought it on a 'walk in, walk out' basis; that is, he bought the house and all its contents. Shortly after the sale, Jack re-purchased the contents for a mere £500. This created ill-feeling and Donald sought the help of his solicitor to challenge the action. It was eventually resolved. In reading through the correspondence, the similarity in tone between Duncan and Donald's manner is striking.

The Perpetual Executors and Trustees Association of Australia finally wound up the Estate of Donald McRae on 28 February 1924. The MacGregor Family Apportionment amounted to £43,060; the same apportionment was made to Mrs A. Forster. Additional costs brought the final figure, assets and liabilities, to £86,534-13-6. However, after debts were paid, an amount of £186-4-10 remained. The children – John, Jessie, Tottie, Cissie, Pearl, Donald and the estate of Margaret (Goodie), – were paid £20-6-11. The commission to the Perpetual Trustees and balance of income at hand totalled £64-3-15.

The enterprising Mr MacGregor

Duncan MacGregor should be remembered for his significant achievements as a pastoralist, intrepid explorer, bushman, conqueror of swampland and judge of stud stock[33]. A dour and stout-hearted Scot who arrived in Australia with limited world experience, his first years in the outback on the Darling River were both confronting and exhilarating. Yet through sheer determination and willpower he fulfilled his ambition to change his life circumstances. He was one of the first to open up the pastoral areas of western Queensland and was a significant contributor to the European exploration of that region. During the 1870s and 1880s his enterprise and entrepreneurship seemed to know no bounds as he accumulated a staggering number of pastoral properties. This was Duncan MacGregor's golden age. At his peak he (with his mother-in-law Christina McRae, in the name of the estate of the late Donald McRae) held property totalling more than 10,000 square miles. This was one-third the size of his native Scotland. For the son of a Scottish tenant farmer, this was an extraordinary achievement.

The Federation Drought, the Great Depression of the 1890s and the Queensland land laws combined to destroy Duncan MacGregor's fortune and he spent much of the rest of his life in legal and financial difficulty as his complex structure of property holdings unravelled. However, he retained his reputation as a renowned and respected authority on the breeding of Shorthorn cattle, Leicester and Border Leicester sheep and Clydesdale horses.

His correspondence makes it clear that strong family bonds existed and he died beloved by his wife, his six surviving children and doting grandchildren.

***

One of Duncan MacGregor's greatest legacies is the collection of his papers held in the State Library of Victoria. After the death of his mother, the Clunie property was sold with all its contents, but John (Jack) MacGregor (1872–1942) then bought all the household items, including the contents of MacGregor's office, and transported them to his home at Baringhup. This is one of the great collections of papers relating to Australia's pastoral history and it was donated to the Library in 1989 by the executors of the estate of the late Duncan Scott MacGregor (1916–89), at the request of MacGregor's grandson Bernard Donald MacGregor (1910–97) and his great-grandson Ian Leckie.

Amongst the contents of Jack MacGregor's home at Baringhup were four oil paintings by the esteemed painter of horses and cattle, Frederick Woodhouse senior. These paintings are inscribed with extracts from MacGregor's Private Herd Book. They have recently been purchased by the Art Gallery of Ballarat and are reproduced in this book.

The other major collection of MacGregor papers is the Leckie Archive. This collection was handed down from Duncan MacGregor's daughter Tottie Pestell (1874–1957) to her daughter Meg Leckie (1907–2006), Ian Leckie's mother. The remainder came from the son of Donald McRae MacGregor (1882–1950), Bernard Donald MacGregor (1910–97), Susan Vale's father. The Leckie Archive contains several significant artefacts, including Duncan's ship-board diary, a cloth-covered Bible, a ready reckoner and a prayer book.

Duncan MacGregor left his mark in his homeland as well as in his adopted country. He erected a gravestone for his mother at Kilmichael Glassary near Inverary, 26 miles from Portsonachan, where the family lived for many years. His name is remembered in Victoria in the Koo-wee-rup and Pakenham areas in McGregor Road and the McGregor Well, Dalmore; and in Queensland the McGregor Channel, the MacGregor Ranges and MacGregor Hill are named in his honour.

MacGregor Family Tree

Duncan MacGregor (1835–1915)   **Margaret McRae (1849–1922)**

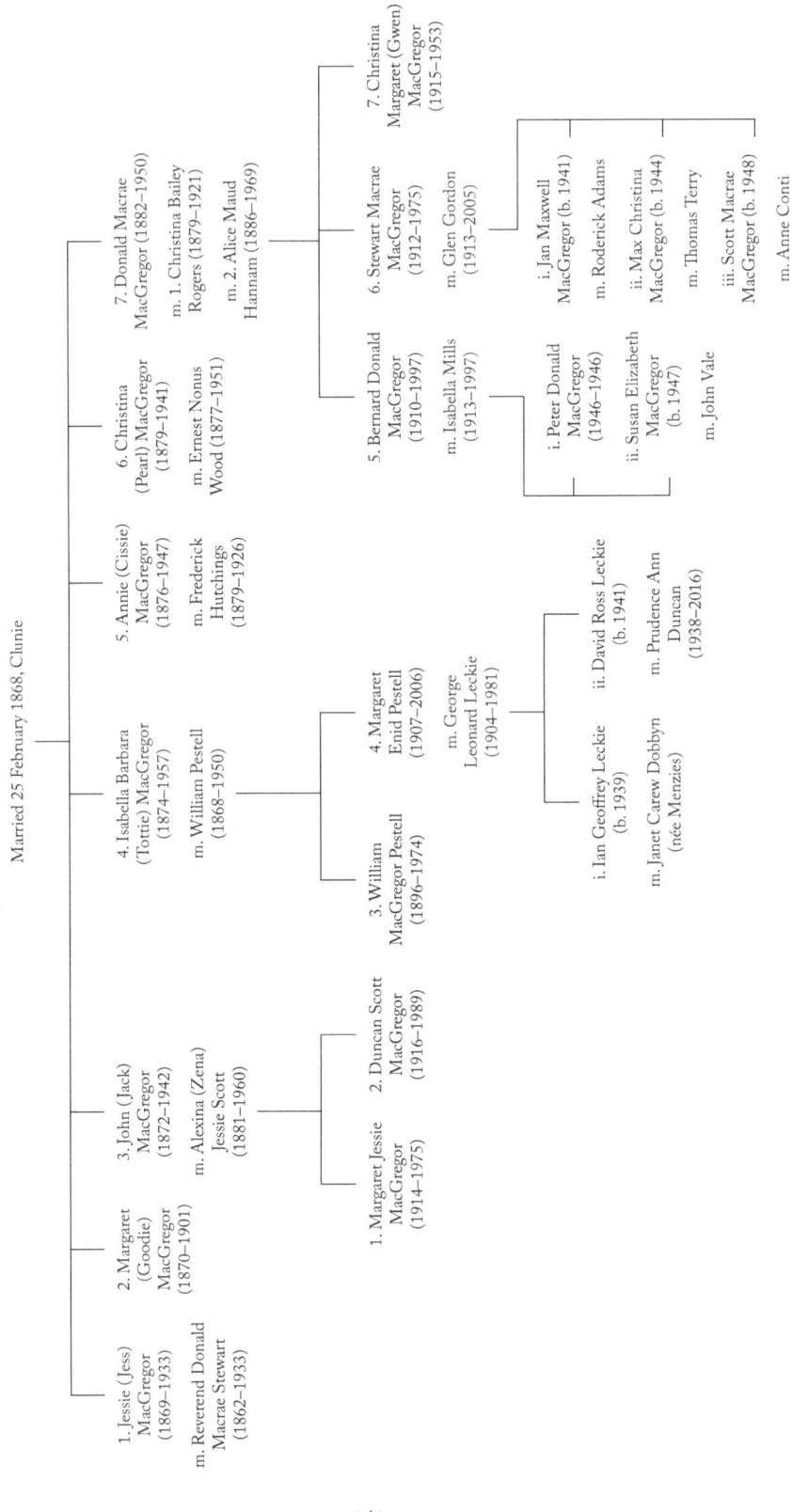

Married 25 February 1868, Clunie

1. Jessie (Jess) MacGregor (1869–1933)
m. Reverend Donald Macrae Stewart (1862–1933)

2. Margaret (Goodie) MacGregor (1870–1901)

3. John (Jack) MacGregor (1872–1942)
m. Alexina (Zena) Jessie Scott (1881–1960)

    1. Margaret Jessie MacGregor (1914–1975)

    2. Duncan Scott MacGregor (1916–1989)

4. Isabella Barbara (Tottie) MacGregor (1874–1957)
m. William Pestell (1868–1950)

    3. William MacGregor Pestell (1896–1974)

    4. Margaret Enid Pestell (1907–2006)
    m. George Leonard Leckie (1904–1981)

        i. Ian Geoffrey Leckie (b. 1939)
        m. Janet Carew Dobbyn (née Menzies)

        ii. David Ross Leckie (b. 1941)
        m. Prudence Ann Duncan (1938–2016)

5. Annie (Cissie) MacGregor (1876–1947)
m. Frederick Hutchings (1879–1926)

6. Christina (Pearl) MacGregor (1879–1941)
m. Ernest Nonus Wood (1877–1951)

    5. Bernard Donald MacGregor (1910–1997)
    m. Isabella Mills (1913–1997)

        i. Peter Donald MacGregor (1946–1946)

        ii. Susan Elizabeth MacGregor (b. 1947)
        m. John Vale

7. Donald Macrae MacGregor (1882–1950)
m. 1. Christina Bailey Rogers (1879–1921)
m. 2. Alice Maud Hannam (1886–1969)

    6. Stewart Macrae MacGregor (1912–1975)
    m. Glen Gordon (1913–2005)

        i. Jan Maxwell MacGregor (b. 1941)
        m. Roderick Adams

        ii. Max Christina MacGregor (b. 1944)
        m. Thomas Terry

        iii. Scott Macrae MacGregor (b. 1948)
        m. Anne Conti

    7. Christina Margaret (Gwen) MacGregor (1915–1953)

Vignettes

Jessie (1869–1933) and Donald Macrae Stewart (1862–1933)

The eldest of Duncan and Margaret MacGregor's seven children, Jessie was born at Clunie, Victoria on 16 December 1869. She was educated privately, was an accomplished horsewoman, and worshipped at the local Presbyterian Church at Darraweit Guim. Jessie was a reliable support and often a comfort for her siblings and parents. Her warm and generous nature is apparent in her correspondence, and letters to her brothers provide insight into her caring personality. Following the tragic death of her sister, Goodie in 1901, she wrote to Jack, then in southern Queensland, about her concern for her mother and made clear her concerns for him too: 'I feel you may be anxious … this has been a dreadful blow … Life seems to be full of sorrow and pain'. The devastation felt by the family is clear as she writes: 'Ciss is in bed and has been there since Thursday. Mother got up for a short time yesterday afternoon. I did not see Pa … I will write again soon and let you know how they are at home'.

When she was 25, on 5 December 1894, Jessie married Presbyterian minister, the Reverend Donald Macrae Stewart at Brunswick Presbyterian Church. Her first posting as a clergyman's wife and helpmeet was at the Ascot Vale Presbyterian Church. It seems clear that from her earliest days as a wife she fully supported her husband's work, contributing to various committees and working for the good of the community.

In 1901, only months before Goodie's death, John MacGregor invited his five sisters – Goodie, Tottie, Cissie, Pearl and Jessie – to become partners in a business he styled 'J. MacGregor & Co.'. In this partnership, six of the seven MacGregor children converted their one-sixth share of the Freehold Dalmore Estate, into a business for the period of five years. Following the death of her mother and the sale of Clunie at Chinton in 1922, Jessie's next real estate venture occurred in 1923 when she purchased land at Riddells Creek. She bought a 43-acre block with a small residence for her horses. In 1929, she and her sister Pearl became joint proprietors of the land. The property was managed by James Winter, one of Duncan's long-term employees who named the property Rannoch in respect of MacGregor's birth place.

While the Macrae Stewart's were childless, they took a great interest in their nieces and nephews and made generous bequeaths to them in their individual Wills. Jessie Macrae Stewart died on 9 March 1933, unaware of the serious nature of her husband's illness. By doctor's orders, he was not told that his wife had pre-deceased him. Jessie Macrae Stewart's personal estate was valued for probate at £12,708.

The son of a Minister of the United Free Church of Scotland, Donald Macrae Stewart was born at Pitlochry, Scotland on 18 October 1862. After graduating from New College Edinburgh, he joined the Black Watch No. 4 Company, 33rd battalion for five years. With his mother, brothers and sisters, the family immigrated to Australia in 1890. Donald's uncle was then a minister of the Presbyterian Church, Toorak. In 1891 Macrae Stewart was appointed minister of the Ascot Vale Presbyterian Church. In 1903 he was transferred to the Malvern Presbyterian Church where he remained until his death. He was instrumental in building the current church.

After the outbreak of the First World War, in 1915, at the age of 52, he enlisted as a commissioned chaplain and was posted to the 21st Battalion 6 Division Infantry. Just weeks after the Gallipoli campaign, on 8 May 1915 the Battalion left Australia and arrived in Egypt in June 1915; they proceeded to Gallipoli in late August. It was an eventful trip; the battalion's transport HMAT *Southland* was torpedoed near the island of Lemnos and was abandoned. They finally landed at ANZAC Cove on 7 September. Donald Macrae Stewart had a relatively quiet time at Gallipoli, as the last major Allied offensives had been defeated in August. After evacuation from Gallipoli in December 1915, the 21st Battalion arrived in France in March 1916. In April, they were the first Australian battalion to commence active operations on the Western Front. During the battle of Pozieres the Battalion was engaged mainly on carrying duties, but suffered its heaviest casualties of the war during the fighting around Mouquet Farm. While serving in Europe, Macrae Stewart was mentioned in despatches on 2 January 1917 by Sir Douglas Haigh,

CIC British Armies, France for conspicuous services with the AIF. He returned to Australia aboard the *Marathon*, arriving on 24 September 1916. Macrae Stewart retained the rank Chaplain-Colonel.

Following his return to Australia, Donald spoke regularly about his war experience. He was appointed Moderator of the Presbyterian Church of Victoria, 1918-19. In this role, he and Jessie travelled extensively throughout the state. As Moderator he regularly lectured on 'A Chaplin's Experience on Active Service'. He also wrote several books, the best known at the time were *The Souter's Lamp and Other Stories*, *Growth in 50 Years – the Jubilee History of the Presbyterian Church in Victoria*, and *The Last Likeness and Other Addresses to Children*.

Reverend Macrae Stewart and the Reverend Gordon Powell were members of the Scotch College Council at the same time. Powell praised his work and the influence he had on his life. In 1972 he wrote: 'Reverend Macrae-Stewart was a very great Christian and had a real influence on my life as I am sure he must have had on the boys of whom he was so fond there in the desert and Gallipoli'. Powell honoured him by naming his son Donald in recognition of his work.

By default, Macrae Stewart became the MacGregor family chaplain; he conducted the marriage services for his three sisters-in-law, Tottie (1896), Cissie (1907) and Pearl (1921).

Donald Macrae Stewart died after a short illness on Tuesday 14 March 1933, just five days after the death of his wife, Jessie on 9 March. His death occurred on the eve of the 30th anniversary of his ministry at Malvern Presbyterian Church. His qualities as a preacher, and the contribution made by his wife, Jessie were acknowledged by the Malvern Presbyterian Church. The congregation voted to erect memorial gates and fencing on the Wattletree Road frontage of the Church in recognition of Macrae Stewart's long and successful ministry. It was also agreed to create a fund of £100 to establish annual prizes in the Sunday school, to be known as the Donald and Jessie Macrae Stewart prizes.

Margaret (Goodie) MacGregor (1870–1901)

Margaret MacGregor was born on 23 August 1870. Although the family can't establish the origin of her pet name, she was always known as Goodie, and this name appears to accurately reflect the personality of Duncan and Margaret's second child.

Like Jessie, Goodie was educated at home and was a competent horsewoman. From correspondence between Goodie and her siblings, we know she enjoyed riding and also taught the children of family friends to ride. She, like her sisters Cissie and Tottie, probably enjoyed the winter hunts and balls at nearby Oaklands.

Goodie was bright and intelligent and always knew the intimate details of the family and their various activities. She kept abreast of local social and political events and had distinct views on local candidates for the Shire's elections.

As a single woman she was in a privileged position. Her main responsibilities seem to have been to encourage her brothers and sisters in their own pursuits as well as to ensure her mother's comfort. Goodie does not appear to have been restricted by social convention when we see how freely she travelled around the state and to events in Melbourne. She also enjoyed spending time at Dalmore, Gowan Lea and Clunie, frequently riding from Coburg to Clunie.

When she was diagnosed with an aggressive and incurable Ovarian Cancer late in 1900, we cannot imagine the devastation her illness must have caused to her family. Painful though the disease was, the feminine nature of the disease, and, in consequence the social stigma attached, must have made the news more agonizing for the family to accept. Because we don't have any correspondence from her during the last year of her life, we can only imagine the terrible time Goodie endured at Fitzgerald's Hospital in Melbourne. Sadly, Goodie died in hospital on 28 November 1901. She was greatly mourned by her family and friends. The family story has always been that Goodie died in a horse riding accident near Dandenong. Until her death certificate was found, the family story has persisted. Goodie died Intestate. With the exception of Donald, along with her five siblings, Goodie held a one-sixth share in the Dalmore Estate. An Affidavit of Administration was issued. Goodie's Real Estate, her one share in Dalmore valued at £4,517 and Personal property of £2,636, was valued at a total of £7,153.

John (Jack) (1872–1942) and Alexina (Zena) (1881–1960) MacGregor

John MacGregor was born on 20 May 1872, Duncan and Margaret's first son. He was probably educated at home and, as would be expected, learned to ride as a boy. In 1889 when he was 17, Jack had his first work experience in Queensland.

It's unclear how Jack spent the intervening years; he may have continued his schooling or occupied his time with his father at Glengyle, Inverauld and Clunie. As early as 1891 he was a member of The Pastoralists Union. In 1896 he began working at Durham Downs. From there he moved to Glengyle, Miranda and Yanko.

When he was 24, Jack's interest in Miss Alexina (Zena) Scott from Tasmania became clear through his correspondence with family members. There is speculation he met her when he travelled to Tasmania with his father. Although the theory cannot be proved, there is evidence MacGregor went to Tasmania to purchase purebred sheep. The pretty and charming Miss Scott frequently stayed with the MacGregor's at Glengyle in Coburg, and that is how the family got to know her.

Farquhar McDonald, the long-term employee and Jack's friend from Durham Downs, wrote to him in 1899 about Miss Scott. Quite apologetically, he wrote:

> I knew nothing about it … that business of letting Donald and I read your letters is only a bit of put on. You keep a bit up your sleeve and have all the good things to yourself. … This little girl asks very interesting questions about you. I was told the other day when I spoke of asking her to go to the play some night that I had better be careful or I might get my head in a sling when I went back to Durham. I have not yet made up my mind to go to Tasmania but if I do go I am afraid there will be war in the camp when I get back to Durham!

After about five years working in the Queensland stations, but with regular holidays in Victoria, in 1901 Jack returned to Victoria permanently to become the manager of Dalmore at Pakenham. In September 1901, together with his sisters Jessie, Goodie, Tottie, Cissie and Pearl he established a company, J. MacGregor & Co. The partnership agreement between the siblings was clear. They were 'in the business of Farmers and Graziers upon their Freehold Estate at Pakenham known as Dalmore for the term of five years.' Donald, who was then only 18 years old, was precluded from becoming a member of this partnership because of his age. Following Goodie's death in November 1901, according to the agreement, the business was carried on by the surviving partners until the partnership was dissolved.

After a 15-year courtship, Jack MacGregor married Zena Scott in Tasmania in 1911. They had two children, Margaret Jessie, born in 1914 and Duncan Scott, born in 1916.

After Margaret MacGregor's death in 1922, Clunie at Chinton was sold, and Jack purchased back from the new owner, as much of the furniture and effects as he was able. A dispute over the distribution of furniture and personal effects led to a furious family argument that was fought for many years.

Jack farmed the Dalmore Estate until the death of his father in 1916. He moved from Gippsland to central Victoria where he purchased another property at Baringhup which he also named Dalmore and successfully farmed it until his death on 14 March 1942. Jack's Will directed that the proceeds of his real and personal estate be paid into a Trust for his widow; the remainder was held in trust for his two children as tenants in common in equal shares. Zena died on 12 November 1960. She too bequeathed all her real and personal property to Margaret and Duncan as tenants in common. Neither Margaret nor Duncan married.

Isabella (Tottie) (1874–1957) and William Pestell (1896–1950)

The third daughter and fourth child of Duncan and Margaret MacGregor, Isabella Barbara MacGregor was always known at 'Tottie'. She was the first child born at Glengyle in Coburg on 11 May 1874. Tottie was born in the same year her aunt, Annie McRae McKenzie, gave birth, out of wedlock, to her first child, Christina.

Tottie, like her sisters was probably educated at home by their governess, Miss Flora Scott. As with her older sisters, she remained at home enjoying horse riding and an active social life until her marriage. Tottie was 22 years old when she married the 28-year old architect from Hawthorn, William Pestell on 25 November 1896. The ceremony took place at her parents' home Glengyle in Coburg and her brother-in-law, the Reverend Donald Macrae Stewart performed the ceremony with Presbyterian rites. Petite in stature, Tottie is described as a woman with a quiet, gentle voice.

In 1901, together with her brother Jack and her four sisters – Goodie, Cissie, Pearl and Jessie – Tottie became a partner in a farming and grazing business their brother Jack styled 'J. MacGregor & Co.'. In this partnership, the five sisters and Jack converted their one-sixth share of the Freehold Dalmore Estate into a business venture.

Tottie and William Pestell had two children: William MacGregor, known as Greg (short for his middle name, MacGregor), was born on 16 October 1897 and Margaret Enid was born on 2 July 1907.

William Pestell, the son of William and Georgina (née Wragg), was born on 5 June 1868 at the Bank of Australasia in Williamstown where his father lived as the manager. In 1883 William junior joined the Victorian Railways. His father died in the same year, his mother had died when he was an infant.

In July 1892, after almost a decade with the Railways, Pestell pursued his interest in the Victorian Voluntary Military Force. Writing to the Army, he established the number and types of courses available in the UK that he might attend. Hoping the Victorian militia would pay for his study, he applied for and was granted leave from the Victorian Railways for 100 days training in the UK during 1893.

On 1 January 1893 he was appointed as a clerk and draughtsman in the Ex-Lines branch of the Railways. Having been granted leave to attend courses in the UK, he departed Melbourne on the *Himalaya* on 14 March 1893. On 30 April he commenced his first course at Chatham; this was followed by a further course at Aldershot in November 1893. After 18 months in England, on 1 March 1894 he returned to Australia. As Lieutenant William Pestell he attended Jessie MacGregor and Donald Macrae Stewart's wedding on 5 December 1894.

Pestell was talented. He gained qualifications in Engineering, Architecture and Surveying. In 1898 he joined a partnership with Gerard Wight, MCE, who was articled to the Victorian Railways' Engineers Department and then to the leading firm of architects, Smith and Johnson. Pestell and Wight were winners of the third prize in the design competition for the new Flinders Street Railway Station. Between August 1900 and July 1907 Pestell was engaged in preparing plans for the construction of the new railway station.

William Pestell served in the First World War. At the age of 47, he enlisted in the Australian Imperial Force Sea Transport Service. He was appointed Major on 23 April 1915, the day he left Melbourne on the HMAT *Suffolk*. He was the senior officer on board with approval to conduct Court Martials. Pestell returned to Australia on the *Ascanius* on 4 October 1915.

William and Tottie's son Greg, (William) MacGregor Pestell, then a 19-year-old draughtsman also at the Victorian Railways, also enlisted in the AIF in 1916 with the rank of Sapper in the 10th Field Company Engineers. He embarked from Sydney on HMAT *Runic* on 22 March 1918.

Returning to the Way and Works Branch of the Victorian Railways in 1917, William Pestell senior was later promoted to Lieutenant Colonel in the Army. He retired from the Army in 1920, retaining the rank of Colonel. In 1933 Pestell retired as Chief Engineer of Ways and Works of the Victorian Railways after nearly 50 years of service. He was an associate of the Royal Victorian Institute of Architects, was a qualified engineer of Victoria and also a local government engineer of New South Wales.

In his retirement, William Pestell became an eminent artist, specialising in watercolour paintings and etchings. During the Second World War he and Tottie held many exhibitions as fund raising events. Their son Greg disappeared from their lives after the First World War and it is only recently that a picture of his life has emerged. Greg married Hazel Bryne in Sydney on 20 July 1929; the couple were childless and divorced in 1954.

William and Tottie's daughter Margaret Enid married George Leonard Leckie on 4 August 1936 at St George's Anglican Church, Malvern. They had two children, Ian Geoffrey, born 2 January 1939 and David Ross, born 27 June 1941.

William Pestell died on 20 November 1950 at the age of 82; Tottie died after a long illness on 14 January 1957, aged 83.

Annie (Cissie) (1876–1947) and Frederick Hutchings (1879–1926)

Cissie MacGregor was born on 7 June 1876 at Glengyle, Coburg, the fourth daughter and fifth of the seven MacGregor children. She was possibly named Annie after her aunt, the infamous Annie McRae. Cissie grew up to be active socially, enjoying the cricket, horse racing, the local hunt at Oaklands and other annual events. When Cissie MacGregor married Frederick Hutchings on 14 September 1907, he was 28 years of age and she was 31. It is not known where they met but it is known they both competed regularly at Oaklands; including at the 1906 hunt.

Frederick Hawthorn Hutchings of Craigievar, Riversdale Road, Hawthorn, was the son of James and Jane (née Jones) Hutchings. He was born on 4 February 1879, the second of four children. His father died in 1884 when he was five years old. Under the terms of her late husband's Will, Jane Hutchings continued to claim an annuity on Hutchings estate even after her marriage in 1891 to the brush manufacturer John Zevenboom. Frederick's mother became his official guardian until her death in March 1893, one month after he entered Geelong Grammar School as a boarder. At the age of 14 he enrolled in the School's Cadet Corps on 15 February 1893 and remained there until May 1897. He eventually achieved the rank of Corporal/Lance Sergeant in the Cadet Corps, although he was described as an 'erratic shot'.

While a student at Geelong Grammar he actively participated in sport, particularly rowing, cricket and football. Hutchings was in the cricket XI in 1895–96, the Inter-Colonial rowing crew 1896–97 and the Senior Fours in 1897. In cricket he 'did his best as wicket-keeper' but was 'an inconsistent batter'. He rowed in the position of bow. The School's Bicycle Club was formed in 1881. Hutchings participated in a race in 1896 and was the Club's Honorary Secretary in 1897, his final year at the school. He may have been more sportsman than scholar, as he is not recorded as the winner of any School prizes.

In 1897 Frederick applied for a commission in the Victorian Military Forces but was not accepted until 1899 when he was attached to the

Metropolitan Garrison Artillery. By 1900 he was part of the Victorian section of the Australian Imperial Regiment, serving at the front of the Second Anglo Boer War. By 1903 he had risen to the rank of Lieutenant. Hutchings contributed to the Calvert and Skene Memorial Tablet Fund which recorded Geelong Grammar School students who had died in the Boer War.

Fred Hutchings volunteered for active service in the First World War on 20 March 1915 at the age of 39, embarking to Egypt on the *Persic* on 28 May 1915. He joined the 13th Light Horse Regiment, C Squadron, rising to the rank of Major. His regiment was later transferred to France, disembarking at Marseilles on 27 June 1916.

Hutchings' experience in the First World War could not have been a happy one. He was removed from C to A Squadron due to his perceived incompetence. Following a report by Lieutenant Colonel Dudley Persse White detailing his poor performance, his services were duly dispensed with. Hutchings agreed with the findings and counter-signed the report. During his absence overseas, Clebeyara Farm was leased and Cissie Hutchings resided at the Occidental Hotel in Melbourne.

It is very likely that Frederick Hutchings was one of the thousands who suffered Shell Shock or what we now call Post Traumatic Stress Disorder. He returned to England from Calais on 30 September 1917 before returning to Australia, at his own expense, on the *SS Niagara* on 6 November 1917. He had been away for 2 ½ years. His appointment with the Army was officially ended on 25 December 1917. It was not a glorious war for Hutchings.

As a child, Tottie's daughter Margaret Pestell recalls her uncle, Fred Hutchings. She referred to him as the 'silly old soldier'. He probably suffered severe stress as a result of his war experience. He died on 4 June 1926 at the age of 47.

Cissie Hutchings died on 26 June 1947 at Bairnsdale District Hospital of cerebral haemorrhage and Arteriosclerosis. She was buried at Springvale. Her real and personal estate was valued at £19,893. Cissie Hutchings owned property, livestock, farming implements, a 1937 Vauxhall coupe, furniture, jewellery, money and a considerable number of bonds. She bequeathed many of her possessions to friends but nothing to her family. Three bequests of £1,000 each were made to Lieutenant Max Wilson Kelsey, Jeffrey David Walker and Dr John Robert Searles and £500 to The Children's Hospital.

The remainder of Cissie's estate was divided in equal shares between the Victorian State Branch of the Returned Sailors, Soldiers and Airmen's Imperial League, the Limbless Soldiers Association of Victoria, the Blinded Soldiers Association of Victoria, the Partially Blinded Soldiers Association of Victoria, Tubercular Sailors Soldiers and Airmen Association of Victoria and the Totally & Permanently Disabled Soldiers Association of Victoria. Cissie recognised the great need to support returned service men and was committed to contribute money to these charities.

Christina (Pearl) (1879–1941) and Ernest Wood (1877–1951)

Christina (Pearl) MacGregor, sometimes referred to as 'that brat Pearl', was the youngest of five daughters. She was born on 28 April 1879 at Glengyle. Pearl had much in common with her sisters, especially their shared interest in horses. Their letters to other family members frequently discuss riding out with one person or the other. She was keenly interested in the price of horses and the pure stock her father bred. It is possible she met her future husband, the veterinary surgeon Ernest Nonus Wood at the nearby Oaklands while enjoying the pleasures of a hunt.

Christina MacGregor remained a spinster until she was 42 years of age; she was the last in her family to marry. On 17 September 1921, at the Presbyterian Church, Malvern she married Ernest Wood who was then 45 years of age. Her brother-in-law, Donald Macrae Stewart conducted the ceremony.

Ernest Nonus Wood, born 1877 in Richmond, was the son of Frederick William Wood and Elizabeth Wood (née Stepts). He was educated at the University of Melbourne. At the age of 39 he enlisted and served in the First World War as a Veterinary Officer with the rank of Captain. He embarked for the Suez on 6 May 1916 on the *Clan Maccorquodale*. Wood served with both the 2nd and 3rd Light Horse. He returned to Australia on 29 April 1918.

Returning to civilian life in late 1918, Wood returned to working with the Victorian Racing Club and the Victorian Amateur Turf Club. He retired as an official of the VRC in February 1949. Described as 'one of Australia's best known veterinary surgeons', he worked at Flemington for more than 50 years. Few veterinary surgeons, it was thought, had gained the confidence of racing men, particularly horse owners. His 'wide knowledge of racing, his expert diagnosis of complaints, and his wisdom and care with horses broken down or hurt endeared him to thousands of horse lovers'.

In September 1929, Pearl became a joint proprietor with Jessie, of Rannoch, the 43-acre property at Riddells Creek Jessie had purchased in 1923.

When she died on 24 June 1941, after almost 20 years of marriage, Christina Wood left an estate valued at £26,863. The valuation of the Riddells Creek property included the land at £700, 3 cows and 20 sheep, furniture and effects, furniture and effects from their Caulfield house, inscribed stock valued at £21,719, cash in the bank, shares in the department store A Horden, and shares in the theatrical company, J.C. Williamson. Pearl bequeathed to her friend, Jean Lockwood £1,000, to her niece Christine MacGregor £1,000 and to her niece Margaret Leckie £700.

Ernest Wood died on 17 December 1951. In his will dated 13 December 1951, he bequeathed Rannoch at Riddells Creek to Margaret Enid Leckie. The bequest was in line with the wishes of Jessie Macrae Stewart's Will that the residue of her estate be divided equally between the children of her brothers Jack and Donald and her sister Tottie. The Leckie's held the property for only one year.

Donald McRae MacGregor (1882–1950), Christina Rogers (1879–1921) and Maud Hannam (1886–1969)

Donald Macrae MacGregor was born on 11 March 1882 at Glengyle, Coburg, the youngest of seven children. Little is known of his education although it is likely he attended the local primary and secondary schools. The files are silent on his and his siblings' education.

On 21 October 1908 Donald, then 26 years of age, married Christina Bailey Rogers, 29. The marriage took place in the drawing room of Christina's brother-in-law's home 'Paringa', overlooking the Eastern Beach at Geelong. Christina was born in Bendigo in 1879; she was the sixth of eight children of David Thompson Rogers and Katherine Sabina Gill Rogers and lived in the family home 'Newburgh' in McIvor Road, Bendigo. Christina's mother Katherine was the daughter of Dr William Bailey and Catherine Gill of Woodend. Her father, David Rogers was born in Newburgh, Fifeshire, Scotland, and came to Australia in 1847; he established a corn merchant business at Barkers Creek, Castlemaine.

In 1912, Donald lost a leg in a wool press accident at Clunie. His leg was buried in the MacGregor grave at the Melbourne General Cemetery on 18 June 1912. When Jack left Dalmore around 1915, Donald and Christina moved into Gowan Lea. The family appear to have moved to Dalmore and lived there from 1917 to 1919 when Jack and Zena moved back into the homestead. Donald, Christina and Gwen were living in Kew in 1919 before moving to 'Melrose' at Harkaway where Christina died in 1921.

Donald worked as an adviser to the Victorian State Government on the Soldier Settlement scheme in the Gippsland region. He was appointed President of the Shire of Cranbourne on 7 September 1918. He was elected a councillor of the Berwick Riding in October 1926 and on 9 December 1926 he was appointed a Justice of the Peace. He resigned as Councillor on 18 March 1932. He also served as President of the Council of Springfield.

Christina (Teen) was described as a 'dark and good looking woman with a contralto voice'. Teen trained as a nurse at the Melbourne Hospital. They lived at Clunie for some years and had three children: Bernard Donald

MacGregor (born 1910), Stewart Macrae MacGregor (born 1913) and Christina Margaret MacGregor (born 1915 at Gowan Lea). Christina was known as Gwen; she suffered from a debilitating condition which meant she was unable to walk. Gwen was confined to a wheelchair. Her two brothers, Bernard and Stewart attended Berwick Grammar School. The family lived at the property 'Melrose' in Harkaway near Berwick. Teen's health deteriorated around 1920 and, to ease the burden of caring for a sick wife, Donald engaged a nurse to care for both Teen and Gwen. Teen died on 14 September 1921 from complications relating to a blood disorder; she is buried in the Berwick Cemetery with Donald MacGregor.

The nurse engaged to care for Teen and Gwen was named Alice Maud Hannam – she was always known as Maud. Born in Yass, New South Wales in 1886, she was a first cousin of Sir Donald Bradman. Maud trained as a nurse at the Coast Hospital, Little Bay, near Sydney. In 1917 she enlisted with the Australia Medical Corps as a trained nurse. On 10 May 1917 she embarked from Sydney on the RMS Mooltan and disembarked at Suez on 19 July 1917 for transit to the 52nd General Hospital Unit in Salonika, Greece where she served for two years on the front as a Staff Nurse. Maud was posted to AIF HQ in London and ultimately returned to Australia in August 1919. She was decorated with the 1914/15 Star, British War Medal and the Victory Medal. Much of her memorabilia has been placed with the Australian War Memorial.

Following her return to Victoria, she was offered the role of nurse with Donald MacGregor at Harkaway and took up that position some months later. Following Teen's death in 1921, she remained with the family to care for Gwen. The two boys were sent to Scotch College as boarders. Maud (then 36) and Donald MacGregor (40 years) married in Ormond on 6 June 1922. They remained childless.

Some years later the MacGregors operated the Lynn Private Hospital in Armadale; Donald died there on 27 August 1950. Maud continued to operate the hospital and care for Gwen. When the hospital was eventually sold, Maud and Gwen moved to Murrumbeena where Gwen died on 10 June 1953, aged 38.

After Gwen's death, Maud travelled extensively and eventually settled in Windsor and died at the Repatriation Hospital, Macleod on 23 April 1969. Her ashes were placed at the Springvale Botanical Cemetery with Gwen.

Annie McRae (1853–1939), Kenneth McKenzie (1842–1892) and Phillip Ernest Forster (1868–1946)

Anna (always known as Annie) McRae was born on 27 March 1853 at Orange in the Parish of Carcoar, County of Bathurst. She was baptised on 15 January 1854. Educated at home, first at Caulpaulin Station on the Darling River and then at Clunie, Chintin, Annie McRae lived a privileged life. From 1867, following the death of her sister in May and her father in July, Annie lived with her mother and sister at Clunie. She was 15 years old when her sister Maggie married Duncan MacGregor.

The McRae family enjoyed an active social life in the Romsey region, surrounded by long-term family friends, the Tom and McDonnell families. They attended church at the nearby Darraweit Guim Presbyterian Church. While the circumstances of their meeting are unclear, Annie McRae formed a relationship with Kenneth McKenzie, a farmer from Clonbinane, some 33 miles (54 km) away from Chintin. In 1874, at the age of 21, she gave birth, out of wedlock, to a daughter, Christina McKenzie. Although a birth certificate or registration of her birth has not been found, McKenzie acknowledged Christina as his daughter. Some time later, and it is unclear when, Annie McRae left her home at Chintin to take up residence with McKenzie who was then working at Ensay in Gippsland. Annie McRae, then 24 years of age married 35-year old Kenneth McKenzie in East Melbourne on 1 May 1877. They returned to live at Clonbinane. The couple had four more children: Donald McRae McKenzie, born 1883; Margaret Flora Isabella, born 1886; Colin Duncan, born 1887 and Kenneth (junior), born 1891. Donald (born 1883) died in a drowning accident at Clonbinane in 1889. He is buried at Campbellfield Cemetery.

Less than one year after the birth of their fifth child, in June 1891 Kenneth McKenzie left Annie and the children at Clonbinane to live with his brother John at Devonshire Road, Elsternwick. In March 1892, Kenneth McKenzie committed suicide by taking a large draught of laudanum. His suicide note explicitly blamed Annie, her unpaid debts and her infidelity, for his suicide. Annie, it seems clear, was already romantically involved with Phillip Forster, a man 15 years her junior. There may have been doubt about the paternity of Kenneth and Annie's fifth child.

The Forster family continued to live at Clonbinane. Their first child, Arthur McRae Forster was born on 3 July 1894. Their second child, Henry Phillip was born on 3 October 1895. And while Annie continued to receive substantial quarterly sums from the Estate of her late father, she could not manage money. In November 1895 a notice in the *Kilmore Free Press* announced that the Court Bailiff was required to sell the 'Goods and Chattels of Annie Forster, of Clonbinane' unless the 'said process had been undertaken already'. The items for sale were household furniture, buggy, horse and cattle, roller, plough and harrow, tools, mangle and pair of scales, etc. Having to sell these items meant she and her husband would have had difficulty farming their land. How they survived this matter is unknown. An ingenious plan was hatched because one year later, on 15 December 1896, Annie made application for a Mining Lease on her land which was later referred to as 'near Wandong'. A 15-year lease was taken out by the Golden Dyke Mine.

Christina McKenzie, Kenneth and Annie's first-born child, was married in 1897. It is interesting to see that her address at the time was Glenden Road, Toorak. Details of her early life, which might shed light on her circumstances, have not been found. Nevertheless, at Scots Church, Albany, Western Australia, she married William Paton Lyall of Kalgoorlie. William Lyall was the third son of the Reverend James Lyall of Adelaide. The marriage notice does not acknowledge her mother, stating instead that she was the 'eldest daughter of the late Kenneth McKenzie, Clonbinane, Wandong, Victoria'. William Lyall died suddenly of apoplexy at Busselton on 17 July 1906, leaving behind his widow, Christina and their son.

Christina McKenzie seems to have suffered a number of nervous breakdowns, the first in June 1925. The end of her life was tragic. Following the death of her husband, William Lyall, Christina married George Olivey of West Perth. Nothing is known of her life until 17 September 1931 when her fully clothed body was found drowned in the Swan River. She had been reported missing the previous week and when found had been dead for one week. Poignantly, the photograph of a child, her son, was found 'with its face turned against her breast' inside her clothing. Reports of her death included the fact that Christina had suffered a nervous breakdown. An inquest into her death was held in the Perth Courthouse on 1 October 1931. Evidence showed that prior to her death she had been in indifferent health and had been in a 'state of acute mental depression'. The cause of death was due to drowning. Her handbag was found on the Point Lewin jetty but there was no evidence to show how she came to be in the water.

Leasing of the Clonbinane land to the Golden Dyke Mine may have provided income to the Forster family. Gold was found in a number of veins. In 1902, an article in the Melbourne *Argus* by their Mining Reporter pointed out that the importance of the dyke structure to the mining of the gold.

By 1900, Annie and Phillip had moved from Clonbinane near Wandong in Central Victoria to Beachleigh, a large property of 20-acres in Frankston Victoria. How this move came about can only be guessed at Beachleigh had been the property of Mrs Thomas Watts who died in July 1899. It appears the Forster's purchased the property in 1900. Annual statements from the Estate of the Late Donald McRae specify Annie's substantial annual income. On the face of it, her income would have been sufficient to purchase this property. Notwithstanding their financial problems, they settled into the district as an article in the local paper reveals. The local cricket team at Frankston boasted about their 'new man, Mr Forster of Beachleigh who has an upcountry reputation'.

The proximity of the house to the sea at Frankston meant that the Forster family were witness to an awful accident in 1903. Six members of a family party holidaying 'in the scrub' by the shore at Frankston were involved in an accident. Two brothers were drowned. A message was sent to Phillip and Annie Forster who arrived on the scene and applied restoratives to the two young men who survived the accident. They called the local doctor and he was able to revive the two.

Despite their relocation to the Mornington Peninsula and the purchase of a large and prestigious residence, in October 1905 Annie Forster found herself in the Insolvency Court in Melbourne. Mrs Forster's estate had been 'compulsorily sequestrated' for a debt of £272/10/- due on four promissory notes. Mr Charles S. Pinkus, broker and financier, had been doing business with Annie for some years and had understood that she had an annual income of £2,000 in her own right. But as he stated to the paper 'there was always something wrong – a child was ill, or a man wanted to go away'. Mr Pinkus reported that on one occasion he went to Clonbinane Station to take the furniture as security. Between July 1901 and September 1905 his firm's transactions with Annie Forster amounted to £1,600. Poor Phillip Forster was dragged into the newspaper report, confirming that his wife's annual income averaged £1,800, but he said ever since their marriage they had both been in a state of chronic impecuniosity'. Although it is stated in the article that Annie sometimes only received £400 per annum, this is blatantly incorrect. Her average income was indeed around £1,800. It may well be that the difference between the two amounts was the money required to pay the debts incurred. As the judge and the writer of the article made clear, 'they ought to be able to live on £400 a year, but could not do so'. It seems the Forster's blamed their impecuniosity on their new residence: 'up to a couple of months ago there were 14 to keep at Frankston'. That is, the parents, five children and seven servants. Phillip's brother Arthur was also living there and receiving an annual income. The couple could not say 'no'; and they could not manage their money. Perhaps as an income earner, they then turned to agisting stock on their land: 'Von Rysdyk' the pedigree trotting stallion was noted in October 1906 to be standing 'this season at "Beachleigh" Frankston'. Annie and Phillip's son Colin is believed to have been a horsebreeder at the Beachleigh property.

One of the seven servants living at Beachleigh with Annie and Phillip Forster was Farquhar McDonald. The highly respected former station manager, old colonist and family friend died at Beachleigh on 2 March 1913. He was 84 years old. The Mornington Standard reported that he was well known in the area and highly regarded. He was buried at Campbellfield near the McRae family.

Not long after the death of Farquhar McDonald, the lavish lifestyle in which the Forster's lived began to decline. During the First World War, in January 1916, fire broke out at Beachleigh, destroying the stables and sheds before it was contained. The family remained at the house. Taking their War service seriously, during 1918 they hosted a major fund-raising event for the local Boys Home

Further bad luck was now dogging the family. In February 1920 a fatal accident took place at Beachleigh. It is possible the house was being used as a convalescent home, although this is not made clear in any of the newspaper reports. All that is reported is that Mr Angus Sharkey was riding on the road near the Mornington racecourse when he was thrown from his horse, falling on his head. The 21-year-old returned soldier received fatal injuries. In 1926, Annie and Phillip sold the property, Beachleigh, to the Children's Hospital as a convalescent home.

An intriguing item of family history is contained in a statement by John Stanton Atkinson dated 26 June 1935. In his statement Atkinson declares that he 'inspected a family Bible' at the residence of Mrs Annie Forster, 37 Victoria Street, Sandringham. For what reason it is unclear, however, he states that he inspected the Bible and recorded the family Register. Beginning with P E Forster, it notes his birth as 25 February 1866. The following names and birth dates are those of all of the children. It is an intriguing mystery why this search was undertaken.

Annie McRae McKenzie Forster died at her home in Sandringham of heart failure at the age of 86 on 30 September 1939. It was noted on her death certificate that she had suffered cholangitis (two months) and myocarditis, arteriosclerosis and senile degeneration for 10 years. She was buried at the Brighton Cemetery. Annie Forster left real estate to the value of £3,631 and personal property of £4,739. Her Will dated 27 August 1927 appointed the Perpetual Trustees, John Atkinson and William Cook as her Executors. Small sums were bequeathed to her children. Her second husband, Phillip Ernest Forster died on 7 January 1946, leaving real estate of £1,235 and personal property of £56/9. Annie and Kenneth's daughter, Margaret Flora McKenzie died on 31 October 1951 with real estate valued for probate at £4,850 and personal property of £3,790.

Bibliography

Books, Articles and Pamphlets

Armstrong, Albert and Campbell G. Ord, *Australian Sheep Husbandry: A Handbook of the Breeding and Treatment of Sheep, and Station Management*, George Robertson, Melbourne, 1882.

Atkinson, Jeff, *The Troublesome American: The story of Charles Ferguson, foreman on the Burke and Wills Expedition*, Carlton Community History Group, Carlton and www.cchg.as.au, 2010.

Australian Bureau of Statistics, *Demographic History of Queensland*, Commonwealth of Australia, Brisbane, 1992.

Bartley, Nehemiah and Knight, J.J. (ed.) *Australian Pioneers & Reminiscences (Illustrated) Together with portraits of some of the Founders of Australia*, Gordon and Gotch, Brisbane, 1896.

Bean, C.E.W., *The Dreadnought of the Darling*, Angus & Robertson, Sydney, Australian Edition 1956.

Beckler, Hermann, *A Journey to Cooper's Creek*, translated by Stephen Jeffries and Michael Kertesz, edited and with an introduction by Stephen Jeffries, Melbourne University Press at the Miegunyah Press in association with the State Library of Victoria, Melbourne, 1993.

Bell, Katherine et al, *Cattle Australia: the story the icons the drivers the big runs*, Murray David Publishing, Belrose West, 2009.

Bolton, G.C., *A Thousand Miles Away: A History of North Queensland to 1920*, Jacaranda Press in association with Australian National University, Brisbane, 1963.

Bonyhady, Tim, *Burke & Wills from Melbourne to Myth*, David Ell Press, Balmain, 1991.

Bourke, Donna, 'What Happened to the Camels of Burke & Wills Expedition?', Issue No. 9, *Provenance: The Journal of Public Record Office Victoria*, 2010.

Bowen, Jill, *Kidman: The Forgotten King: The true story of the greatest pastoral landholder in modern history*, Angus & Robertson, North Rhyde, 1989.

Boyes, Rosemary, *The Hume Highway a Pot-Pouri of Stories and Scenes. Today and Yesterday*. National Library of Australia, 1978.

Breckwoldt, R., Boden, R. & Andrew, J. (eds), *The Darling*, Murray-Darling Basin Commission, Canberra, 2004.

Broome, Richard, *Coburg, between two creeks*, Lothian, Melbourne, 1987.

Brown-May, Andrew & Swain, Shurlee (eds), *The Encyclopaedia of Melbourne*, Cambridge Press, Melbourne, 2005.

Burke and his Companions, The Victorian Exploring Expedition; from its Origin to the Return from Carpentaria and the Death of Burke, Wills and Gray, from Starvation; and Burke's and Wills' Journals, King's Narrative, Howitt's Diary, The Herald Office, Melbourne, 1861.

Cash, Damien, 'Robert O'Hara Burke (1821–61), *Oxford Companion to Australian History*, Oxford University Press, South Melbourne, 1998.

Cashin, Paul & McDermott, C. John, ''Riding on the Sheep's Back': Examining Australia's Dependence on Wool Exports', *The Economic Record*, Vol. 78, No. 242, September 2002.

Cathcart, Michael, *Starvation in a Land of Plenty. Wills' Diary of the Fateful Burke and Wills Expedition*, NLA Publishing, Canberra, 2013.

Cathcart, Michael, *The Water Dreamers: The Remarkable History of our Dry Continent*, Text Publishing, Melbourne, 2009.

Centenary of Darraweit Guim State School No. 878, 1867–1967: A brief history of the School and the District, Darraweit Guim, 1967.

Chapman, Andrew and Lee, Tim, *The Long Paddock*, The Five Mile Press, Scoresby, 2014.

Clark, Ian D. and Cahir, Fred, *The Aboriginal story of Burke and Wills: Forgotten Narratives*, CSIRO Publishing, Collingwood, 2013.

Clune, Frank, *Dig: A Drama of Central Australia*, Angus & Robertson Limited, Sydney, 1937.

Colwell, Max, *The Journey of Burke and Wills*, Paul Hamlyn, Sydney, 1971.

Cowal Society, *Sketch of Explorations by the late John McKinlay in the Interior of Australia 1861–62, being a paper read before the Cowal Society, October 27, 1878*, and published at the request of the Society, Glasgow, 1878. Reproduced for the Libraries Board of South Australia from a copy held in the Public Library of South Australia, Adelaide, 1962.

Crawford, R.M., *Australia*, Hutchinson University Library, London, 1961.

Davison, Graeme, *The Rise and Fall of Marvellous Melbourne*, Melbourne University Press, Carlton, 1984.

Davison, Graeme, Hirst, John & Macintyre, Stuart (eds), *The Oxford Companion to Australian History*, Oxford University Press, Melbourne, 1998.

De Serville, Paul, *Port Phillip Gentlemen*, Oxford University Press, Oxford, 1980.

De Serville, Paul, *Pounds and Pedigrees, The Upper Class in Victoria 1850–80*, Oxford University Press, Oxford, 1991.

Edmond, Martin, *The Supply Party: Ludwig Becker on the Burke and Wills Expedition*, East Street Publications, Adelaide, 2009.

Ellis, M.H., *The Beef Shorthorn in Australia*, Sydney & Melbourne Publishing Company, Sydney, 1932.

Exploring expedition from Victoria to the Gulf of Carpentaria, under the command of Mr Robert O'Hara Burke: containing journals of Howitt, King, Wills, Burke, Wright and Brahe; communicated by the Colonial Office.

Fiddian, Marc, *Trains, Tracks, Travellers: A History of the Victorian Railways*, South Eastern Independent Newspapers, Pakenham, 1997.

Fitzgerald, Ross, *A History of Queensland from the Dreaming to 1915*, University of Queensland Press, St Lucia, 1982.

Fountain, Paul, *Rambles of an Australian Naturalist*, John Murray, London, 1907.

Garden, Don, 'The Federation Drought of 1895–1903, El Niño and Society in Australia', Chapter 13 in *Common Ground: Integrating the Social and Environmental in History*, Cambridge Scholars Publishing, 2010.

Garden, Don, *Droughts, Floods & Cyclones: El Niños that shaped our colonial past*, Australian Scholarly Publishing, North Melbourne, 2009.

Garden, Don, *Victoria A History*, Nelson, Melbourne, 1984.

Glover, Janet R., *The Story of Scotland*, Faber & Faber, London, 1960.

Greaves, Bernard, *The Story of Bathurst*, Angus & Robertson Publishers, Sydney, 1976.

Gunson, N., *The Good Country – Cranbourne Shire*, J.W. Cheshire, Melbourne, 1968.

Hardy, Bobbie, *West of the Darling*, Jacaranda Press, Milton, 1969.

Harvey, H.J., *Exploration North: A Natural History of Queensland*, Richmond Hill Press, South Yarra, 1978.

Hassan, Riaz, *Suicide in Australia*, Oxford University Press, South Melbourne, 2000.

Hatfield, William, *I Find Australia*, Oxford University Press, London, 1937.

Hawgood, Jacinta, Milner, Allison & De Leo, Diego, 'Farmer suicide: data from the Queensland Suicide Register (QSR) and psychological autopsy case studies', Australian Institute for Suicide Research and Prevention, https://www.griffith.edu.au/__data/assets/pdf_file/0004/428809/Final-Farmer-suicide-poster.pdf

Hyslop, Anthea, 'Epidemics', Graeme Davison, John Hirst and Stuart Macintyre, *The Oxford Companion to Australian History*, Oxford University Press, Melbourne, 1988.

Hood, Col, *Droving down the Cooper*, Rosenberg Publishing, Sydney, 2010.

Holthouse, Hector, *Illustrated History of Queensland*, Rigby, Adelaide, 1978.

Hope, Jeannette & Lindsay, Robert, *The People of the Paroo River: Frederic Bonney's Photographs*, Environment, Climate Change & Water, New South Wales, 2010.

Howitt, Alfred, *Finding Burke and Wills: Personal reminiscences of Central Australia and the Burke and Wills expedition, with a glance at Benjamin Herschel Babbage's 1858 expedition*, The State Library of South Australia, 2007.

Hunter, James, *Scottish Exodus: Travels Among a Worldwide Clan*, Mainstream Publishing, Edinburgh and London, 2007.

Idriess, Ion L., *The Cattle King*, Angus & Robertson Limited, Sydney, 1936.

Inglis, Andrea, *Beside the Seaside: Victorian Resorts in the Nineteenth Century*, The Miegunyah Press, Carlton, 1999.

Kishere, Shirley, *Lancefield History Trail Our Early Beginning*, Romsey & Lancefield Districts Historical Society, Romsey, 2013.

The Journal of the National Agricultural Society of Victoria, Melbourne 1885.

Kelley, R.B., 'Studies on the Breeding Performance of Ewes' *Council for Scientific and Industrial Research, Bulletin* No. 205, Volume XXI, Melbourne, 1946.

Lee, Timothy, *Wanganella and the Merino Aristocrats*, Hardie Grant Books, Richmond, 2011.

McKinlay, John, *Sketch of Explorations by the late John McKinlay in the Interior of Australia, 1861–62*, Aird & Coghill, Glasgow, 1863.

McHugh, Evan, *The Drovers: Stories behind the heroes of our stock routes*, Viking an imprint of Penguin Books, Camberwell, 2010.

McHugh, Evan, *Outback Stations: the life and times of Australia's biggest cattle and sheep properties*, Viking an imprint of Penguin Books, Camberwell, 2012.

McLaren, Ian, *The Victorian Exploring Expedition and Relieving Expeditions 1860–61: The Burke and Wills Tragedy,* (Presidential address to the Society) Reprinted from *The Victorian Historical Magazine,* 116 issue, November 1959, Vol. XXIX, No. 4, 1960.

Macmillan, David S., *Scotland and Australia 1788–1850: Emigration, commerce and Investment*, Oxford at the Clarendon Press, Oxford, 1967.

Mahood, Marie, *Legends of the Outback*, Central Queensland University Press, Rockhampton, 2002.

Mahood, Marguerite 'Melbourne *Punch* and its Early Artists', *The La Trobe Journal*, No. 4, October 1969.

Maiden, Sandra J., *Menindee First Town on the River Darling*, The Sunnyland Press, Red Cliffs, 1989.

Matthews, Stephen and Kemp, David, *The Pipes and Drums, Scotch College Melbourne: A History*, Scotch College, Melbourne, 2007.

Meston, Archibald, *Geographic History of Queensland*, Government Printer, Brisbane, 1895.

Mitchell, Peter, *Romsey: A Veritable Garden of Eden*, West Bourke Books, Romsey, 2004.

Mitchell, T.L., *A Journey into the Interior of Eastern Australia; with descriptions of the recently explored region of Australia Felix and of the present colony of New South Wales*, Volume 1, T. & W. Boone, London, 1859.

Moorehead, Alan, *Cooper's Creek*, A Four Square Book, Sydney, 1965.

Murgatroyd, Sarah, *The Dig Tree: The Story of Burke & Wills*, Text Publishing, Melbourne, 2002.

Murgatroyd, Sarah, *Dig 3 ft NW The Legendary Journey of Burke & Wills*, Text Publishing, Melbourne, 2002.

Noble, J., *Port Phillip Panorama*, The Hawthorn Press, Melbourne, 1975.

Parson, Ian, *The Australian Ark: A history of domesticated animals in Australia*, CSIRO Publishing, Collingwood, 1998.

Pearson, Michael & Lennon, Jane, *Pastoral Australia: Fortunes, Failures and Hard Yakka: A historical overview 1788–1967*, CSIRO Publishing, the Department of the Environment, Water, Heritage and the Arts and the Australia Heritage Council, 2010.

Pearson, S.E., The South West Corner of Queensland, University of Queensland, 1937.

Peck, Harry H., *Memoirs of a Stockman*, Stock & Land Publishing Company, 4th reprint (Limited Edition), Melbourne, 1972.

Peck, Harry H., *Memoirs of a Stockman*, Stockland Press, 1942.

Phillips, John, *Reminiscences of Early Australian Life 1893*, A Transcription by Ian Itter, Swan Hill, 2014.

Phoenix, Dave, *Following Burke and Wills Across Australia: A Touring Guide*, CSIRO Publishing, Clayton South, 2015.

Prentis, Malcolm D., *The Scots in Australia: A Study of New South Wales, Victoria and Queensland, 1788–1900*, Sydney University Press, Sydney, 1983.

Prentis, Malcolm D., *The Scottish in Australia*, A.E. Press, Melbourne, 1987.

Prentis, Malcolm D., *The Scots in Australia*, University of New South Wales Press, Sydney, 2008.

Randall, W.R., *A Voyage up the Darling and Barwan Rivers in 1859*, Centre for Library Studies, Riverina-Murray Institute of Higher Education, 1986.

Rea, Beresford, *Up and Down the Sydney Road*, Georgian House, Melbourne, 1958.

Reardon, Mitch, *The Australian Geographic Book of Corner Country: Where outback Queensland, NSW and SA meet*, Australian Geographic Pty Ltd, Terrey Hills, 1998.

Reid, John, *When Memory Turns the Key: The History of the Shire of Romsey*, The Shire of Romsey History Book Committee, Romsey, 1992.

Reynolds, Henry, *Frontier: Aborigines, Settlers and Land*, Allen & Unwin, Sydney, 1987.

Reynolds, Henry, *The Other Side of the Frontier: Aboriginal resistance to the European invasion of Australia*, UNSW Press, Sydney, 2006.

Roberts, Stephen H, *History of Australian Land Settlement (1788–1920)*, Macmillan & Co. Ltd in association with Melbourne University Press, Melbourne, 1924.

Serle, Geoffrey, *The Golden Age: A history of the Colony of Victoria 1851–1861*, Melbourne University Press, Carlton, 1968.

Tipping, Marjorie, *Ludwig Becker: Artist & Naturalist with the Burke & Wills Expedition*, Melbourne University Press on behalf of The Library Council of Victoria, 1979.

Tolcher, H.M., *Drought or Deluge: Man in the Cooper's Creek Region*, Melbourne University Press, Carlton, 1986.

Tulloch, David J., *100 Years of Wentworth: 1859–1959*, Wentworth Shire Council, Wentworth, 1959.

Turnbull, Marian, *John King: The story of the only member of the Burke and Wills Expedition to cross Australia from south to north and return to Melbourne alive*, Carlton Community History Group, Carlton, 2011.

Watson, Don, *Caledonia Australis: Scottish highlanders on the frontier of Australia*, Collins, Sydney, 1984.

Watson, Michael J., *The Story of Burke and Wills: Sketches and Essays*, William P. Linehan, Melbourne, 1911.

Wills, William, (ed.), *Successful Exploration Through the Interior of Australia, from Melbourne to the Gulf of Carpentaria from the Journals and letters of William John Wills*, Richard Bentley, London, 1863.

White, Gabriel & Meyer, Martin, *Beyond the Cooper: Burke and Wills – Some Missing Links*, Preshil Camping Club, Kew, 1992.

Woodhouse, Fay, *Significance Assessment: Harewood Homestead Museum*, Hindsight Consulting Historians, 2011.

Manuscript Collections

W.B. Atkinson, Shipboard Diary, Voyage to Australia on board the *Hornet* 1857, Box 3421/3, W.B. Atkinson, MS 12599, State Library of Victoria.

Leckie Collection of Personal Papers belonging to Donald McRae, Duncan MacGregor and descendants, North Balwyn.

Duncan MacGregor, MS12914, State Library of Victoria.

Stewart, Shipboard Diary on the Marco Polo, June 1857.

William Lyall Collection, MS SEQ 8282, MS 7916; MS 10014; State Library of Victoria.

Theses and Unpublished Manuscripts

Cunningham, G., 'The Draining and Settlement of the Koo-wee-rup Swamp', unpublished Honours Thesis, Department of History, Monash University, 1972.

Key, L.M., 'Historical Geography of the Koo-wee-rup District', unpublished MA Thesis, University of Melbourne, 1967.

Macwhirter, Patricia, 'Harewood, Western Port: Woven from Stardust: A ten-billion-year view from an Australian Verandah, unpublished PhD thesis, University of Melbourne, 2005.

Notes

Chapter 1

1. 1 June 1857, Letter of Introduction, Alex MacKinnon, Minister, Folder 1.1, Box 1, MS12914, SLV.
2. Malcolm D Prentis, *The Scots in Australia: A Study of New South Wales, Victoria and Queensland, 1788–1900*, Sydney University Press, Sydney, 1983, p. 16.
3. Don Watson, *Caledonia Australis: Scottish highlanders on the frontier of Australia*, Collins, Sydney, 1984, p. 65; R.J.W. Selleck, 'Education', and Marjorie Theobold 'Educational History', *The Oxford Companion to Australian History, op. cit.*, pp. 205–8; Wayne Hudson 'Republicanism', *The Oxford Companion to Australian History, op. cit.*, pp. 555–6. D.W.A. Baker, 'John Dunmore Lang (1799–1878)', *Australian Dictionary of Biography*, http://adb.anu.edu.au/biography/lang-john-dunmore-2326; Prentis, *The Scots in Australia*, 1983, p. 58.
4. Malcolm Prentis, *The Scots in Australia*, UNSW Press, Sydney, 2008, pp. 29, 34.
5. Perth, Fortingal (part of) Enumeration District 8. Registrar General for Scotland Census Information, Parish of Fortingal, 6 June 1841.
6. Family Tree taken from Old Parish Register, Fortingall, 355/A3 and Old Parish Register, Killan 361/3. Leckie Archive.
7. Parish of Killin, Quoad Sacra – Parish of Strathfillan, District 6, District of Weem. Formerly part of the Parish of Killin as lies between the Bridge of Wear and farm of Cornush, together with the Inn of Tyndrum, both included but exclusive of Clifton. Census Statistics, 3 April 1851, Duncan MacGregor aged 16 'scholar at home'.
8. 20 May 1857, Letter of Introduction, Reverend John Campbell, Shire of Strathfillan, Perthshire, Folder 1.1, Box 1, MS12914, SLV.
9. 1 June 1857, Letter of Introduction, Alex MacKinnon, Minister, Folder 1.1, Box 1, MS12914, SLV; 2 June 1857, Letter of Introduction, Michael Grieves, Folder 1.1, Box 1, MS12914, SLV.
10. 23 May 1857, American and Australian Packet Office, London to Duncan MacGregor, Folder 1, Box 1, MS12914, SLV.
11. MacGregor Tree, Leckie Collection.
12. http://en.wikipedia.org/wiki/Marco_Polo_%28ship%29
13. 'Shipping Intelligence', 4 September 1857, *Argus*, p. 4.
14. http://museumvictoria.com.au/discoverycentre/websites-mini/journeys-australia/
15. http://en.wikipedia.org/wiki/Great_capes#/media/File:ClipperRoute.png

16 Duncan MacGregor, 'Memorandum or Journal on board the ship "Marco Polo" which sailed from Liverpool on the 7th June 1857', transcribed from shipboard diary by Ian G Leckie, Great-grandson of Duncan MacGregor, May 1994, Leckie Archive.

17 'James Cooper Stewart Records the voyage from Liverpool to Melbourne on the clipper Marco Polo', State Library of Victoria virtual exhibition Life on the Goldfields.

18 Duncan MacGregor Journal, p. 1.

19 Stewart Journal, p. 2.

20 W.B. Atkinson, Shipboard Diary, Voyage to Australia on board the *Hornet*, 1857, p. 2, Box 3421/3, MS12599, SLV, p. 2.

21 PROV, Index to Unassisted Inward Passenger Lists to Victoria 1852–1923. Campbell, Fiche 130, page 004; Stewart, Fiche 130, page 007.

22 Duncan MacGregor, journal, 8 June 1857.

23 http://www.slsa.sa.gov.au/fh/passengerlists/Journey.htm

24 Stewart Journal, p. 4.

25 'Privies and Hygiene' Museum Victoria http://museumvictoria.com.au/discoverycentre/websites-mini/journeys-australia/

26 Journal, 12 June 1857.

27 Journal, 13 and 14 June 1857.

28 Journal, 15 June 1857.

29 *Ibid*.

30 Journal, 18 June 1857.

31 Journal, 19 June 1857.

32 Journal, 21 June 1857.

33 Stewart Journal, 21 June 1857.

34 Journal, 28–29 June 1857.

35 Index to Unassisted Inward Passenger Lists to Victoria 1852–1923, PROV.

36 Stewart Journal, 18 June 1857.

37 Journal, 30 June 1857.

38 Journal, 31 June 1857.

39 Stewart Journal, 4 July 1857.

40 Stewart Journal, 1–3 September 1857.

41 'Shipping', Melbourne *Age*, Friday 4 September 1857, p. 4.

42 Marguerite Mahood, 'Melbourne Punch and its Early Artists', *The La Trobe Journal*, No. 4, October 1969, p. 65.

43 Graeme Davison, *The Rise and Fall of Marvellous Melbourne*, Melbourne University Press, Carlton, 1974, p. 11.

44 'Appendix 1 Population Census', March 1857, Geoffrey Serle, *The Golden Age: A History of the Colony of Victoria 1851–1861*, Melbourne University Press, Carlton, 1968, p. 382.

45 David Goodman, 'Gold', Andrew Brown-May & Shurlee Swain, *The Encyclopedia of Melbourne,* Cambridge University Press, Port Melbourne, 2005, pp. 309–10.

46 Serle, *The Golden Age: A History of the Colony of Victoria 1851–1861*, p. 43.

47 Don Garden, *Victoria A History*, Nelson, Melbourne 1984, pp. 80–1.

48 Serle, *op. cit.*, p. 44.

49 'Appendix 2 Migration Arrivals', Serle, *ibid.*, p. 383.

50 'Appendix 3 Unassisted Migration', Serle, *ibid.*, pp. 386–7.

51 Garden, *op. cit.*, pp. 84–5.

52 Atkinson, Shipboard Diary, *op. cit.*, 'Finis'.

53 Garden, *op. cit.*, p. 89–90.

54 'Melbourne Punch and its early artists', *La Trobe Journal*, No. 4 1969, p. 65.

55 Garden, *op. cit.*, p. 86.

56 By the late 1850s the number was almost 20 million. Garden, p. 86.

57 B.R. Davidson and Boris Schedvin quoted in Paul Cashin & John C. McDermott, "Riding on the Sheep's Back: Examining Australia's Dependence on Wool Exports', in *The Economic Record*, Vol. 78, No. 242, September 2002, p. 249.

58 5 January 1858, John MacGregor to Duncan MacGregor, Ewich, Folder 2.5, Box 1, MS12914, SLV.

59 7 September 1858, Annie MacGregor to Duncan MacGregor, Folder 2.5, Box 1, MS12914, SLV.

60 1 March 1859, Kate MacGregor to Duncan MacGregor, Folder 2.5, Box 1, MS12914, SLV.

61 26 May 1937, Donald MacGregor to Messrs R &J M Brown, Glasgow, Leckie Archive.

62 5 January 1858, John MacGregor to Duncan MacGregor, Ewich, Folder 2.5, Box 1, MS12914, SLV.

63 R.V.B. and A.S.K. (No. 149), 'Pastoral Pioneers Donald Campbell', first published in *Argus*, 14 August 1934 and later in *The Australasian*, 6 October 1934. Republished in *The Australasian*, 24 October 1936, p. 4.

64 'Donald Campbell', *ibid.* He also applied for a 620 acre pre-emptive right at Tarrangower. Ken James, 'The Surveying career of William Swan Urquhart, 1845–1864', *Provenance: the Journal of Public Record Office Victoria*, Issue No. 8, 2009, p. 9 and Endnote 54, PROV, VPRS 1330/P0, Unit 1, Item 54/162, Urquhart to Assistant surveyor Turner, 1 August 1854.

65 Lachlan W. McBean, *Lachlan McBean 1810-1894 Pastoral Pioneer*, Lismore, 1994, p. 18 and *The Australasian Pastoralists' Review*, 15 February 1894, p. 577.

66 'Lachlan McBean (1810-1894), http://oa.anu.edu.au/obituary/mcbean-lachlan-678

67 James McNee to Duncan MacGregor, 12 November 1859, Folder 2.5, Box 2, MS12914, SLV.

68 John MacGregor to Duncan MacGregor 28 June 1860, Folder 2.5, Box 2, MS12914, SLV.

69 Greg Dening, *Readings/Writings*, Melbourne, 1998, p. 166 quoted in Peter Freeman Pty Ltd, *Former Kinchega Station Sites – Kinchega National Park Conservation Management & Cultural Tourism Plan*, Volume 1, 2002, p. 18.

70 8 March 1968, 'Early Days of Pakenham and Dalmore', *The Gazette*, Pakenham, p. 7; Gerard Cunningham, 'The Draining and Settlement of the Koo-wee-rup Swamp' unpublished Honours Thesis, Monash, 1972, p. 19; L.M. Keys, 'Historical Geography of the Koo-wee-rup District', unpublished MA Thesis, Melbourne, 1967; J. Ann Hone, 'Duncan MacGregor (1835–1916), *Australian Dictionary of Biography*, Melbourne University Press, Carlton 1974, pp. 157–8.

71 Unauthored, undated note on paper in box 2, Folder 2.5, MS12914, SLV. Although slightly different wording, the statement that he 'piloted Burke and Wills Expedition on part of its journey' is quoted in Cunningham thesis, Key thesis.

72 Phoenix, p. 122; Becker, p. 203.

73 Phoenix, p. 133, pp. 137–44.

74 Anon., 'Bedourie pub: An Old Queensland ballad', Bill Wannan (ed.), *The Heather in the South: Lore Literature and Balladry of the Scots in Australia*, Landsdowne, Melbourne, 1966, pp. 188–9.

75 David Phoenix (author of *Following Burke and Wills Across Australia*, CSIRO Publishing, Clayton South, 2015), correspondence with Ian Leckie, 1 July 2016.

76 Harry H. Peck, *Memoirs of a Stockman*, Stock & Land Company, Melbourne, 1972, p. 115.

77 Annie MacGregor to Duncan MacGregor, 25 Gayfield Square, Edinburgh, 12 May 1862 and Margaret MacGregor to Duncan MacGregor, Ewich, Folder 2.5, Box 2, MS12914, SLV.

78 Sandra J. Maiden, *Menindee First Town on the River Darling*, Sunnyland Press, Red Cliffs, 1989, p. 175.

79 *Ibid.*, pp. 175–6.

80 *Ibid.*, p. 177.

81 Jeanette Hope and Robert Lindsay, *The People of the Paroo River: Frederic Bonney's Photographs*, Department of Environment, Climate Change & Water NSW, Sydney South, 2010, p. 9.

82 *Ibid.*, p. 21.

83 4 March 1941, Fredric Bonney to Duncan MacGregor, Letter no. 42, Folder 2.1, Box 2, MS12914, SLV.

84 Hope and Lindsay, *op. cit.*, p. 87.

85 Folder 1.1, Box 1, Duncan MacGregor: personal documents; family history, MS12914, SLV.

86 His birth was recorded in the Parish baptism register 8/10/1816, MacRae, Donald (OPR Births 072/00 0010 0044) Kintail.

87 https://en.wikipedia.org/wiki/Sir_Alexander_Matheson,_1st_Baronet, accessed 29.12.2015.

88 'Pioneering on the Darling', *The Australasian*, 25 March 1922, p. 5.

89 *James Pattison*, arrived 11 December 1838, http://srwww.records.nsw.gov.au/ebook/list

90 The *Norval*, picked up the passengers from the James Pattison. *James Pattison*, http://srwww.records.nsw.gov.au/ebook/list

91 http://museumvictoria.com.au/discoverycentre/websites-mini/journeys-australia/

92 The *Norval*, *op. cit.*

93 'Pioneering on the Darling', *The Australasian*, 18 March 1922, p. 2.

94 David Macmillan, *Scotland and Australia, 1788–1850: emigration, commerce and investment*, Clarendon Press, Oxford, 1967, pp. 291–3.

95 Gavin Long, 'Ranken, George (1793–1860)' *Australian Dictionary of Biography*, http://adb.anu.edu.au/biography/ranken-george-2572

96 Bernard Greaves (ed.), *The Story of Bathurst*, Angus & Robertson, p. 57.

97 Marriage Certificate, No. 1234, Vol. 76.

98 The Gordon Family History website reveals, *James Moran* Family Groups lists. Item 21 lists Roderick McKenzie, of Loch Broom, farmer, 50, his wife 46 and 4 children who nominated their religion as Presbyterian. http://www.gordonfamilyhistory.com.au/ships/famgroups.html

99 *Ibid.* http://www.gordonfamilyhistory.com.au/ships/famgroups.html

100 Baptism Records, Roderick 1/11/1844 No. 421, Vol. 48; Isabella 17/3/1847 No. 544, Vol. 49; Margaret 20/6/1849 No. 811, Vol. 50; Anna 27/3/1853 No. 1109, Vol. 52, Registry of Births, Deaths and Marriages, New South Wales. Registry of Births Deaths and Marriages, Sydney, 18 May 2015.

101 Don Watson, *Caledonia Australis*, *op. cit.*, p. 64.

102 Bernard MacGregor, talk to Book Collectors, 1969.

103 Malcolm Prentis, *The Scots in Australia: A Study of New South Wales, Victoria and Queensland, 1788–1900*, Sydney University Press, 1983, p. 69.

104 John McRae, Death Certificate No. 42, Schedule B, Death Certificate in the District of Kalkallo in the Colony of Victoria.

105 Folder 1.5, Donald McRae Accounts, Box 1, MS12914, SLV.

106 Crown Lands Offfice, Register, p. 1785 Item 113, 2 July 1855, Albert District, Donald McRae 'Bonley Run £75, Kulpaulin (sp.) £75 Netallie £75' and Maiden, *op. cit.*, p. 19.

107 'Crown Lands Beyond the Settled Districts, New Runs' Government Gazette, 3 June 1856, No. 18, Bonley, 94 ½ square miles, 640 cattle; Netallie, 80 square miles, 640 cattle, Culpaulin, 100 square miles, 640 cattle', p. 1617 and p. 1785.

108 Lands Department New South Wales.

109 Maiden, *op. cit.*

110 15 May 1863, Gibson to McRae Culpaulin Station, Duncan MacGregor Papers, 1857–1938, MS 12914, Box 1, Folder 5.

111 http://adb.anu.edu.au/biography/sturt-evelyn-pitfield-shirley-4663, accessed 30 December 2015.

112 *Victoria and its Metropolis: Past and Present*, p. 466.

113 'Richard Gibson (1831–1886)', *Traralgon Record*, 17 August 1886, p. 3, republished on Obituaries Australia website, http://oa.anu.edu.au/obituary/gibson-richard-16025, accessed 24 February 2015.

114 John E Barry, 'Some Famous Rides', *Western Herald*, Bourke, NSW, 27 March 1953, p. 5 previously published in the *Brisbane Observer* on 1 January 1906.

115 Archives in Brief 60, Commissioners of Crown Lands, https://www.records.nsw.gov.au/state-archives/guides-and-finding-aids/archives-in-brief/archives-in-brief-60

116 Ross Fitzgerald, *A History of Queensland from the Dreaming to 1915*, University of Queensland Press, St Lucia, 1982, p. 133.

117 *Ibid.*, p. 134.

118 *Ibid.*, p. 136.

119 11 October 1866, Post Master and Land Agent, Mount Murchison to Donald McRae, Folder 1.5, Box 1, MS12914, SLV.

120 21 February 1867, Dal Campbell & Co. to Donald McRae, Caulpaulin, Folder 2.5, Box 2, MS12914, SLV.

121 19 March 1867, Neil Macdonald to Dal Campbell, Folder 2.5, Box 2, MS12914, SLV.

122 Gibson to McRae Culpaulin Station, 9 March 1864, Duncan MacGregor Papers, 1857–1938, Folder 5, Box 1, MS12914, SLV.

123 *Ibid.*

124 Glen was also a composer. He is remembered for *Glen's Highland Schottische* (1875) and *New Highland Schottische* (1881). See http://sydney.edu.au/paradisec/australharmony/register-G.php. My thanks to Noel Wright, Scottish Resource Centre, for this information. Correspondence with author 23 November 2015.

125 11 April 1866, Dal, Campbell & Co., Melbourne to Donald McRae, Esq., Caulpaulin Station, Darling River via Wentworth. Duncan MacGregor Papers, 1857–1938, Folder 5, Box 1, MS12914, SLV.

126 Gavin Long, 'William Tom (1791–1883)', http://adb.anu.edu.au/biography/tom-william-2737

127 Peter Mitchell, *Romsey A Veritable Garden of Eden*, West Bourke Books, Romsey, 2004, pp. 295–6; John Reid (ed.), *When Memory Turns the Key: The History of the Shire of Romsey*, The Shire of Romsey History Book Committee, Joval Publications, Romsey, 1992, p. 128.

128 Lands Victoria, Volume 2641 Folio 528012.

129 A memoir 'Chintin Grange and its People' was written for the McDonnell family in 1980 and traces the lives of the families living at Chintin, Chintin Grange, Glengarry, Glengyle and Clunie.

130 Clarkefield Station is on the Sunbury to Woodend Line. This line opened on 8 July 1861. On 25 April 1862, the Woodend to Kyneton extension opened; on 21 October 1862, the Kyneton to Bendigo extension opened, and on 19 September 1864 the Bendigo to Echuca extension opened. Marc Fiddian, *Trains, Tracks, Travellers: A History of the Victorian Railways*, South Eastern Independent Newspapers, Pakenham, 1997, p. 159.

131 *Centenary of Darraweit Guim State School*, Darraweit Guim, 1967.

132 'Clunie', Macedon Ranges Cultural Heritage and Landscape Study, p. 739.

133 'Home with a Past', *Age*, 14 November 1970, p. 29.

134 16 May 1975, Mona Lyall to Bernard MacGregor, Leckie Archive.

135 Small notebook found in Folder 'Notebooks 1860/61, 1866, 1868', Box 8, MS12914, SLV.

136 *Ibid.*

137 1 June 1867, Duncan McRae to unknown recipient, Folder 2.7, Box 2, MS12914, SLV.

138 Certificate Of Marriage between Duncan MacGregor, Sheep farmer and Bachelor, and Margaret McCrae, Spinster, in the District of Lancefield, No. 32 in Register, on 25th February 1868 at the residence of the mother of the Bride, Clunie House, Chintin. Folder 1.1, Box 1, Duncan MacGregor: personal documents; family history, MS12914, SLV.

139 Mona Lyall tletter, *op. cit.*, Leckie Archive.

140 26 April 1868, Duncan McRae to 'Dear Sir', Caulpaulin. Folder 1.5, Box 1, Donald McRae accounts and correspondence, MS12914, SLV.

141 8 June 1868, Duncan McRae to Neil Macdonald, Folder 1.5, Box 1, MS12914, SLV.

Chapter 2

1 VPRS 28/P0, Unit 75; VPRS 28/P1, Unit 15; VPRS 7591/P1, Unit 29; File No. 6/920, PROV.

2 Will of Donald McRae Esq., VPRS 7591, P1, Unit 29, PROV.

3 VPRS7591/P1/Unit 29; VPRS28/P0/Unit 75; VPRS28/P1/Unit 15, PROV.

4 Letter from McIntosh, dated 27 August 1867, Attachment 'B' to Affidavit dated 30 October 1867; Letter from Smith dated 9 September 1867, Attachment 'C', Affidavit dated 30 October 1867.

5 Will of Donald McRae, No. 920, PROV.

6 Death Notice, Donald McRae, *Argus*, 8 November 1864, p. 4.

7 Christina McRae, 17 June 1868, Folder 2.4, Box 2, MS12914, SLV.

8 'Miscellaneous Accounts – Caulpaulin Station River Darling 26th January 1869', Folder 3.5 Durham Downs Miscellaneous Accounts, Box 3, MS12914, SLV.

9 Duncan MacGregor Notebooks 1870s, Folder 8.1, Box 8, MS12914, SLV.

10 http://adb.anu.edu.au/biography/clarke-william-john-1902

11 Ronald McNicoll, 'Riddell, John Carre (1809–1879)', *Australian Dictionary of Biography*, http://adb.anu.edu.au/biography/riddell-john-carre-4476/text7307, published first in hardcopy 1976, accessed online 9 September 2015.

12 J. Ann Hone, 'Hamilton, Thomas Ferrier (1820–1905)', *ADB*, http://adb.anu.edu.au/biography/hamilton-thomas-ferrier-3704/text5809, published first in hardcopy 1972, accessed online 9 September 2015.

13 http://adb.anu.edu.au/biography/black-niel-3003

14 Hugh Anderson, 'Clarke, William John (1805–1874)', *ADB*, http://adb.anu.edu.au/biography/clarke-william-john-1902/text2247, published first in hardcopy 1966, accessed online 9 September 2015.

15 J. Ann Hone, 'Amess, Samuel (1826–1898)', *ADB*, http://adb.anu.edu.au/biography/amess-samuel-2882/text4121, published first in hardcopy 1969, accessed online 9 September 2015.

16 Parish of Kerrie, Plan undated, but indicating MacGregor's ownership of Allotment 18, and Allotments 42, 43 and 44.

17 MacGregor Notebooks, Box 8, MS12914, SLV.

18 Dr Val Noone, Gaelic scholar, email, 10 September 2015.

19 'Farming at Riddell's Creek', *Australasian*, Saturday 3 June 1876, p. 24.

20 *Ibid.*

21 *Ibid.*

22 *Ibid.*

23 *Ibid.*

24 Harry H. Peck, *Memoirs of a Stockman*, Stock & Land Publishing, Melbourne, 1972, p. 114.

25 Memorandum of Agreement dated 21 June 1876 between Mr Duncan Sinclair and Messrs Aitken, Lilburn & Co. of Glasgow Managing owners of ship 'Loch Ness', Folder 2.8, Box 2, MS12914, SLV.

26 26 September 1876, *Tribune*, Hobart, p. 2.

27 *Argus*, 6 April 1878, p. 10, 13 April 1878, p. 10 and 11 May 1878, p. 3.

28 Peck, *op. cit.*, p. 114.

29 http://web.archive.org/web/20031003045653/; http://www.arts.monash.edu.au/ncas/multimedia/gazetteer/list/coburg.html

30 Richard Broome, *Coburg: Between Two Creeks*, Coburg Historical Society, Pascoe Vale South, 2001, pp. 40, 43 quoted in Historica, *City of Moreland Thematic History*, 2010, p. 18.

31 http://collections.museumvictoria.com.au/items/76047

32 http://www.arts.monash.edu.au/ncas/multimedia/gazetteer/list/coburg.html

33 *Argus*, Friday 3 October 1919, p. 6; *Victoria and its Metropolis Past and Present, Vol. 11B, The Colony and its People in 1888*, McCarron Bird Publishing, Melbourne, 1888, p. 492.

34 Richard Broome, *op. cit.*, pp. 64, 137.

35 *Brunswick Coburg Star*, 8 September 1916, p. 4.

36 Ledger 7.1 Glengyle Station Accounts 1873–1891, Box 7, Ledgers 1–7, MS12914, SLV.

37 *Pastoral Leases, Unsettled Districts: An Act to Consolidate and amend the Laws relating to the Pastoral Occupation of Crown Lands in the Unsettled District Act, Assented to 14 September 1869*, p. 1122; see also Duncan MacGregor, 'The Crisis in the Far West', 26 January 1901, *Brisbane Courier*, p. 14.

38 Ion L Idriess, *The Cattle King: The Story of Sir Sidney Kidman*, Angus & Robertson, Sydney, 1936, pp. 103–5.

39 *Ibid.*, p. 108.

40 Letters to Duncan MacGregor from Duncan Campbell and N Macdonald 1872–1877, Folder 2.6, MS12914, SLV.

41 *Ibid.*

42 16 July 1872, McDonald to MacGregor, Folder 2.6, MS12914, SLV.

43 14 January 1873, Macdonald to MacGregor, Folder 2.6, Box 2, MS 12914.

44 'Untitled transcript of dealings with Neil Hugh Macdonald and David and Robert Mailer 1872–1885', Miscellaneous legal documents, Box 3, MS12914, SLV.

45 Untitled notes 1872–1885, *op. cit.*, Box 3, MS12914, SLV.

46 9 May 1874, 'Arrival of the Steamship Northumberland Fifty-One days' Passage', *Weekly Times*, Melbourne, p. 9; 7 May 1874, *Launceston Examiner*, p. 3; 12 May 1874, *Sydney Morning Herald*, p. 4.

47 MacGregor Notebook 1874/75, Folder 8.3, MS12914, SLV.

48 Application No. 15, Received 29 January 1874; Application No. 23, Received 5 March 1874.

49 Application No. 15, Neil Hugh Macdonald, Name of Run: Durham Downs, p. 15.

50 http://www.kidman.com.au/properties/1/glengyle accessed 31.05.2016.

51 Miscellaneous legal document, Box 3, MS12914, SLV.

52 19 December 1875, Duncan Campbell to Duncan MacGregor. Folder 2.5, Box 2, MS12914, SLV.

53 S. Roberts, *History of Australian Land Settlement*, Melbourne, 1968, p. 247; J.M. Powell, *The Public Lands of Australia Felix*, Melbourne, 1970, p. xxii.

54 Gerard Cunningham, 'The Draining and Settlement of the Koo-wee-rup Swamp', unpublished Honours Thesis, Department of History, Monash University, 1972 and Lesley Keys, 'Historical Geography of the Koo-wee-rup District', unpublished Master of Arts thesis, School of Geography, University of Melbourne, 1967.

55 William Lyall's record of the purchase indicates MacGregor paid £5,338 not £5,085 as Cunningham has stated. MS7916, William Lyall 1821–1888, Part 2, Copy 2, *'Extracts taken from the diaries of William Lyall Esquire of "Harewood" Westernport Victoria by his Granddaughter Bertha Irene Ricardo, Part II'*, p. 192.

56 Cunningham, p. 15.

57 *Ibid.*, pp. 15–16; Keys, p. 59.

58 Cunningham, p. 17; 'Koo-wee-rup' Swamp', *Daily Telegraph*, Melbourne, 28 April 1880.

59 Keys, p. 34.

60 Cunningham, p. 19.

61 *Ibid.*, p. 20.

62 *Ibid.*, p. 22.

63 'Rich Farming and Fattening Land', *Argus*, 30 April 1932, p. 3.

64 Folder 4.5, Mrs McRae, Cluny, 1867 to 1890, Box 4, MS12914, SLV.

65 Marriage Certificate No. 7 in the Register, Marriage solemnized in the District of Bourke.

66 Ensay Station, https://en.wikipedia.org/wiki/Ensay,_Victoria

67 *Sydney Morning Herald*, 19 August 1878, p. 3.

68 'Chronic Impecuniosity: Could not live on £1,800 per year', *Age*, 27 October 1905, p. 7.

Chapter 3

1 J. Ann Hone, Duncan MacGregor (1835–1916), *ADB, op. cit.*

2 Evan McHugh, *The Drovers: Stories Behind the heroes of our stock routes*, Viking, Camberwell, 2010, p. 9; 'Breeds of Beef Cattle', www.agriculture.vic.gov.au/livestock/beef/breeds; 'First Fleet Cattle', www.firstfleetfellowship.org.au/library/first-fleet-cattle

3 'History of beef cattle in Australia', www.drakensberger.com.au accessed 09.02.2016.

4 McHugh, *op. cit.*, p. 11; Shorthorn, en.wikipedia.org/wiki/Shorthorn

5 McHugh, *op. cit.*, p. 11.

6 *Ibid.*

7 'The Shorthorn in Australia: A Fascinating Story', *Sydney Mail*, 20 July 1932, pp. 37-8.

8 G.R. Quaife, 'Robert McDougall (1813–1887)', *Australian Dictionary of Biography*, Volume 5, Melbourne University Press, 1974, p. 150; 'Emigrated first to Canada; arrived Melbourne 1842', Re-Member (Former Members) Parliament of Victoria, http://www.parliament.vic.gov.au/re-member/details/546-mcdougall-robert; Index to Assisted British Immigration 183901871, 'Robert McDougall, Age 28, February 1842, Ship, *The Manlius*, PROV, Book 2/3, p. 85.

9 P.L. Brown, 'Learmonth, Thomas (1818–1903)', *Australian Dictionary of Biography*, Vol. 2, Melbourne University Press, 1967, pp. 100–1.

10 McDougall, *ADB, op. cit.*, p. 150.

11 http://adb.anu.edu.au/biography/black-niel-3003; Jerimiah Ware was the brother-in-law of Thomas Dowling who owned Jellalabad station near Darlington and built up a fine merino stock using Larra stud stock from Tasmania. http://adb.anu.edu.au/biography/dowling-thomas-323

12 McDougall, *ADB, op. cit.*, p. 150.

13 M.H. Ellis, *The Beef Shorthorn in Australia*, Melbourne, 1932, p. 74.

14 Wills & Probate papers for Robert McDougall, VPRS7591/P2/Unit 126; VPRS28/P2/Unit 224.

15 McDougall, *ADB, op. cit.*, p. 150.

16 'Mr Robert Clarke and Bolinda Vale', in M.H. Ellis, *The Beef Shorthorn in Australia*, Melbourne, 1932, pp. 182–3.

17 'Mount Derrimut Subject and Correspondence Files [1855–1878], University of Melbourne, Faculty of Agriculture and Forestry (1905–), University of Melbourne Archives.

18 'The Late Mr Robert Clarke', *Australasian*, 27 April 1918, pp. 4–5.

19 'Dalmahoy Campbell & Co.'s Melbourne Stock Report – 25 October', 31 October 1871, *South Australian Register*, p. 4.

20 'The Wares: Pastoral Pioneers', *Australasian*, 3 April 1937, p. 4.

21 *Australian Sheep Husbandry*, p. 16.

22 15 October 1857, *Argus*, p. 5.

23 5 August 1858, *Argus*, p. 1.

24 W.J.T. Clarke, Letter to the Editor, *Argus*, 20 September 1858, p. 1.

25 'Lincolnshire Sheep', *Star*, Ballarat, 22 January 1864, p. 4.

26 'Farming at Darraweit Guim', *Australasian*, 24 June 1876, p. 24.

27 Duncan MacGregor, 'Description of Border Leicester', 11 March 1911, Leckie Collection.

28 Hank Nelson, 'Horses', *Oxford Companion to Australian History*, pp. 325–6.

29 Commonwealth Clydesdale Horse Society of Australia, p. 1.

30 Duncan MacGregor, 'Description of Border Leicester', 11 March 1911, Leckie Collection.

31 Duncan MacGregor, 'The Horse – Particular Description of a Clydesdale Horse', p. 3, undated, Leckie Collection.

32 Certificate of Title, Volume 144 Folio 161 (p. 2), issued 19 August 1872, NSW Land and Property Information (NSW LP3).

33 Ledger Book – wages 1875–1878, Folder 6.3, Box 6, MS12914, SLV.

34 Durham Downs Ledgers 1874–1885, Folder 4.4, Box 4, MS12914, SLV.

35 5 February 1878, *Evening News*, p. 3.

36 'Queensland', *South Australian Chronicle and Weekly Mail*, 24 August 1878, p. 6.

37 'Important Sale of Pure-bred Shorthorn cattle … on Thursday 23rd May', *Argus*, 6 April 1878, p. 10.

38 'Stock and Station Report', *Western Champion*, Blackall/Barcaldine, 3 June 1881, p. 2.

39 27 February 1883, Wigugomrie, Deed of Partnership, Folder 3.1, Box 3, MS12914, SLV.

40 'Fat Stock Report', *South Australian Register*, 4 December 1885, p. 3.

41 Western Grazier's Correspondent (Wilcannia) quoted in 'Stock and Station Report', *Western Champion*, 3 June 1881; 'Stock Report', *Riverine Grazier*, 21 July 1883, p. 2.

42 'Pastoral News, Stock Movements, and Markets', *Maitland Mercury and Hunter River General Advertiser*, 19 September 1885.

43 Hone, *op. cit.*

44 Minute Book, Berwick Shire Council, 24 April 1880, quoted in Cunningham, p. 24.

45 Cunningham, p. 24.

46 Schedule B, Deaths in the District of Drouin in the Colony of Victoria, Item 20, Annie Brown.

47 Agreement dated 8 November 1881, Folder 3.1, Box 3, MS12914, SLV.

48 8 November 1871, Agreement between D. Mailer and D. MacGregor, Foldeer 3.1, Box 3, MS 12914, SLV.

49 The Melbourne solicitors Brahe & Gair acted for Duncan MacGregor and his family throughout Duncan's professional life. Originally Macgregor, Ramsay and Brahe, the firm opened in Melbourne in 1856. In later years it became Macgregor & Brahe, Brahe & Gair, and today it is Garland, Hawthorn, Brahe. John Macgregor (no relation) was a member of the Legislative Assembly from 1862 to 1874. Robert Ramsay was a member of the Legislative Assembly in 1870 and remained in politics until his death in 1882. William Alexander Brahe was appointed Consul for Prussia in 1868, a position he held for 25 years.

50 *Geelong Advertiser*, 23 February 1886, p. 4.

51 *Border Watch*, Mt Gambier, 23 June 1886, p. 2.

52 'Durham Downs Station', *Newcastle Morning Herald and Miners' Advocate*, 26 June 1886, p. 10.

53 'The estate of the Late Robert McDougall', Folder 1.9, Box 1, MS12914, SLV.

54 VPRS7591/P2, Unit 126, No. 34/994, PROV.

55 G.R. Quaife, 'McDougall, Robert (1813–1887)', *Australian Dictionary of Biography*, National Centre of Biography, Australian National University, http://adb.anu.edu.au/biography/mcdougall-robert-4086/text6527, published first in hardcopy 1974, accessed online 4 May 2016.

56 Catalogue of the Arundel Herd of Pure Booth Shorthorns to be sold by Public Auction at Arundel on Thursday, December 1, 1887 by Powers Rutherford & Co., Ryan & Hammond, A.S. King & Co., Pearson, Rowe, Smith & Co., SLV.

57 3 May 1899, J.R. Thompson to Brahe & Gair, Folder 1.9, Box 1, MS12914, SLV.

58 19 May 1899, Brahe & Gair to Thompson, Folder 1.9, Box 1, MS12914, SLV.

59 2 March 1900, Opinion of Counsel, Folder 1.6, Box 1, MS12914.

60 Schedule B., Deaths in the District of Coburg. No. 987, Christina McRae.

61 Christina McRae, VPRS 28/P0/444, VPRS/P2/234, VPRS 7591/P2/133, PROV.

62 7 March 1892, Brahe & Gair, Melbourne to Thomas Bunton, Esq., Brisbane, Folder 1, Box 1, MS12914, SLV.

63 *Ibid.*

64 H.B. Higgins, http://adb.anu.edu.au/biography/higgins-henry-bournes-6662; Edward Russell, http://adb.anu.edu.au/biography/russell-edward-

fitzgerald-13180

65 Counsels Opinion, H.B. Higgins, 1 Selbourne Chambers, 26 September 1888, Box 1, Duncan MacGregor correspondence, MS12914, SLV.

66 The Estate of the Late Donald McRae, 1886–1900, Mrs MacGregor's half share, Folder 1, Box 1, MS12914, SLV.

Chapter 4

1 Living with Drought, Australian Bureau of Meteorology, accessed 20.02.2016.

2 'Drought in Australia', 1301.0 – Year Book Australia, 1988, http://www.abs.gov.au/AUSSTATS/abs

3 *Ibid.*

4 Office of Economic and Statistical Research, *Queensland Past and Present: 100 Years of Statistics 1896-1996*, Queensland Government, 2009.

5 Bureau of Meteorology, *Results of Rainfall Observations Made in Queensland*, Government Printer, Melbourne, 1914, quoted in *Queensland Past and Present*, p. 29.

6 John Cameron to Duncan MacGregor, 8 January 1866, Folder 1, Box 1, MS12914, SLV.

7 Dalmahoy Campbell & Co., *Argus*, 21 November 1866.

8 'Melbourne Live Stock Market', *Mount Alexander Mail*, 23 November 1866, p. 2.

9 Glengyle Accounts, Box 5, MS12914, SLV; *The Queenslander*, 24 August 1877.

10 Alexander Campbell to Duncan MacGregor, 16 February 1877, Folder 1, Box 1, MS12914, SLV.

11 T.M. Tolcher, *Drought or Deluge: Man in the Cooper's Creek Region*, Melbourne University Press, Carlton, 1986, p. 217.

12 *Ibid.*, p. 218.

13 *Ibid.*

14 Tolcher, *op. cit.*, p. 206.

15 'The Drought in Queensland', *Sydney Morning Herald*, 25 October 1888, p. 10.

16 Don Garden, *Droughts, Floods & Cyclones: El Niños that shaped our colonial past*, Australian Scholarly Publishing, North Melbourne, 2009.

17 Don Garden, 'The Federation Drought of 1895–1903, El Niño and Society in Australia', Chapter 13 in *Common Ground: Integrating the Social and Environmental in History*. Cambridge Scholars Publishing. 2010, p. 270–2; Don Garden, *Droughts, Floods & Cyclones: El Niños that shaped our colonial past*, Australian Scholarly Publishing, North Melbourne, 2009; Daniel McKay, 'Dust and Bluster: An historical evaluation of the political discourse on drought in Australia' Burgmann Journal, II, 2013, pp. 33–9.

18 *Burra Record*, 25 May 1898 quoted in Garden, 2009, p. 276.

19 Garden, *op. cit.*, 'The Federation Drought of 1895–1903, El Niño and Society in Australia', p. 275.

20 *Ibid.*

21 Jenny Lee, 'Depressions', in Graeme Davison, John Hirst and Stuart Macintyre (eds), *The Oxford Companion to Australian History*, Oxford University Press, South Melbourne, 1998, pp. 183–4.

22 G.H. Knibbs, 'Suicide in Australia: a statistical analysis of the facts', *Journal and Proceedings of the Royal Society of New South Wales*, pp. 225–46, quoted in Riaz Hassan, *Suicide in Australia*, Oxford University Press, South Melbourne, 2000, p. 44.

23 3 September 1896, Margaret MacGregor to Jack, Folder 2.1, Box 2, MS12914, SLV.

24 'Weddings', *Australasian*, Saturday 8 December 1894, p. 39.

25 3 September 1896, Margaret MacGregor to Jack, Folder 2.1, Box 2, MS12914, SLV.

26 25 November 1896, unidentified newspaper cutting in Leckie Archive.

27 Conveyance record no. 56839, Lands Victoria.

28 27 January 1897, Margaret to Jack MacGregor, Folder 2.1, Box 2, MS12914, SLV.

29 Garden, *op. cit.*, x.

30 11 April 1898, Farquhar McDonald to Jack, Folder 2.4, Box 2, MS12914, SLV.

31 27 October 1897, Farquhar McDonald to Jack, Folder 2.4, Box 2, MS12914, SLV.

32 11 April 1898, Farquhar McDonald to Jack, Folder 2.4, Box 2, MS12914, SLV.

33 3 September 1896, Cissie to Jack MacGregor, Folder 2.3, Box 2, MS12914, SLV.

34 27 January 1897, Margaret to Jack MacGregor, Folder 2.1, Box 2, MS12914, SLV.

35 10 June 1897, Margaret to Jack MacGregor, Folder 2.1, Box 2, MS12914, SLV.

36 1 July 1897, Margaret to Jack MacGregor, Folder 2.1, Box 2, MS12914, SLV.

37 4 August 1897, Margaret to Jack MacGregor, Folder 2.1, Box 2, MS12914, SLV.

38 1 June 1897, Duncan to Jack, Folder 2.2, Box 2, MS12914, SLV.

39 1 and 2 June 1892, Duncan to Jack MacGregor, Folder 2.2, Box 2, MS12914, SLV.

40 http://www.parliament.vic.gov.au/re-member/details/386-gair-mackay-john-scobie; http://www.parliament.vic.gov.au/re-member/details/430-harper-robert

41 14 October 1897, Goodie to Jack, Folder 2.3 Box 2, MS12914, SLV.

42 Saturday 16 October1897, *Argus,* p. 12, Notice of Election results.

43 23 November 1897, Cissie to Jack, Folder 2.1, Box 2, MS12914, SLV.

44 13 January 1898, Jessie to Jack, Folder 2.2, Box 2, MS12914, SLV.

45 20 January 1898, Pearl to Jack, Folder 2.1, Box 2, MS12914, SLV.

46 http://www.depi.vic.gov.au/fire-and-emergencies/managing-risk-and-learning-about-managing-fire/bushfire-history

47 7 February 1898, 'Along McDonald's Track'; 'The Bush Fires Position of Korumburra'; 'The Warragul Outbreak'; and 'Yallock Village Settlement', *Argus*, p. 6.

48 Longstaff's canvas 'Gippsland, Sunday Night, February 20th, 1898' was purchased by the National Gallery of Victoria, http://adb.anu.edu.au/biography/longstaff-sir-john-campbell-7230

49 10 February 1898, Pearl to Jack, Folder 2.2, Box 2, MS12914, SLV.

50 20 April 1898, Pearl to Jack, Folder 2.2, Box 2, MS12914, SLV.

51 28 April 1898, Cissie to Jack, Folder 2.2, Box 2, MS12914, SLV.

52 12 May 1898, Goodie to Jack, Folder 2.2, Box 2, MS12914, SLV.

53 *Ibid.*

54 'To Stand at "Inverauld" near Riddell's Creek', *Australasian*, 16 September 1899, p. 3.

55 Artesian Basin Protection Group, The Great Artesian Basin, http://www.gabpg.org.au/great-artesian-basin, accessed 27 June 2016.

56 25 April 1899, Farquhar McDonald to Jack, Folder 2.3, Box 2, MS12914, SLV.

57 8 November 1899, Goodie to Jack, Folder 2.2, Box 2, MS12914, SLV.

58 Peter Burness, 'Boer War', in Davison, Graeme, Hirst, John & Macintyre, Stuart (eds) *The Oxford Companion to Australian History*, Oxford University Press, Melbourne, 1998, pp. 78–9.

59 8 November 1899, Goodie to Jack, Folder 2.2, Box 2, MS12914, SLV.

60 1 February 1900, Farquhar McDonald to Jack, Folder 2.3, Box 2, MS12914, SLV.

61 1 July 1900, Farquhar McDonald to Jack, Folder 2.3, Box 2, MS12914, SLV.

62 13 February 1901, Farquhar McDonald to Jack, Folder 2.3, Box 2, MS12914, SLV.

63 Correspondence re Dalmore Estate, Folder 9.1, Box 9, MS12914, SLV.

64 Undated letter from Jessie to Jack, November 1901, Folder 2.3, Box 2, MS12914, SLV.

Chapter 5

1 Duncan MacGregor, 'The Crisis in the Far West', *Brisbane Courier*, 26 January 1901, p. 14 and 'The Crisis in the Far West II', *Brisbane Courier*, 4 June 1901, p. 6.

2 24 February 1903, 'Stupendous Losses by the Drought', *Morning Bulletin*, Rockhampton, p. 4.

3 'Measuring Worth', https://www.measuringworth.com/australiacompare/result.php?year_source=1903&amount=1023912&year_result=2015 Accessed 14/07/2016.

4 15 July 1901, Farquhar McDonald to Jack, Folder 2.3, Box 2, MS12914, SLV.

5 30 April 1902, Farquhar McDonald to Jack, Folder 2.3, Box 2, MS12914, SLV.

6 2 June 1902, Farquhar to Jack, Folder 2.3, Box 2, MS12914, SLV.

7 Notebook 1900–1901, Box 8, MS12914, SLV.

8 Duncan MacGregor, 'Crisis in the Far West', *Brisbane Courier*, 26 January 1901, p. 14.

9 *Ibid.*

10 Duncan MacGregor, Leckie Archive, 'Crisis in the Far West II', *Brisbane Courier*, 4 June 1901, p. 6.

11 Duncan MacGregor, Notebook c. Folder 8.9 a-c, Box 8, MS12914, SLV.

12 6 June 1903, K. Larson to D. MacGregor, Leckie Archive.

13 23 March 1904, Annie Forster to Duncan MacGregor, Folder 1.9, Box 1, MS12914, SLV.

14 24 December 1907, Brahe & Gair to MacGregor, Folder 1.9, Box 1, MS12914, SLV.

15 28 February 1908, Folder 1.9, MS12914, SLV.

16 Original Assets of the Estate of the Late Donald McRae, 29.02.1908, Folder 1.9, Box 1, MS12914, SLV.

17 27 January 1910, Rucker & MacKenzie to Brahe & Gair, Leckie Archive.

18 *Ibid.*

19 1 and 3 August 1910, Brahe & Gair to MacGregor.

20 1 December 1910, Perpetual Trustees to MacGregor, Leckie Archive.

21 4 August 1910, Perpetual to John MacGregor, Mrs I. Pestell, Mrs J. Stewart, Mrs A. Hutchings, Miss C. MacGregor, Executors Miss M. MacGregor (deceased), Leckie Archive.

22 17 November 1910, Russell & Mears to Mrs MacGregor, Leckie Archive.

23 9 December 1910, Price & Price to John MacGregor, Leckie Archive.

24 17 April 1914, Russell & Mears to John MacGregor, Leckie Archive.

25 Harry H. Peck, 'Duncan MacGregor, Bushman, Cattle Judge', 20 December 1939.

26 *Ibid.*

27 'About People', *Age*, 29 January 1916, p. 11; 4 February 1916, *Romsey Examiner & General Advertiser*, p. 2; 5 February 1916, *Kilmore Advertiser*, p. 2.

28 Quoted in J. Ann Hone, 'MacGregor, Duncan (1835–1916)', *Australian Dictionary of Biography*, Volume 5, Melbourne University Publishing, Carlton, 1974, pp. 157–8.

29 5 February 1916, *Kilmore Advertiser*, p. 2; *Age*, 29 January 1916, p. 11; *Romsey Examiner & General Advertiser*, 4 February 1916, p. 2; 'Western Cattle Ways', Argus, 19 November 1932, p. 4; 'Early Days of Pakenham and Dalmore', *Pakenham Gazette*, 8 March 1968, (n.p.).

30 Hone, *ADB, op. cit.*, pp. 157–8.

31 Bernard Donald MacGregor, talk to Australian Book Collectors Society, 1969, Leckie Archive.

32 The Last Will and Testament of Margaret MacGregor of Darraweit Guim, Widow, dated 12 October 1921. Leckie Archive.

33 Hone, *ADB, op. cit.*

Index

Aboriginal people 15–16, 21–2, 28, 53, 78, 95

Black, Niel 45, 73–4
Bonney, Frederic 21–2, 78
Burke & Wills vii, 16–18, 108

Cameron, Duncan 12
Cameron, John 93–4
Campbell, Alexander 16, 63, 88, 95, 105
Campbell, Dalmahoy 27–30, 32, 74, 94
Campbell, Duncan 18, 63–4, 80–1
Caulpaulin Station 14, 23, 27–8, 30, 32, 34–5, 37–8, 41–3, 51–2, 56, 69–70, 77–9, 83, 94, 158
Charleville, Queensland 54, 58, 61
Chintin, Victoria 18, 32–3, 37, 43, 45, 49–51, 85, 107, 137, 158
Clarke, Robert ix, 45, 73–4
Clarke, W.J.T. 45, 73, 75
Clunie Station 17–18, 32–3, 37, 42, 44–5, 49–50, 61, 67–8, 73, 79, 85, 106–7, 109–11, 113, 120, 125, 137, 139–41, 144, 146–7, 156, 158
Cooper Creek vii, 17–18, 53, 55–8, 60, 63, 65, 95–6, 120–1, 126

Dalmahoy Campbell & Co. 27–8, 74, 94
Dalmore, Pakenham 66–7, 71, 76, 79, 100, 106, 108–11, 115–16, 120–1, 123, 128, 131–5, 137, 139, 141, 144–8, 156

Durham Downs Station, Queensland 17–18, 54, 56, 58, 60, 62–5, 70, 78–9, 81, 85–6, 100, 103, 105, 107, 111–13, 117–20, 146

Forster, Phillip 99, 129, 158–62

Gibson, Richard 28–30, 32, 39, 41
Glengyle, Coburg 49–51, 54, 58–9, 89, 100–2, 107, 116, 146, 148, 151, 154, 156
Glengyle Station, Queensland 17–18, 42–3, 62, 64, 69–70, 83–6, 88, 94–5, 100, 103, 107, 110, 112–13, 117–19, 146
Golden Dyke Mine 159–60
Gowan Lea, Pakenham ix, 67, 132–3, 135, 144, 156–7

Hannam, Alice Maud 140, 156–7
Hutchings, Frederick 135, 140, 151–2

Innaminka, South Australia 17
Inverauld, Riddells Creek, Victoria 44, 46–8, 52, 64, 71, 73, 75–6, 79–80, 85, 88, 109–11, 119–20, 146

Lang, Reverend John Dunmore 2, 25
Liaran, Scotland 2–3, 59, 72

Macdonald, Neil Hugh 31, 38, 54–60, 62–3, 86
MacGregor, Annie (Cissie) 26, 51,

101–4, 106, 109, 111, 113–16, 135, 137–8, 140–1, 143–4, 146, 148, 151–3
MacGregor, Christina (Pearl) 51, 101–2, 104, 108–9, 111, 113, 115–16, 135, 137–8, 140–3, 147–8, 154–5
MacGregor, Donald 13, 51, 81, 102, 104–5, 116, 120–2, 133–7, 139–40, 144, 147, 155
MacGregor, Duncan *passim*
MacGregor, Isabella Barbara (Tottie) 51, 59, 68, 101–2, 111, 115, 133–5, 137–41, 143–4, 146, 148–50, 152, 155
MacGregor, Jessie 44, 49, 51, 100–1, 104, 106, 108–11, 113, 116, 133, 135, 137–8, 140–4, 147–9, 154–5
MacGregor, John (Jack) 49, 51, 54, 81, 100–10, 112–16, 120–1, 133–5, 137–41, 146–8, 155–6
MacGregor, Margaret (Goodie) 49, 51, 101, 103–4, 106–13, 115–16, 121, 133, 138, 140–1, 144–8
MacGregor, Margaret (née McRae) 13, 15, 23, 25–7, 36–7, 49–2, 59, 68–9, 89, 91, 104, 106, 111, 133, 140–1, 144, 146–8
Mailer, David 37, 50, 52, 54, 56–9, 62–5, 79, 84–6
Mailer, Robert 50, 52, 54, 56–8, 62–4, 79, 86
Marco Polo (ship) 3–9
McDonald, Farquhar 81, 103, 107, 111–15, 119–22, 146
McDougall, Robert 45, 71–4, 80, 87–9, 101, 136
McKenzie, Kenneth 68–9, 79, 91, 98–9, 158–9, 162
McNee, James 14
McRae, Anna (Annie), *also* Annie McKenzie, Annie Forster 25, 41, 49, 67–9, 79, 89, 91–2, 98–9, 102, 129–30, 133, 148, 158–62

McRae, Christina (née McKenzie) 26–7, 30–1, 34, 37, 39–41, 51, 59, 61, 64, 67–8, 79, 83, 85, 89–90, 138
McRae, Donald vii, ix, 15–16, 23–32, 34, 36–7, 39–42, 52, 61, 67, 69, 83, 89–92, 94, 129, 130, 133, 138, 160
Meba Downs Station, Queensland 80, 100, 115, 117–18
Menindee, New South Wales 15, 17–20, 28, 32, 79
Miranda Station, South Australia and Queensland 80, 100, 113, 117–18, 146
Morton, Richard and Septimus 74
Mount Margaret Station, Queensland 17–18, 30–1, 35, 38, 42–3, 51–2, 54–8, 61, 63–4, 69–70, 78, 83–4, 90, 95
Mount Murchison Station, Darling River 13, 20–3, 31, 34, 78, 93–4

Pastoral
  business 100, 105
  district 30, 77
  history 21, 139
  industry vii, 1, 20, 30, 136
  land 11, 64
  lease 15, 24
  property 1, 13, 39, 62, 97, 138
  purpose 29, 52
  pursuit 33, 54
  station 23, 30, 54, 77–8
Pastoralism 11, 30
Pastoralist vii, 1, 11, 19, 25–6, 28, 32, 34, 70, 72, 75, 80, 96–97, 100, 112, 125, 127, 138, 146
Pestell, William 102, 135, 140, 148–50
Presbyterian
  Church 25, 37, 68, 100–1, 141–3, 154, 158
  clergyman 2

faith 1
minister 2, 141
rites 148
Presbyterianism 20

Rannoch, Riddells Creek, Victoria 44, 154–5
Reid, Ross and William 20–1, 23, 31, 34, 93
Riddells Creek, Victoria 44–8, 52, 64, 70–1, 73, 80, 109, 111, 119, 142, 154–5
Rogers, Christina (Teen) 140, 156–7

Scott, Alexina (Zena) 101–3, 112, 114, 140, 146–7
Scott, Flora 103, 137, 148
Stewart, Donald Macrae 100–2, 109–10, 135, 140–3, 148–9, 154

Strathfillan, Parish of 3–4

Thargomindah, Queensland 55, 63, 114

Ware, Jeremiah 73–4
Wentworth, New South Wales 21, 36–7
Wigugomrie/Carcory Stations, Queensland 62, 81, 85
Wilcannia, New South Wales 19, 27, 64, 136
Winter, James 44–5, 47, 109, 142
Wood, Ernest Nonus 135, 154–5
Woorooma Station, New South Wales 13–15
Wright, William 16–18

Yanko Station, Queensland 81, 100, 103–4, 107, 110, 117–19, 146